Perspectives on Evangelical Theology

PERSPECTIVES ON EVANGELICAL THEOLOGY

Papers from the
Thirtieth Annual Meeting
of the
Evangelical Theological Society

Kenneth S. Kantzer
Stanley N. Gundry
Editors

BAKER BOOK HOUSE
Grand Rapids, Michigan

CONTENTS

PART ONE
Systematic Theology

Contributors

Klaus Bockmuehl. D.Theol., University of Basel. Professor of Theology and Ethics, Regent College.

Harold O. J. Brown. Ph.D., Harvard University. Associate Professor of Systematic Theology, Trinity Evangelical Divinity School.

John Jefferson Davis. Ph.D., Duke University. Assistant Professor of Theology, Gordon-Conwell Theological Seminary.

Wilber T. Dayton. Th.D., Northern Baptist Theological Seminary. Professor of Biblical Literature and Historical Theology, Wesley Biblical Seminary.

Bruce A. Demarest. Ph.D., University of Manchester. Associate Professor of Systematic Theology, Conservative Baptist Theological Seminary.

Millard J. Erickson. Ph.D., Northwestern University. Professor of Theology, Bethel Theological Seminary.

Gerhard F. Hasel. Ph.D., Vanderbilt University. Professor of Old Testament and Biblical Theology, Andrews University.

E. Margaret Howe. Ph.D., University of Manchester. Associate Professor of Philosophy and Religion, Western Kentucky University.

Morris A. Inch. Ph.D., Boston University. Professor of Theology, Wheaton College.

Fred H. Klooster. Th.D., Free University of Amsterdam. Professor of Systematic Theology, Calvin Theological Seminary.

Gordon R. Lewis. Ph.D., Syracuse University. Professor of Systematic Theology and Christian Philosophy, Conservative Baptist Theological Seminary.

Richard N. Longenecker. Ph.D., University of Edinburgh. Professor of New Testament, Wycliffe College, University of Toronto.

William W. Menzies. Ph.D., University of Iowa. Professor of Biblical Studies, Evangel College.

John Warwick Montgomery. Ph.D., University of Chicago; D.Theol., University of Strasbourg. Professor at Large, Melodyland Christian Center.

Clark H. Pinnock. Ph.D., University of Manchester. Professor of Theology, McMaster Divinity College.

Earl D. Radmacher. Th.D., Dallas Theological Seminary. Professor of Systematic Theology, Western Conservative Baptist Seminary.

O. Palmer Robertson. Th.D., Union Theological Seminary (Richmond). Associate Professor of Old Testament Theology, Westminster Theological Seminary.

Robert L. Saucy. Th.D., Dallas Theological Seminary. Professor of Systematic Theology, Talbot Theological Seminary.

David P. Scaer. Th.D., Concordia Seminary (St. Louis). Professor of Systematic Theology and New Testament, Concordia Theological Seminary (Fort Wayne).

Ronald J. Sider. Ph.D., Yale University. Associate Professor of Theology, Eastern Baptist Theological Seminary.

Preface

The Evangelical Theological Society (ETS) met for its thirtieth annual meeting December 27–29, 1978, on the campuses of Trinity Evangelical Divinity School and Trinity College in Deerfield, Illinois. In the three-day conference more than seventy papers were read and discussed. The general theme was "Evangelical Theology: Where Are We and Where Are We Going?" with special emphasis on systematic and biblical theology.

This meeting marked a significant milestone in the history of the society which has now grown to a membership of 1,200. Not only did the attendance testify to the vitality of the society (388 paying registrants and about 500 in attendance at some plenary sessions), but the papers presented for discussion were noteworthy for the breadth of viewpoints represented and the depth of discussion and insight into the issues addressed. "Evangelicalism" is currently very visible and the "in thing" on the North American scene. Evangelical theologians, historians, and biblical scholars would be the first to admit that too much that goes by that label is shallow and shoddy. But evangelical scholarship is alive and well, coming to grips with the tough questions of the present and facing the future. The program of the Thirtieth Annual Meeting of the ETS is one testimony to that fact.

It has been customary on the anniversaries that are multiples of five for a volume to be published incorporating the best of the papers presented at the anniversary meeting. As editors we are embarrassed by the large number of quality papers we were unable to include in this collection because of space limitations. We were confronted with a situation in which nearly every participant left us a copy of his/her paper. We are most appreciative of that cooperation, but this wealth of material at our disposal meant that we could only use one in three papers; we had some hard choices to make. In the final analysis quality was not the only consideration; indeed, some papers every bit as fine as any in this volume had to be excluded. Our choices also reflect that the major emphasis of the meeting was systematic theology and secondarily biblical theology. Other considerations prominent in our thinking were that selected papers should address contemporary issues in evangelical theology and that they should reflect at least some of the theological diversity present within the Evangelical Theological Society. It is most appropriate that this volume be published under the title, *Perspectives on Evangelical Theology*.

The executive committee of the ETS chose us as co-editors of this project since we as program chairman (Kantzer) and president (Gundry) had worked most closely with the program as a whole. But we would be remiss if we did not acknowledge the members of the program committee who met together often for the overall planning of the program. In addition each man was responsible for the details of programming in the different subject areas. Although we take the responsibility for the final selection of papers and editing, Alan Johnson, Walter Kaiser, Donald Tinder, and Paul Feinberg were not only members of the program committee but are in a very real sense associate editors of this volume. We thank them for their work.

Kenneth S. Kantzer
Stanley N. Gundry
Editors

PART ONE

SYSTEMATIC THEOLOGY

The Task of Systematic Theology

Klaus Bockmuehl

Many will agree there exists an alienation between much of evangelicalism and systematic theology.

In this respect evangelicals are not so different from liberal Christians. A true liberal thinks dogma is disgusting because it seems to impede his personal liberty of mind. He equips himself with the Sermon on the Mount, takes a sharp turn where the NT gets dogmatic, and steers right through into ethics and social welfare work.

Evangelicals (present-day representatives of Reformed Orthodoxy honorably excluded) are not so different when it comes to doctrine. If they feel a theological responsibility at all, they set out from Scripture, preferably from Paul, then demand a personal experience of faith which is to undergird a life of sanctification. They seem to avoid systematic theology altogether because in the past at times it has been seen to be dominated by philosophy or found to be "dead orthodoxy" as opposed to real life. Consequently, the evangelical party will perhaps produce some Bible theologians, an occasional church historian, but hardly any worker in systematic theology, although systematic theology—as is clear from history—has had the habit of setting the course for much of theology and the church.

With the considerations following I shall try to help overcome the existing estrangement between evangelicals and systematic theology. I propose to first deal with the task of systematic theology in general, then with its tasks today as I see them.

THE TASK OF SYSTEMATIC THEOLOGY IN GENERAL

A Job Description

Speaking about the task of systematic theology in general, I suggest a preliminary distinction between the job that needs to be done and the name that has been given to it.

What actually is the task of systematic theology? Let me try a job description: systematic theology is a service for the church, in the church. It is to produce a summary of Christian doctrine, an ordered summary or synopsis of the themes of teaching in Holy Scripture. We are to collect the different, dispersed propositions on essential themes or topics of the OT and the NT and put them together in an order that fits the subject-matter in hand. Furthermore, we are to do this in the light of the history of theology which very much is a history of the interpretation of important biblical passages.

I refer to the example of how the very first textbook of dogmatics was produced during the early years of the Reformation. Philipp Melanchthon, to follow up his own lecture course on Romans, prepared and published his "Loci communes." He called it an index, a "nomenclatura" (list of concepts), a table of the main subjects of Paul's letter.[1] With this method he felt he was more faithful to the text of Holy Scripture than ever so many commentaries which were full of human assumptions. As to the order or sequence of subjects, he followed Paul's own line of argument, observing (as later did Calvin)[2] that Paul himself was a systematic thinker.

To use a contemporary comparison: the task of systematic theology is like the work of men at the actual assembly point of a production line in an appliance factory where the different parts are collected, controlled in terms of their completeness, both in themselves and in their sum, assembled, then sent out for distribution.

Some Purposes of Systematic Theology

What, then, is systematic theology good for? Appliances are for application. Similarly, in spite of what might be thought by some, systematic theology is not primarily a speculative science (as Thomas

---

[1]Melanchthon's *Werke*, II. 1. *Loci communes* of 1521, ed. H. Engelland (Gütersloh: Bertelsmann, 1952) 4.

[2]Cf., e.g., Calvin's reflections on Rom 8:30 in his *Institutes*, III. xiv. 21.

Aquinas would have it)[3] but a *sapientia eminens practica* (Hollatz)[4] which aims at practice and even includes its own theory of practice, i.e., ethics. Systematic theology is a part of Christian service and cannot be done properly in the spirit of *l'art pour l'art*.

Emil Brunner has spoken of three historical roots and intentions of systematic theology: biblical, catechetical, apologetic.[5] The first was to develop a summary or comprehensive order of biblical teaching for general practical purposes in the church, e.g., for the very "domestic use" of confirmation of a soul in anguish (Melanchthon).[6] Karl Barth named two other aspects of this first purpose: systematic theology has the critical task of examining the church's actual proclamation by the standards of Scripture, and positively, of presenting the church with a general paradigm of biblical proclamation.[7]

The first of the two, I believe, is just as much needed in terms of a critical examination of the exposition of Scripture that is going on in the church. Insofar as systematic theology is concerned with the completeness of the sum of parts, it has to see to it that the church gets the whole message of Scripture and not only the darling doctrines and the almost inevitable systematizations or abbreviations of the expositors. Usually this has been argued the other way around: for the task of the exegete to stop the systematic theologian from taking off to speculative flights. But exegetes and systematic theologians here have to serve each other. Especially avowed biblicists can become very dogmatic, if only through their use of terminology and concepts. This therefore applies to evangelicalism with its tendency to emphasize and develop particular themes of Scripture, ignoring others. It is just as true for confessional theologies with their tradition to emphasize a "centre of Scripture," thus relegating other materials to the periphery. Systematic theology faces the need to teach the whole of doctrine, encyclopedically. Its approach should therefore be welcomed as a necessary perspective and corrective for evangelicals.

Barth's other aspect was the presentation of a paradigm of procla-

---

[3] *Summa Theologica* I. 1, 4. Sacra doctrina is "magis ... speculativa quam practica, quia principalius agit de rebus divinis quam de actibus humanis."

[4] In the opening sentence of David Hollatz's *Examen theologicum acroamaticum* (1707) (Darmstadt: Wiss. Buchgesellschaft, 1971), 1. 1.

[5] E. Brunner, *The Christian Doctrine of God*, Dogmatics, I (Philadelphia: Westminster, 1950) 9–11.

[6] In the dedicatory epistle to the reader of the *Loci communes* of 1559, 165.

[7] K. Barth, *Church Dogmatics*, I. 1 (Edinburgh: T. & T. Clark, 1936) 279–81 and I.2 (Edinburgh: T. & T. Clark, 1956) 853ff.

mation. This, then, applies particularly to that continuing task of the church's proclamation, namely teaching, *didache,* the follow-up of evangelism, the work of confirmation and deepening of the faith. Brunner noted it as the second historical root of dogmatics: the need to establish a catechism. In the introduction to a later edition of his "Loci communes" Melanchthon argued for an ordered presentation of the doctrinal material of the Christian faith in terms of psychology of learning. Man, he said, has been created to learn by way of numbers and order, distinguishing the beginning, the middle, and the end.[8] Dogmatics, then, is an enlarged catechism (see Calvin's *Institutes*), a presentation of doctrine in the light of those questions that may have come up, serving the instruction and confirmation of the believer.

The third historical root and intention of systematic theology is in the area of apologetics, the confirmation of the church as a whole. Here the creeds are an early, nuclear form of systematic theology. Their purpose is both apologetic (toward the outside) and unifying (within the membership of the universal church). That is why Melanchthon gave his book the title "Loci communes"—themes commonly held—not the opinions of an individual theologian. On the side of apologetics systematic theology has addressed itself to the task of encounter with heresies, ideologies, and other religions.

These different tasks of systematic theology in general all show that it is goal-oriented, a science for application. As with the other ministries of the church, systematic theology, too, must be exercised singlemindedly for the one goal: the advance of the gospel.

The Term *Systematic Theology*

I have spoken of the aim of systematic theology to provide the church with an ordered summary or synopsis of important subjects of biblical teaching. I have also suggested that it would include the fields of dogmatics, ethics, and apologetics, in this order. Indeed, both ethics and apologetics are—in different ways—part of dogmatics in the wider sense of the word. So we might have chosen to speak of "The Task of Dogmatics" instead of "of Systematic Theology." Paul Tillich, however, has suggested that the term *dogmatic* is no longer usable today because of its negative overtones in general usage due to the "demonic activities of states and churches" in the past.[9] That is

---

[8]Melanchthon, *Loci* (1559) 167.
[9]P. Tillich, *Systematic Theology* (Chicago: Univ. of Chicago, 1951), 1. 32.

why he calls his three-volume synthesis "Systematic Theology." A better reason for the choice of the term might be the fact that we generally have come to use *dogmatics* in the narrower sense, meaning *credenda* but not *agenda*. *Systematic theology* would cover both dogmatics and ethics. As we employ the term, a number of distinctions nevertheless need to be made and have been made. Karl Barth refused to speak of dogmatics as a "system" because he associated *system* with closedness, compulsion, arbitrariness, and the development of a whole from a single principle.[10] In another place, however, and in small print he conceded that there might be "something like a system," a system, as it were, in quotation marks—because of the need to express the coherence and definiteness of the biblical message.[11] Tillich in turn showed that indeed not every system is a deductive system, and himself set up a system which was not at all a system in terms of a *summa* or a totality of content but the treatment of a number of questions in a systematic form or fashion, i.e., with the same method or approach.[12]

So obviously there can be closed systems and open systems (the same distinction is also being made by philosophers), there are systems of content, and there is systematic procedure. As in all sciences, the subject-matter—in the case of systematic theology the biblical material—must be allowed to decide the most appropriate form of its rendering. Of systematic theology it will demand openness. That openness is needed for at least two eschatological reservations, one objective, and one subjective: the history of God's deeds of mercy (Rom 12:1) which is the subject-matter of systematic theology, is not yet complete, *and* our present knowledge of it is as yet imperfect (1 Cor 13:10). Therefore I do not think that we should speak of a system of theology in the proper sense, just as we should not speak uncritically of a "whole" of doctrine but only of an entirety of parts of the revelation given. "Systematic theology" can only mean: to report a history in the proper order of sequence of its details, and report it fully insofar as it has already taken place.

Perhaps we can best explain the terminological options by way of using a Kantian antithesis. Immanuel Kant defined a "system" (and by it he very much determined our understanding of the term) as an architectural design where the completeness and the definite order of the parts of a coherent whole are determined by a principle, *a priori*. He set it against the concept of an "aggregate" which was to be under-

---

[10]Barth, *Dogmatics*, I. 2. 861ff.
[11]Ibid., 868f.
[12]Tillich, *Systematic Theology*, 1. 58f.

stood as a heap or accumulation by chance of individual entities.[13] Now the history of God's deeds of mercy as the subject-matter of systematic theology (done by human beings with their limitations) is neither the one nor the other. It would best be compared with an *organism,* a coherent, orderly *body* of members, all with different functions and places, but all linked to each other and to the whole, a body that still can grow. This actually was the medieval understanding of "system": *systema* could describe the members of a church together, similar to the New Testament concept of *soma,* the church as a "body" of believers.[14]

How, then, shall the different "members" of this body of doctrine be ordered? Melanchthon named his method *historica series,* the historical sequence.[15] He had in mind the sequence of the books of Scripture. His formula might perhaps be used more profitably denoting the sequence of God's deeds of mercy in the history of salvation, his acts and works. The order of topics in systematic theology would then be a sequence of themes in terms of the history of God's deeds—which is very much the plan that we see the early creeds of the church proceed by.

Is there a difference from biblical theology? In my present understanding, the borderline between biblical and systematic theology is fluid. In years past, the biblical data have been gathered (if at all) in terms of the theologies of biblical authors (G. von Rad as against W. Eichrodt). This procedure was suggested by the traditio-historical approach to Scripture. If that were all the biblical disciplines would be willing to provide, it would make the systematic effort absolutely mandatory for the practical purposes of the church's teaching. More recently, however, we see the perspective of biblical theology being taken up again. If, then, theological themes are being followed right through Scripture again, the question of their overall order and mutual relationship becomes the more visible. Of course, exegetes, careful as they are, would probably stop short of systematizing their themes and perhaps put them into an alphabetical order, as did Hermann Cremer with his famous *Dictionary of New Testament Greek,* the forerunner of Kittel. But with this method the awkwardness remains that one would, e.g., begin with "Atonement" which as such presupposes God's commandment and man's sin. Therefore a logical (which

---

[13]I. Kant, *Critique of Pure Reason,* "Transcendental Doctrine of Method," chap. 3 (B 860).

[14]G. Gloege, "Systematische Theologie," I. Begriff, *Die Religion in Geschichte und Gegenwart,* ed. K. Galling (Tubingen: Mohr, 1962), 6. col. 584.

[15]Melanchthon, *Loci* (1559) 170.

is also the historical) sequence is needed in addition to the presentation of biblical theology, and so is also the incorporation of the perspective of the history of doctrine, if only as a history of interpretation of Scripture.

PRESENT TASKS OF SYSTEMATIC THEOLOGY

As I address this particular subject I am aware that I am treading on controversial grounds in making statements on today's situation, but theology cannot be taught completely irrespective of the situation surrounding it. I shall address three areas of our life: culture or society at large, theology, and the church.

On the public horizon, it seems to me that today, in an age of affluence and consequent practical materialism, we are witnessing the almost complete rule of secularism. This is true for the media, and for the public philosophy of education. It also surfaces in the overall rule of immorality, and in the lack of integrative power of our Christian proclamation. The recent mass-suicide of Jonestown is in part also the end-product of our public weakness of theology and thus falls to our responsibility. One might address the situation with the fundamental, simple words of the prophet (Jer 18:7), "Suddenly I declare concerning a nation or kingdom that I will pluck up and break down and destroy it, but if that nation turns from its evil, I will repent of the evil that I intended to do to it." In the West we stand under the horizon of God's wrath over a society overflowing with evil. But who will speak about it? In a continent which in many places kills every second child before birth? Which leads children to prostitution, then makes a film about it and gets its intellectuals to propagate it as "artistically highly commendable"? In a continent which notoriously refuses to hear anything of God's commandments? This cannot go on much longer. And nobody should imagine that geographic distance from the Soviet Union as a possible means of scourge is a dependable safety margin against God's judgment. In the field of theology, we are in a state of confusion. In general one might say that theology today is torn apart by two different centrifugal forces, on the one hand the trend into practical politics with all considerations of doctrine abandoned, on the other hand "the evaporation of substance in sublime reflexion of reflexion,"[16] a theological mannerism and intellectual playfulness that

---

[16]G. Ebeling, "Der Lebensbezug der Theologie," *Was ist los mit der deutschen Theologie? Antworten auf eine Anfrage,* ed. H. N. Janowski and E. Stammler (Stuttgart: Kreuz, 1978) 12.

loses both doctrine and practice. Both trends witness to the impact of affluence on theology. Much of today's theology is a theology of accommodation to the spirit of "We never had it so good," with its domesticated concept of God and no judgment on human nature. Theology's overall message to the public seems to be: Yes, there still is a God, but we can promise he won't interfere. As to detail, I think one cannot be far wrong in saying that the last major influence felt in North America was that of Paul Tillich and his depersonalization and ontologization of God.

Concerning the church: in addition to the adverse effects of affluence showing also here, there is—as a positive note—the great number of new Christians, many of them evangelicals, but at the same time an incredible lack of teaching, and consequently, the rule of subjectivism and so a constant threat of disintegration of the church.

On the basis of these observations I suggest there are three major tasks of systematic theology today:

The Task of Teaching

First, as to the horizon of the church: systematic theology must dare to be itself again, and to be active as such. It must encourage and itself exercise the ministry of teaching in the church. It must reactivate its catechetical function in order to confirm both churches and individual believers so that they are not being driven around by alien doctrines and finally destroyed. Making disciples (Matt 28:19) is not a matter of a one-time proclamation. It requires the intensive stage of teaching to follow up the extensive work of evangelism. This is the proper NT order. "If you want to go wide, you have got to go deep." Think of what quantity and substance of teaching the very young churches of Paul were supposed to digest! Failing to provide teaching as the continuation of mass evangelism today, means—as John Wesley put it—begetting children for the devil. This after-work is a consistent problem for our generation. What we need is theological substance instead of preoccupation with gimmicks and technique.

Recovery of Biblical Dynamism for Systematic Theology

The second task addresses the horizon of theology. It is a concern of form, however decisive. Tillich's ontological theology is only the latest offshoot of a tradition of static theology informed by Greek concepts of thought and language. For this tradition Dionysius the pseudo-Areopagite, the Neo-platonic philosopher of the sixth century A.D. posing as a pupil of Paul, is responsible more than anyone else.

This manner of thinking needs to be replaced by a new dynamism in systematic theology. The basic task before us is to exchange the inherited structure of "Is"-sentences, of sentences made up by predicate nouns and copula, a structure characteristic of Greek metaphysics and its propositions on being, for straight verb predicate sentences which can render act, deed, history, as found in Scripture. We need to learn from the Hebrew forms of thought and language instead of from the Greek, or anyway, we must make sure that we get a better formal equivalent for the content of biblical teaching which is the history of God's deeds of mercy, and not a set of timeless ideas.

I concede that as we in the West still seem to think and speak in categories similar to those of the ancient Greeks perhaps there is then a—secondary—hermeneutical task to translate the established categories of biblical teaching into this other framework of thought forms. Nevertheless, the first job now is to recover the biblical dynamism. It would mean, e.g., for the doctrine of God that we suspend the traditional language of God's nature and attributes as possibilities, and instead speak of God as revealed in his actual deeds. Had it been known, for instance—the so-called Reformational discovery—that according to biblical language God *is just* because he *makes just* (or: in making just, Rom 3:26), it would have saved Luther and the universal church a lot of trouble. Similarly it is clear that the much-abused Johannine statement "God is love" (1 John 4:8) is shorthand only for the verb sentence "God so loved the world that he gave his only Son" (John 3:16; cf. 1 John 4:9).

Similarly, it has long been a concern to reform the doctrine of Christ, interpreting it more in terms of Christ's way and works than of his "natures" and "states." Further, it is high time that in pneumatology we begin to deal with the work of the Holy Spirit instead of with his place within the Trinity only. Also, the doctrine of the church needs this kind of reform: an emphasis not so much on the church's eternal nature and predicates but on its life and commission: the church as a co-operative of people (Rom 16).

This need of dynamism goes for ethics, too. Here the Reformation already went part of the way, turning away from the dominion of the Greek concept of "virtue" which describes the being of a person, to the biblical ethics of God's commandments which address the acting of a person. This, however, seems to me to have been a half-way reform only. The Reformers faithfully reinstalled the biblical creation ethic, the ethics of the preservation of life. Today, in addition we need to recover the New Testament redemption ethics, the ethics of restoration of life, both spiritual and physical, the *causative* ethos of Jesus who equated doing good with saving life (Mark 3:4) and taught ethics by way of the parable of the Good Samaritan. Only such a dynamic, functional ethos will overcome the alleged dilemma of norm and situation proclaimed by the "New Morality." And only thus will we be able to at last accommodate in Christian ethics the task of mission and the work of extramural charity, an inclusion strangely lacking in almost all textbooks of Protestant ethics today.

It is clear that this dynamism envisaged for systematic theology would mean an overall closer contact with Scripture. So one of the basic concerns that evangelicals have for systematic theology is being heeded.

A Call for the Reversal of the Decision for Secularism

The third task of systematic theology today is pitched against the public horizon, the horizon of society. It has been said that all theology must be task-oriented, practical, instructed to serve the advance of the gospel. It is here that the apologetic function of systematic theology comes into focus, or rather its "eristic" function (E. Brunner),[17] that is to say, in dealing with the ideologies of the day systematic theology cannot be reduced to defense; it must go on the offensive.

At this point we face the need of not only a formal, but a material reorientation, a reorientation of emphasis in theology. In the opening paragraphs of his doctrine of God, Karl Barth gave the following definition of the task of dogmatics: "Dogmatics, in each and all of its divisions and subdivisions . . . can first and last as a whole and in part, say nothing else but that *God is.* According to the measure that it does this, it serves the church . . . and decides about its own scientific value or lack of value. In every train of thought, in every sentence which directly or indirectly serves the purpose of saying this, dogmatics does what it ought to do."[18] Theologians of a conviction quite different from that of Karl Barth today make similar statements about the essence of theology. Gerhard Ebeling, one of the leading minds of existentialist theology, recently called for theology to recover the basic distinction between earthly life and life eternal, world and God, distinctions without which theology would soon become superfluous.[19]

"To say nothing else but that God is"—to this must be added, or it is its necessary implication, that God is—*Lord.* In the history of ideas it is not so much the existence but the lordship of God which is being contested. Shrewdly, Karl Marx observed: "Is God sovereign, or is

---

[17]Brunner, *Doctrine of God,* I. 98–101.
[18]Barth, *Dogmatics,* II. 1 (Edinburgh: T. & T. Clark, 1957) 258.
[19]Ebeling, "Der Lebensbezug der Theologie," 12ff.

man? One of the two is an untruth, even if an existing untruth."[20] Therefore, in the present situation of an overall rule of secularism and its confession to the sovereignty of man, systematic theology must step down to this basic level and publicly assert and encourage to assert the lordship of God: that we let God be regnant again. It means to announce God truly as God to a generation forgetful of this fundamental fact.

If systematic theology has the task, among others, to encounter the ideologies and so gets the primary feel of the intellectual climate outside theology, it is in a position as good as any to call for a counter-attack on secularism, for a reversal of the decision for godlessness, not only as an intellectual, but a moral and existential stance.

This must be seen, too, in the horizon of the social consequences of atheism. The OT is very serious about God as the guarantor of human brotherhood (e.g. in Lev 25). Only where people relate to God will there come healing into the world. This is taken up in the NT: Romans 3 twice points out the relation: where there is no fear of God there will be no peace among men. That is a perspective which should make theology again aware of its vast responsibility. We are dealing with a matter not only of the life or death of theology, but of the life or death of millions of people for which Christian theology holds the key.

The rediscovery of theology's public responsibility must result in a change of attitude in theology itself. It is in theology and the church first of all, I believe, that a large scale swing-back to the will of God is called for. Let God be God and let theology be *theo*logy again and not merely anthropology! The reversal of the "secularization of Christianity" (Eric Mascall) needs to take place first in theology.

As we understand this perspective we will have to focus all our energies on it, reconsider our order of priorities and restructure our work. Much theological work which we do today (and which witnesses to our too small and personal aims) may become redundant. Other, useful work will be done with a new, unifying vision. The larger horizon must determine the single steps of our theological advance. For a reversal of today's theological trend or for at least the establishment of a publicly visible, biblical alternative to the theologies informed by secularism, we need to change and unite.

For evangelical theologians it would mean to surrender their factional interests and outlook. They have a tendency to, as has been aptly said, speak in an intramural fashion, addressing intramural

---

[20]K. Marx-F. Engels. *Collected Works* (New York: International Publishers, written in 1843), 3. 28.

questions. Evangelicals need to break their barriers of concern. They must not be concerned only with the life of their own denomination or of the church as such, but with the spiritual state of humanity as the object of God's love. We all need to shed our small horizons. I believe our destiny is to pick up the battle against the philosophy of the lordship of man.

It may have been noticed that my topic was not "The Task of Evangelical Systematic Theology." Perhaps systematic theology can never function properly as a factional concern. Truth is indivisible, and "to first seek the Kingdom of God and his righteousness" is the duty not only of evangelical theologians.

Summing up, may I repeat this paper's major concerns:

—for systematic theology, the biblical concern of a new dynamism,
—for theology in general, the systematic concern for an unmutilated, encyclopedic presentation of the themes of biblical theology,
—for the church, the theological concern for an overall emphasis on teaching and the confirmation of faith,
—for society today, the Christian concern for the proclamation of God's lordship in the horizon of humanity, beginning with a large scale swing-back to the will of God in theology and the church.

I am aware of the fact that the fulfillment of these demands is not a matter of desperate human effort, but of prayer. Prayer, therefore, is not only an important topic, but the elementary and ultimate task of the systematic theologian, and it is a confession of the lordship of God in its own right.

2

Process Trinitarianism

Bruce A. Demarest

THE CURRENT THEOLOGICAL CHALLENGE

One of the most significant contemporary challenges to biblical orthodoxy is being mounted by the burgeoning Anglo-American movement known as process theology. Darwin's work in biological evolution, Einstein's theory of relativity, the development of quantum mechanics and field theory, and the dominant empirical, pragmatic, and pluralistic outlook of modern philosophy have all contributed to the ascendency of the twentieth-century phenomenon called dipolar theism or process theology.

A. N. Whitehead (1861–1947), son of a vicar of the Church of England and later a prominent philosopher at Cambridge and Harvard, developed the dynamic, evolutionary model which undergirds the process view of reality. If Whitehead is the acknowledged patriarch of process philosophy, Charles Hartshorne (1897–), who taught at the University of Chicago from 1928 to 1955, has become the prominent process philosopher of religion. Following Hartshorne a line of process thinkers have emerged at the University of Chicago, the most prominent of whom are H. N. Wieman, Bernard Meland, Bernard Loomer, Daniel Day Williams, and Schubert Ogden. Most recently the work of John B. Cobb, Jr., and David Griffin have made the Claremont Graduate School a second leading center of process theology. Norman Pittenger, a Canadian Anglican lecturing at Cambridge, together with J. A. T. Robinson, Peter Hamilton, and David Pailin, have developed process approaches to theology on the other side of the Atlantic. Evolutionists in the Roman Catholic camp who traditionally have followed Teilhard de Chardin are showing fresh interest in the Whiteheadian approach to naturalistic theism. In process theology, then, we encounter a significant theological system which displays the uncommon label, "Made in America." Those with only a cursory knowledge of current theological literature are aware that faculties of religion and mainline theological seminaries are rapidly buying into the Whiteheadian process system.

Process theology, or neo-classical theism, believes that it offers modern scientific man a theological option more viable than classical theism, neo-orthodoxy, existentialism, or "death-of-God" nihilism. Whiteheadians argue that the so-called absolute and immutable creator God of theism, who allegedly is unrelated to time and irrelevant to the world, is at best a deistical construction. Pittenger brashly describes the God of theism as "the entirely transcendent, remote, miracle-mongering, absolute, impassible, unrelational idol."[1] Modern science has successfully de-Hellenized the old supernaturalism by demonstrating that our self-sufficient universe can manage quite well without a transcendent First Cause, Cosmic Moralist, or Controlling Power.

Neo-orthodoxy's postulate of the radically Other Deity who relates to the world only by paradox and contradiction represents the antithesis of the process vision of the organismic unity of all reality. Moreover, empiricism and positivism have shown that the nonverifiable propositions of neo-orthodoxy are meaningless. Their sheer irrationality dooms them to oblivion. The fate of Barthianism is more perilous than that of classical theism.

Process theology is sympathetic to existentialism's emphasis on engagement and decision (in Whitehead's jargon, awareness to a subjective aim) as determinative for the shaping of a radically open future. Yet neo-classical theists reject existentialism as an adequate philosophical representation of reality. Whereas existentialists differentiate human experience from everything else (e.g., nature), process thinkers view experience as the essence of reality. Moreover, after the Bultmannians have demythologized the biblical witness, one is still left with a creator God beyond nature who confronts man as sovereign and judge.[2]

---

[1]N. Pittenger, *God's Way With Men* (London: Hodder and Stoughton, 1969) 37, 38.

[2]As Pittenger notes, "We still have God who in some fashion moulds and moves nature, history and man, and who can and will achieve his purposes, both in time and over time." *The Word Incarnate: A Study in the Doctrine of the Person of Christ* (New York: Harper, 1959) 36.

Finally process theology polemicizes against secular nihilism whose worldview allows no place for God. Modern nihilists are atheists in the commendable sense that they have smashed the idols of traditional theism.[3] Yet they erringly overlook the sacred reality embedded in the warp and woof of the universe which imparts purpose and direction to the whole.

AN OVERVIEW OF NEO-CLASSICAL THEISM

Process theology, or naturalistic theism, subscribes to a one-order view of the universe. Consistent with Eastern philosophy and the modern secular outlook it rejects the traditional Western metaphysical dualism between matter and spirit, natural and supernatural, the creature and the Creator. One cannot differentiate between what is temporal and thus accessible to the senses, and what is timeless and inaccessible to the senses. Reality is a single, structured spatio-temporal process consisting of a series of becomings and perishings with new becomings emerging from what has perished. The title of Whitehead's monumental essay, *Process and Reality* (1929), suggests that what is actual is that which is in process.

The ultimate "stuff" of the universe, then, consists not of bits of matter or elemental particles, but sub-atomic moments of experience which Whitehead termed "actual occasions" or "occasions of experience." In the Whiteheadian vision, the basic units of reality are societal energies or charges of experience, up to ten of which are said to occur in one second of human consciousness. These momentary occasions succeed one another with such rapidity that analysis of a single energy-event is impossible.

But reality is not only dynamic, it is profoundly interrelational and societal. Nothing exists in isolation; everything in the universe profoundly affects everything else. The dynamics of the interaction simplify thus. Each actual occasion "prehends" (i.e., grasps or feels) prior actual occasions and incorporates the antecedent moments of experience into its own universe, thus forming a creative and novel synthesis. Immediately the new occasion serves as an experience to be prehended by succeeding actual occasions. The former experience perishes, yet is immortalized in the flow to novelty. The incorporation of antecedent thrusts, drives, and aims into a novel synthesis is called "concrescence." Enduring objects familiar to us such as electrons, atoms, or cells represent a series of actual occasions. More complex

---

[3]Pittenger, *God's Way*, 38.

organisms such as the human body, which are unities of more fundamental elements, are called societies of actual occasions, or nexus.
Again, reality is both processive, interrelational, and organismic.

In order to account for purpose and order in the emergence of
novelty, Whitehead was obliged to posit Deity in the evolutionary
schema. The causative agent which provides the initial aim or inten-
tional purpose for each actual occasion is defined as God. God
functions as the "lure" of the process which draws each occasion to
fulfillment. In addition, God is envisaged as the final effect or *telos* of
the cosmic process. Even at this preliminary stage of our outline of the
process vision it is evident that God is not an eminent self-existent
being, but in Whitehead's words, God is "the chief exemplification" of
processive reality. The becoming God is the creative energy immanent in the evolutionary advance. A full explication of the process
vision of God awaits a brief consideration of how knowledge of God is
gained in the Whiteheadian scheme.

We have noted that divine reality is prehended or felt in a series of
drops or moments of ecstatic experience. It follows that awareness of
God is an intrinsic and inescapable ingredient of human experience.
Cobb and Griffin thus affirm, "There are not actual entities that first
are self-contained and then have accidental relations to God. God-
relatedness is constitutive of every occasion of experience."[4] Apprehension of God's reality cannot be avoided by the very nature of
the process definition of reality as a richly variegated organic unity,
understood as a continuum of moments of experience. One recalls
Whitehead's comment addressed to the theist who posits that God
discloses himself supernaturally from without, "The pure conservative is fighting against the essence of the universe."[5]

Process epistemology in fact involves the correlation of an empirical
analysis of the character of the universe (its order, coherence, and
intelligibility) together with an experience of sacred reality from
within the flow of the creative advance. Thus human knowledge involves both the "accidents" and the sheer necessities of human experience. But the bottom line reads that God is known not indirectly or
inferentially, but as the personal agent confronts, senses, feels, and
interprets reality through a series of momentary drops of experience.
All of humankind thus participates in a common, equally valid religious experience of sacred reality. As Hartshorne insists, God is "a

---

[4]J. Cobb and D. Griffin, *Process Theology: An Introductory Exposition*
(Philadelphia: Westminster, 1976) 29.

[5]A. Whitehead, *Adventures of Ideas* (New York: Macmillan, 1933) 354.

universal datum of experience."[6] To be human is *de facto* to experience the reality of God.[7]

It follows, as an aside, that process theologians define revelation in terms of the experienced perception of the human agent. Pittenger suggests that special revelation is "that which is extraordinary or unusual in our experience."[8] Special revelation in the process system is man interpreting his experiences and attempting to grasp the significance of his own life.

But the Whiteheadian prehensions or nonsensuous perceptions of sacred reality are largely subconscious and prereflective. As Cobb and Griffin argue, "Consciousness presupposes experience, and not experience consciousness."[9] This prethematized psychic knowledge buried beneath the level of consciousness, although intuitively realized, remains conceptually unformulated. The pre-thematized experiences which never reach formulation are similar to the submerged hulk of an iceberg. Those few perceptions of Deity which rise to conceptual expression correspond to the iceberg's exposed tip. The thematized doctrines of the world's religions represent human attempts to express deeply experienced reality in formal language. Historical, cultural, and perspectival differences among people account for the divergent conceptual formulations of the universally experienced sacred reality. Process theology thus upholds the primacy of the subconscious, prereflective experience over against formal propositionalized doctrines. The experienced reality, it is argued, defies objective formulation. The doctrine of the Trinity, for example, is a fragile attempt by the Christian tradition to thematize its ecstatic experience of God. Muslims, Hindus, and Buddhists conceptualize the experienced sacred reality in terms of other no less valid models. In fact, given the reflective, spiritual outlook of the Eastern world, Chris-

---

[6]C. Hartshorne, *A Natural Theology for Our Time* (Lasalle, IL: Open Court, 1967) 2.

[7]Process epistemology involves a radical empiricism. The quest for knowledge begins with an analysis of sense data but moves on to weigh the evidence from moments of personal religious experience. Comments Whitehead, "Nothing can be omitted, experience drunk and experience sober, experience sleeping and experience waking, experience drowsy and experience wide awake, experience self-conscious and experience self-forgetful, experience anxious and experience carefree, experience anticipatory and experience retrospective, experience happy and experience grieving." *Adventures of Ideas*, 290, 291.

[8]Pittenger, *Word Incarnate*, 22.

[9]Cobb and Griffin, *Process Theology*, 17.

tians in the West should be prepared to alter their doctrinal models in the light of the emerging experiences of Hindu Yoga or Zen Buddhist meditation. In short, process theology concedes the tentativeness of any specific doctrine and cautions the Christian tradition not to plead the normativeness of a rigidly trinitarian form of logic.[10] But let us return to the Whiteheadian conception of God.

The process vision of Deity, shaped by the empirical dictum, "God is what God does," envisages God as dynamic, creative Act. Argues Cobb, "If we can think of God as an energy-event, as an occurrence of thinking, willing, feeling and living, then we are close to the heart of the biblical faith."[11] Given the Whiteheadian premise that what is most real are energy-events and that God is the chief exemplification of reality, it follows that God is a very special kind of energy-event.[12] Pittenger speaks of God as the chief exemplification of the living, dynamic, energizing force in the universe.[13] R. C. Miller of Yale Divinity School identifies God with the cosmic evolutionary process "by which we are made new . . . and by which we are lured into feelings of wonder, awe, and reverence."[14]

A crucial question to be faced is whether the God of process theology is a *personal* reality. Whitehead responds negatively, insisting that God, while altogether real, is nevertheless an actual entity, or an exemplar moment of experience. The crux of Whitehead's thesis is that God is not a being distinct from other beings, but that God is organically related to the whole of reality defined as energy-event. Whitehead's vision resembles Tillich's immanentalistic and quasi-pantheistic notion of God as Being-itself, which is identified with the total reality of the universe. Pittenger argues that the process God transcends personal categories, although he is the ground and source of the personal.[15] Cobb, on the other hand, tries to rescue process

---

[10]For further discussion of the relationship between subconscious experience of reality and consciously formulated beliefs see Cobb and Griffin, *Process Theology,* 30–40.

[11]J. Cobb, "The World and God," in Cousins, ed., *Process Theology* (New York: Newman, 1971) 158.

[12]J. Cobb, *God and the World* (Philadelphia: Westminster, 1969) 71.

[13]N. Pittenger, "Bernard E. Meland, Process Thought, and the Significance of Christ," in Cousins, ed., *Process Theology,* 205.

[14]R. C. Miller, "Empiricism and Process Theology," *Christian Century* 93 (Mar. 24, 1976) 286.

[15]Pittenger, "Meland, Process Thought, and the Significance of Christ," 205.

theology from pantheism by insisting that God is more a living person than an actual entity.[16] It is difficult to conceive of God defined in terms of energy-event or power of creative transformation as possessing qualities of personality, such as intellect, volition, and will. Attempts to interpret the processive power in nature in personal categories fall short of the warmly personal God of the Bible.

Process theology further postulates a dipolar Deity who is both being and becoming, primordial and concrete. Classical theism, of course, is monopolar in its assertion that God is a God of unqualified absoluteness and perfection. In the dipolar Whiteheadian scheme, God is necessary yet contingent, abstract yet concrete, transcendent yet immanent, eternal yet temporal.

According to Whitehead, God as primordial is above the process as the structure of possibility, the organ of novelty and the principle of limitation. This conceptual pole of Deity is the basis for the actualizing of all possibilities. In providing the process with its subjective aims, God as primordial is the lure for feeling and the eternal urge for desire which draws the process towards value, order, and fulfillment.

The consequent or concrete pole describes what God is at any moment in the emergent process. Since neither the world nor God reaches static perfection, there is a real becoming in God. Whitehead could say that "the actuality of God must also be understood as a multiplicity of actual components in process of creation."[17] In fact, the reality of God is shaped by physical prehension of all other actual occasions. In other words, the world passes into God's consequent nature, where its values are actualized for the emergent process. God, conceived of as a concrete actuality, thus "is temporal, relative, dependent, and constantly changing."[18] It follows that the process Deity is not in control of the world as all-determining causation and possesses incomplete knowledge of future contingencies.

Significantly, the real God of process theology is God in his concrete actuality. Pittenger concedes that "the distinction between 'abstract' and 'concrete' or 'primordial' and 'consequent' . . . is only for the purpose of analysis and discussion. The *real* God—by which is meant God as he is actually known—is the concrete, active, dynamic reality who does this or that."[19] God as primordial is a philosophical abstraction.

---

[16]J. Cobb, *A Christian Natural Theology* (Philadelphia: Westminster, 1965) 188ff.

[17]A. Whitehead, *Process and Reality* (New York: Macmillan, 1929) 532.

[18]Cobb and Griffin, *Process Theology*, 47.

[19]N. Pittenger, *Alfred North Whitehead* (Richmond: John Knox, 1969) 35.

The real God is the relative, immanent reality which is identified with the creative process operative in the universe.[20]

Finally, process theology defines the relation between God and the world as panentheism. God is not identified with the universe (pantheism), but only with those features which promote order, purpose, and love. Nor is God an entity distinct from the universe (classical theism). As part of the total natural structure of things, "God literally contains the universe"[21] so that every part of it exists in Deity. God is in all and all is in God, where God is 'cosmic wholeness,' 'universal Love,' and the modally all-inclusive or nonfragmentary reality surpassible only by himself. Whiteheadians promote the panentheist model in an attempt to affirm the divine transcendence while insisting that God is continuously and inextricably related to the natural order.

THE DIVINE TRIUNITY IN PROCESS THEOLOGY

Whiteheadians concede that process theology is in a state of process. Dipolar theism never descended upon the theological world as a full-blown, coherent system. Although process thinkers have long struggled with the question of God, only in the last decade or two have attempts been made to formulate a Whiteheadian Christology. Moreover, relatively little attention has been given in process circles to the Holy Spirit. And until Pittenger's 1977 essay, *The Divine Triunity*, Whiteheadians had produced no systematic explication of the Trinity. It is to the unfolding process interpretation of the classical doctrine of the Trinity that we now turn.

Whitehead's interaction with the person of Jesus was only occasional and unsystematic. It is clear that Whitehead was genuinely impressed by Jesus' impact upon the course of human history. Not without justification time divides at the emergence of the Nazarene upon the human scene. Whitehead judged that Plato's wisdom and the quality of Jesus' life served as powerful catalysts in the development of Western civilization.[22] Although God was somehow imma-

---

[20]Pittenger, for example, defines God's transcendence as "his inexhaustibility of resource, his indefatigability in bringing the occasions to fulfillment, and his faithfulness to his overarching purpose." *The Holy Spirit* (Philadelphia: United Church, 1974) 29.

[21]C. Hartshorne, *The Divine Relativity* (New Haven: Yale University, 1948) 90.

[22]Whitehead, *Adventure of Ideas*, 212.

nent in Jesus, Whitehead attributed no particular distinctiveness to the relation.

Hartshorne, whose chief interest was the formulation of a Whiteheadian philosophy of religion, laid the initial foundations for later process interpretations of Christ. Comments Hartshorne:

> I have no Christology to offer, beyond the simple suggestion that Jesus appears to be the supreme symbol furnished to us by history of the notion of God genuinely and literally "sympathetic" (inconceivably *more* literally than any man is), receiving into his own experience the sufferings as well as the joys of the world.[23]

Although Jesus is no more ontologically divine than any other creature, he is the most profound exemplification of the God who suffers sympathetically with the universe. Jesus' "uniqueness" consists in that the living God was imaged in him with a clarity and decisiveness not found in other men. Traditional formulae such as "Jesus was God," or "the divinity of Jesus" are ambiguous and misleading. "The most they can do is to name a mystery which is felt rather than thought; and people may well feel differently about ways of phrasing the mystery."[24]

John B. Cobb, Jr. argues that the substantialist model of the relationship between God and Jesus must be abandoned, for two entities (such as God and man) cannot occupy the same place at the same time. The old relation of substances must give way to the new model of an experiential relation in which societies of actual occasions or momentary experiences merge in creative synthesis. Cobb details the differences between the substantial and processive approaches thus:

> In the case of two substances, they must be conceived as having their essential being first and then coming into relation subsequently. The relation is external to their being. But in the case of the two experiences, the second cannot come into being except as a process of reactualizing and completing the first. The second momentary experience has no essential being that does not include the effective presence within it of the first. The presence of the first is constitutive of the second.[25]

The logos motif lies at the heart of the process vision of the relation between God and Jesus. For Cobb, the logos is both transcendent and

---

[23]C. Hartshorne, *Reality as Social Process: Studies in Metaphysics and Religion* (Boston: Beacon, 1953) 24.

[24]Ibid., 152.

[25]J. Cobb, *Christ in a Pluralistic Age* (Philadelphia: Westminster, 1975) 74.

immanent. In its transcendence the logos is timeless and infinite. As the source of purpose, the organ of novelty, the lure for feeling, the logos is God in his primordial nature. The immanent logos functions as the lure toward optimal creative transformation. It provides each entity with its subjective aim or basic impulse towards actualization. To the extent that the creature allows the logos to incorporate elements from the past in a novel synthesis, creative transformation takes place. Cobb defines this event of creative transformation lured and energized by the latent logos as the Christ.[26] Christ, then, is the immanence of the logos—the power of creative transformation.

The logos, of course, is immanent in all men, in all traditions, in all faiths and unfaiths. But Cobb differentiates the man Jesus from other incarnations of the logos. Jesus is a paradigm instance of incarnation in that he allowed the logos to fully constitute his subjective aim. In Jesus there was no tension, no opposition, of his "I" to God. Whiteheadians claim that this process construction avoids the logical fallacy of ontologically equating Jesus with God. Immanence, Cobb notes, does not mean identity. The name Christ "does not designate deity as such but refers to deity as graciously incarnate in the world."[27]

As an aside, Cobb notes that other religious figures may have possessed an existence-structure similar to that of Jesus. Gotama the Buddha probably incarnated the logos redemptively. Herein lies the possibility of an authentic religious pluralism. But since Christ is that openended process of creative transformation, there exists a genuine religious pluralism without relativism.

Professor Norman Pittenger, a Canadian Anglican who lectures at Cambridge and who calls himself "a Catholic and a modernist,"[28] has become increasingly identified in recent years with the process movement. Pittenger cites the presence of "imperfections, inaccuracies, over-emphases, and under-emphases, perhaps even misleading ideas and implications"[29] in the traditional doctrinal formulations.

The assertion that Christ is the incarnation of the second person of the eternal Trinity perverts the intent of the earliest Christian writings. Jesus was no "divine intruder" who descended to earth from another realm. He was the human son of Mary and Joseph who labored at a carpenter's bench in Nazareth. Jesus' selfhood was shaped by a constellation of environmental and relational occasions in the

---

[26]Ibid., 76.
[27]Ibid., 66.
[28]Pittenger, *Word Incarnate,* xiv.
[29]Ibid., xvi.

historical process. Selfhood, affirms Pittenger, "is a specific... routing or series of occasions in which there is a continuity which includes the memory of the past, the relationships of the present, and the projective aim toward the future."[30]

The logos, for Pittenger, is not the psychological center of Jesus' person, but the Self-Expressive Action of God toward and with the creation.[31] There is always and everywhere an interpenetrative activity between God and the world. The activity of the Word which normally is diffused throughout the universe, at a particular time and place focused in Jesus. Jesus' significance lies in the fact that he functioned as the human vehicle for the divine activity. Argues Pittenger,

> At every point in the existence of Jesus, the divine activity is operative, not in contradiction of the humanity nor in rejection of any part of it but in and through it all—in teaching, preaching, healing, comforting, acting, dying, rising again. . . . He is indeed the personalized instrument for the Self-Expressive Activity of God.[32]

Pittenger's immanentalistic functionalism carries over to other Christological formulations. The hypostatic union is defined as "the *coincidence* of the divine and human acts, the act of God and the act of man."[33] The Deity of our Lord is in the Self-Expressive Activity of God in and through him. The "scandalous assertion" of Christianity is that God was there in Christ, active, at work, incarnate, enmanned.[34] In sum, Christ is not identical with Jesus, but refers to Deity experienced as graciously incarnate in the world.

Pittenger, unlike Cobb, holds that Jesus differed from the rest of humanity in degree rather than in kind. If Jesus were dissimilar in kind his solidarity with the human family would be compromised. Jesus' obedience to God's intention for him is the key to the speciality of the church's Lord. Because Jesus allowed his subjective aim or directionality to be shaped by God, he represents the distinctive, decisive, definitive man. Concludes Pittenger, "the uniqueness of Jesus Christ can only be seen in his speciality, his supreme and decisive expression of that which God always and everywhere is 'up to' in his

---

[30]N. Pittenger, *Christology Reconsidered* (London: SCM, 1970) 79.

[31]Pittenger, *Word Incarnate*, 183.

[32]N. Pittenger, "The Incarnation in Process Theology," *Rev Exp* 71 (Winter 1974) 52, 53.

[33]Pittenger, *Word Incarnate*, 181.

[34]Ibid., 179.

world."[35] The foregoing does not suggest that history displays no approximations to Jesus. In reality, Socrates, Plato, the Buddha, and Confucius all were instruments of the divine activity.

Process theologians readily acknowledge the difficulty of achieving a trinitarian formulation within a process conceptuality. Hartshorne refers to the doctrine of the Trinity as a none too successful attempt to express the sociality of God. Cobb finds it necessary to modify radically the classical trinitarian construction. Insists Cobb, "Process theology is not interested in formulating distinctions within God for the sake of conforming with traditional Trinitarian notions."[36]

Cobb argues that the dipolar God is immanent in the world as creative love (the logos). This is an immanence of God in his primordial nature, and denotes the Christ. Second, God is immanent in the world as responsive love. This is an immanence of God in his consequent nature, and denotes the Spirit.

Cobb concedes that his formulation involves but two "persons": God as creative love (Christ) and God as responsive love (Spirit). How then is a trinitarian formula achieved? To the two "persons," God as creative love and God as responsive love, there should be added the unity in which the two persons are cojoined in the one God. The result is thus a trinity. Yet Cobb concedes that "the unity is not another person in the same sense that the other two are persons."[37] What Cobb in effect has postulated is the existence of creative and responsive modes to an immanent reality. But of course neither Scripture nor the church witness to a thoroughgoing immanentalism, albeit with operational distinctions. However, process thinkers such as Cobb are unimpressed with the primary datum of Scripture and the secondary datum of the witness of the historic church. Their ultimate referent is the philosophical scheme of Whitehead.

Norman Pittenger, in his two recent books, *The Holy Spirit* (1974) and *The Divine Triunity* (1977), has interacted more than any other process thinker with the problem of the divine unity and multiplicity. Pittenger's explication of the Trinity, although differing in details from Cobb's, involves a similar immanentalistic monism. Pittenger claims that "the immanent operations of God could all be styled ... the work of the spirit of God, the wisdom of God, or the word of God."[38] A distinction needs to be made, however, between

---

[35]Pittenger, "Meland, Process Thought, and the Significance of Christ," 214.

[36]Cobb and Griffin, *Process Theology*, 110.

[37]Ibid., 109.

[38]Pittenger, *Holy Spirit*, 40.

God's working *upon and with* nature, history, and humanity, and God's more internal activity felt *within* the human spirit. The former, God's Self-Expressive Act, denotes the Word which achieved maximum actualization in Jesus. The latter, God's Self-Responsive Movement, connotes the Holy Spirit, the power of divine love, which elicits in the faithful the response of obedience, worship, and love for God. Again the Holy Spirit is God in his responsive mode of activity.

Pittenger argues that the early church never intended to speak of three "consciousnesses" in God. There is but one God who is profoundly dynamic and social. This God in continuous relationship with the world displays his reality in a threefold creative activity.

The triadic character of the divine reality begins to emerge more clearly. The Father, as the source of genuine novelty, provides each entity with its initial aim. The Word, or Son, is the self-expression of God in humanity and especially in Jesus of Nazareth. The Word lures each occasion to maximal fulfillment; it provides the thrust for the realization of the initial aim of all possibility. The Spirit "is the 'responding,' the conforming, the returning of the 'amen' of God through the whole creation and in deity itself."[39] The Spirit prompts assent to the divine actualization of novelty and advance. Pittenger's trinitarian pattern can be summarized thus: the Father is Creative Source, the Son is Self-Expressive Act, and the Spirit is Responsive Movement.[40] Pittenger styles his God concept as triunitarian rather than trinitarian, for he judges the former term less suggestive of heretical tritheism.

Pittenger next makes the logical leap that what is true of God's relationships with the creation is true of God himself. Thus, "the relationships God sustains with his world are reflective of an immanent relationship in his own life—that is, he is best symbolized for us as 'Three in One,' not as sheer and unqualified singularity."[41] God is thus declared to be triunitarian in his nature because he is so in his actions with the creation.

Consistent with the Whiteheadian principle that God is immediately perceived in human experience, Pittenger argues that a threefold experience of God constitutes the basic data for the triune conceptuality. A threefold experience of facts corresponds to the threefold facts of experience. Through the experiences of mundane life a *vestigium Trinitatis* is intuited: namely, God in creative fatherhood is love, God in self-expressive activity is love, and God as enabling response to that

---

[39]Ibid., 59.
[40]Ibid., 124.
[41]Pittenger, "The Incarnation in Process Theology," 57.

activity is love.[42] Pittenger argues that if we conclude that the doctrine of the Trinity is not explicitly affirmed in the NT, yet Christians of all ages have experienced a threefold awareness of God—God over us, God with us, and God in us. A remarkable fit, therefore, is claimed between the realities of religious experience and the insights of process philosophy. If the process formulation of the Trinity proves less than satisfying at the rational level, Pittenger argues this is so because the ultimate reality of Love is marked by great mystery. Western thought needs to cultivate the "feeling tones" of Asian cultures to apprehend the triadic character of Love in all its mystical fulness.[43]

Pittenger, like Cobb, rejects the classical ontological formulation of the Trinity, arguing instead for a triunity of relational activity. God *is* what God *does*. Pittenger concedes that the early Christian theologians did the best they could given the Greek categories of substance and being with which they worked. Unfortunately they missed the truth that God is always dynamic, creative, and socially related. The inadequate classical formulations of the Trinity must yield to new models based on the modern, evolutionary vision of reality expounded by Whitehead and his disciples.

CRITIQUE OF PROCESS TRINITARIANISM

Norman Geisler offers an excellent philosophical critique of process thought in the volume, *Tensions in Contemporary Theology*.[44] Our own comments focus more specifically on the process explication of the Divine reality.

On the positive side, process theology's emphasis upon God as dynamically active and related can only be applauded. The God Christians worship is not a static Sovereign, a remote Ruler, or a detached Deity who dwells in isolation beyond the clouds. God is dynamically related to his creation. Although sovereign and transcendent, God is also profoundly immanent, involved, and operative in the human arena. God not only loves, empathizes, and cares for his people, but he "lures" them to greater participation in his own life. The God of the Bible is not an "impassible idol" (Pittenger) who fails to suffer along with the sufferings of his creatures. Perhaps the classi-

---

[42]N. Pittenger, *The Divine Triunity* (New York: United Church, 1977) 66.

[43]Pittenger's appeal to mystical ultimacy rather than rational verification is set forth in *Divine Triunity*, 51–9.

[44]Ed. by Stanley N. Gundry and Alan F. Johnson (Chicago: Moody, 1976), 237–84.

cal tradition (and surely the Barthian reformulation) has overemphasized the divine transcendence to the neglect of the divine immanence. Theists can agree with process theology, even as Paul agreed with the Greek poets, "In him we live and move and have our being" (Acts 17:28).

But process theology is open to serious criticisms. First of all, Whiteheadians labor under the delusion that biblical theism's conception of God is identical to Aristotle's Unmoved Mover, the unrelated, impassive, unconcerned Deity of the Greeks. Such an understanding is a parody of biblical theism's true commitment. The Christian faith emerged out of the matrix of Judaism with its conception of God as a living, active being relentlessly operative in the ordinary events of nature and the supernatural display of miracles. The God of the Jewish-Christian tradition is changeless in being, attributes, and purposes, but in his dealings with the creation God does enter into changing relations. Thus, the divine immutability in no wise implies that God is unconcerned, inactive, or unrelated. Calvin chided the Epicureans as "pests with which the world has always been plagued, who dream of an inert and idle God."[45] It is wholly irresponsible to replace the God of theism with a finite, evolving Deity in order to affirm relatedness to the world. Biblical faith unhesitatingly affirms that the perfection of God includes creative interaction consistent with His changeless character and purposes.

Second, process theology has falsely bought into the modern embargo on ontology. To a man Whiteheadians argue that God cannot be objectified as an existent or a substantial self. Selfhood becomes a mere flux or stream of events. It follows that in process theology no ontological relation can be established between Jesus, the Spirit, and God. In its affirmation that reality consists of energy-events or occasions of experience, we observe the modern empiricist's denial of the idea of substance as that which underlies an entity's changing qualities.

But is it unreasonable to insist that the God who acts and who may be experienced is the God who *is?* The Whiteheadian scheme has no tool at its disposal to account for God's essential identity through the course of the creative advance. If we consider God at the beginning, the middle, and the end of the process, there must be something which accounts for the identity of Deity through the course of the change. Substance-attributes language, which talks of attributes coextensive with being, provides a conceptuality for describing how God can remain uniquely himself through the continuum of his changing

---

[45]J. Calvin, *Institutes*, I. xvi. 4.

dynamic acts. To be sure, God's being cannot be detached from his actions. But neither can God's actions be detached from his being without drifting into a serendipity syndrome.[46]

Far from being peculiarly Aristotelian, ontological affirmations constitute the warp and woof of the biblical testimony to the triune God. In the OT God revealed himself to the concrete and functional Hebrew mindset as Yahweh, the Absolute Existent who in his fundamental nature is radically other than man. Our Lord himself, in describing his relationship to God the Father, employed ontological language—"I and the Father are one" (John 10:30).[47] The Jewish solution to the ontological problem raised by our Lord is evident: stoning the One who claimed to be equal to God in essence and being.

The apostolic teaching, received directly from Jesus, likewise utilized ontological categories. Paul, who was hardly a Greek metaphysician, spoke in Romans 1:20 of God's "eternal power and deity" ($\theta\epsilon\iota\acute{o}\tau\eta\varsigma$). In Philippians 2:6 he referred to God's "form" or underlying reality ($\mu o\rho\phi\acute{\eta}$).[48] In Colossians 2:9 the Pauline expression "the whole fulness of deity" ($\pi\hat{\alpha}\nu\ \tau\grave{o}\ \pi\lambda\acute{\eta}\rho\omega\mu\alpha\ \tau\hat{\eta}\varsigma\ \theta\epsilon\acute{o}\tau\eta\tau o\varsigma$) is descriptive of the divine essence.[49] The writer of Hebrews defined Christ in precise ontological categories, both to his divinity ($\chi\alpha\rho\alpha\kappa\tau\grave{\eta}\rho\ \tau\hat{\eta}\varsigma\ \acute{v}\pi o\sigma\tau\acute{\alpha}\sigma\epsilon\omega\varsigma\ \alpha\grave{v}\tau o\hat{v}$; Heb 1:3)[50] and as to his humanity (Heb 2:14). We are justified in concluding that a clear transcendent metaphysical focus exists in the biblical documents. Brunner is right, therefore, in speaking of "the Eternal Divine Being" who is to be "contrasted with the ceaseless flux of earthly becoming."[51]

---

[46]Cf. Geisler's comment: "How can something continue to come from nothing, being from non-being, unless there is an unchanging Being beyond the process of change . . . that grounds the change?" "Process Theology," in Gundry and Johnson, eds., *Tensions*, 278.

[47]Gerald Bray argues convincingly that it was Jesus himself rather than the disciples or the early church who made the shift from a predominantly Jewish functional to an ontological Christology. "Can We Dispense With Chalcedon?" *Themelios* 3 2NS (Jan. 1978) 4.

[48]Moulton and Milligan state that $\mu o\rho\phi\acute{\eta}$ "always signifies a form which truly and fully expresses the being which underlies it." *Vocabulary of the Greek New Testament* (Grand Rapids: Eerdmans, 1974) 417.

[49]D. Guthrie, "Colossians," *New Bible Commentary,* rev. ed. (London: Inter-Varsity, 1970) 1147.

[50]G. Braumann defines $\acute{v}\pi\acute{o}\sigma\tau\alpha\sigma\iota\varsigma$ as "substance, essential nature, essence, actual being. The word is used concretely for what stands under, the basis of something." *New International Dictionary of New Testament Theology* (Grand Rapids: Zondervan, 1975–78), 1. 703.

[51]E. Brunner, *The Mediator* (Philadelphia: Westminster, 1948) 400.

If a meaningful trinitarianism is to be sought, the transcendent ontological foundations upon which the soteriological edifice is built must not be discarded. The Whiteheadian redefinition of metaphysics, articulated to conform to modern humanistic evolutionism, produces a fruitless monism of event where God is no more than the energy latent in the universe.

Thirdly, in a system in which God himself is a product of the process absolutes are entirely wanting—all is relative. Process thinkers concede that to be real is to be actual. In the Whiteheadian scheme, process *is* reality. There is no going behind actual entities to more ultimate reality. It is difficult to escape the conclusion, then, that God is not dipolar at all. The primordial pole of God, which possesses no actuality, in fact possesses no reality. The attempt to impose upon the system a transcendent, timeless anchor in the form of the primordial nature smacks of a desperate attempt to forestall the system's collapse into radical immanentism and pantheism. But attempts by the Whiteheadian empiricists to postulate the reality of a pure abstraction fails. God as primordial cannot be induced from the data of experience.

Thus the real God of process theology is a finite and temporal entity contingent upon the process of nature and history. Given a God who is eternal Becoming, ultimacy collapses into eminent relativity (Ogden). Control of the world of future possibilities is no longer a prerogative of Deity. Pittenger concedes that process theology lives with the loss of all absolutes. "A processive conception . . . requires of us that we give up our human demand for absolutes of the totally unchanging sort and for the kind of perfection which allows no room for development and growth."[52] In a system of naturalistic pantheism God has been reduced to the factor of order and value within the evolutionary process.

The question arises why process theology bothers to postulate God at all. If Deity is merely the impersonal driving force latent in the universe, if science has shown that the world is self-sufficient and requires no supreme being to subsist, why introduce God into the system?[53] The answer must be that imbedded in the hearts of those who deny the God of the Bible is a compelling witness to his reality.

---

[52] Pittenger, *Holy Spirit*, 19.

[53] Cobb at bottom eliminates God altogether from his process system. Thus Cobb defines theology independently of any reference to God as a "coherent statement about matters of ultimate concern that recognizes that the perspective by which it is governed is received from a community of faith." *Christian Natural Theology*, 252.

Thus, even though God may be denied at the theoretical level, at the religious level he cannot be dispensed with altogether. John Hick writes in this vein, "The distinctive religious attitude today sees religion as an activity which has value independently of any alleged connection with a divine creator and redeemer."[54] Having created from naturalistic premises a relatively consistent non-theistic vision of the universe, process theology should lay all its cards out on the table and eliminate God entirely.

In its formulation of God, process theology displays striking parallels to several classical religious and theological systems. The Whiteheadian scheme first bears significant similarities to Buddhist thought. In its emphasis on immanence, its rejection of substance undergirding the flow of experience, and its vision of reality as totally interdependent and interrelated, process thought shares common ground with Buddhism. Whiteheadians, in fact, often project their task as that of reshaping the Christian faith in the light of the wisdom of Buddhism. Cobb and Griffin thus argue:

> While continuing to submit itself to creative transformation in its assimilation of new aspects of Western culture, Christianity needs to open itself to still more radical transformation through the Asian religions. The task is to be carried out individually with each of these great Ways, but the conversation with Buddhism is particularly urgent and fruitful.[55]

And again:

> The encounter with Buddhism can lead to a creative transformation of process theology that does not deny its insights but incorporates them in a larger whole. Perhaps it can adopt from Buddhism the art of meditation while transforming it into an instrument of a new form of Christianity.[56]

Process theology also evinces parallels to the thought of the prechristian Stoics. Stoicism, like dipolar theism, represents a pantheistic system which posits the essential oneness between parts of the universe conceived of as a network of interlocking causes. At the heart of Stoic thought was the logos, the law of nature and reason. The logos was envisioned as the divine power for change which pervades all reality. Both Stoicism and process theology thus construct their re-

---

[54]J. Hick, *Faith and Knowledge* (2nd ed.; Ithaca, NY: Cornell University, 1966) 162.

[55]J. Cobb and Griffin, *Process Theology*, 137.

[56]Ibid., 140.

spective systems about the inanimate logos—the power of creative transformation latent in the universe.

In the Christian era "process" theology was foreshadowed by the third-century movement known as Dynamic Monarchianism. The Monarchians argued that the doctrine of the Trinity, which differentiated the personhood of Father, Son, and Holy Spirit, compromised the unity of the Godhead. Like the Whiteheadian tradition, the Dynamic Monarchians affirmed that the logos, as an impersonal power (δύναμις) lacking substance, indwelt and energized the man Jesus who thus became the special instrument of the divine working. When the divine wisdom from above rested upon the man Jesus, only then did he become the Christ or the Son of God. The union between God and Jesus, actualized by the latter's will, was a mere moral union.

The Monarchian Trinity postulated that Father, Son, and Holy Spirit are not ontologically one. Rather, the Father is God who created all things, the Son the man energized by the logos, and the Spirit the grace which indwelt the apostles.[57] The early church rightly branded Paul of Samosata and other Adoptionists as heretics.

Process thought, in fact, follows a checkered course from Oriental religion, through the pantheism of the Greeks and Spinoza (who equated God with nature), through the immanental and evolutionary monism of Hegel, and finally through the experientialism of nineteenth-century romantic liberalism.

But process trinitarianism falters in its vision of a generally impersonal and becoming Deity which is undifferentiated from the universe. It is pantheistic in its insistence that reality is a manifestation of a single, impersonal entity defined as energy-event. Calvin remarked that "the idea that God is the soul of the world, though the most tolerable that philosophers have suggested, is absurd."[58] With the collapse of the primordial nature God is totally immanent, temporal, contingent, and relative. The God of process theology is shorn not only of personality, but also of aseity, eternity, infinity, omniscience, and omnipotence. The process Deity is not the causative agent of creation, nor the sovereign sustainer of the universe, nor the providential protector of human destiny. In short, the God of process theology is not the God of the Bible.

---

[57]See J. N. D. Kelly, *Early Christian Doctrines* (London: Adam and Charles Black, 1968) 118. Kelly further argues that Paul of Samosata "was prepared to use the officially accepted Trinitarian formula, but only as a veil to cover a theology which was nakedly unitarian." Ibid.

[58]Calvin, *Institutes*, I. xiv. 1.

The process explication of the Trinity falters on its erroneous interpretation of the logos. Ironically, it has slavishly followed pagan wisdom (Heraclitus, Plato, the Stoics) in defining the logos as the *impersonal* principle of order and actuality in the universe. The early Christian fathers borrowed the logos category from the Greek world. But they did so apologetically to correlate the biblical revelation with glimpses of truth granted to the Greek philosophers. But, both Scripture (John 1:1-4, 14) and the church fathers (Ignatius, Origen, Tertullian) regard the logos as a personal being who subsisted with God from eternity past prior to his disclosure in time. The logos, then, is the living, personal bridge spanning the chasm between God and man. Once the early Christians encountered Jesus Christ in the flesh and in the power of the Spirit they abandoned forever any notion that the logos was an impersonal principle or power.

Thus Jesus Christ is more than a man in whom the logos was functionally immanent. Jesus is more than a symbol of the God immeasurably sympathetic with the world (Hartshorne). He is more than the personalized instrument of God's Self-Expressive Activity (Pittenger). He is more than a homo sapiens raised up to be the instrument of the divine work (Robinson). Jesus is more than the active actuality of God displayed within the limits of a human life (Pailin). The presence of God in Christ cannot be restricted to immanental activity, but includes a unity of being as well as purpose and work (John 10:30; Col 1:19; 2:9). Jesus Christ represents the ontological union of God the Word and the Man from Nazareth. Scripture portrays Christ as the second person of the eternal Godhead who left the Father's presence to become man (Phil 2:6-8; 2 Cor 8:9). Jesus is not so much a "routing of occasions" as one routed from heaven by the Father's love to pursue an errand of saving mercy. The incarnation of the eternal Word cannot be diluted to the immanence of an impersonal force. Biblical theism, moreover, insists that God displayed himself in Jesus as he displayed himself in no other figure. There is a once-happenedness in God's manifestation in Jesus of Nazareth.[59]

Similarly, Scripture provides no ground for defining the Holy Spirit merely as the immanent manifestation of divine power which elicits a creaturely response. The Holy Spirit is a personal *hypostasis*, not merely a mode of the divine working (Matt 3:16; Acts 5:3, 4). The

---

[59]Gabriel Facre argues that the process explication of the relation between God and Jesus "is too static and conservative a view for this revolutionary event." See "Cobb's Christ in a Pluralistic Age," *Andover Newton Quarterly* 17 (Mar. 1977) 314.

biblical record attests the existence of a profoundly personal "I-Thou" relationship between the Spirit, Son, and Father (John 14:16, 17, 26). The Holy Spirit is more than the power of Self-Responsive Love, but a personal center of divine consciousness who loves.

Process theology, as we have seen, postulates a triunity of relational activity—a merely functional triunity—where Word and Spirit are two aspects or modes of the divine working. Scripture, on the other hand, postulates three personal centers of existence within the unity of the divine Being. The Father who is God, the Son who is God, and the Spirit who is God are together one divine Reality. Three personal centers of consciousness within the divine unity is both the biblical pattern (Matt 28:19; 1 Cor 12:4–6; 2 Cor 13:14) and the ecclesiastical pattern as reflected in the Old Roman and Nicene creeds.

Whiteheadians object that three persons cannot at the same time be one person, as three billiard balls cannot occupy one spot. The analogy and hence the objection prove invalid, for theism never affirms the contradiction that three persons are at the same time one person. The three personal centers of the Godhead consist of one essence, as the three billiard balls are of one substance, be it plastic, resin, or wood.

The Christian, however, embraces in faith the doctrine of the Trinity as a truth directly revealed by God. The Christian theist is not offended by whatever mystery exists in the classical formula, but rests on the noncontradictory data of revelation which receives ample confirmation from historical and experiential evidences. Thomas Watson, the Puritan, claims that:

> The Trinity is purely an object of faith. The plumbline of reason is too short to fathom the mystery; but where reason cannot wade, there faith must swim. . . . This sacred doctrine, though it be not against reason, yet is above reason.[60]

If the doctrine of the Trinity transcends discursive reason it is because of human finitude and the crippling effects of sin upon the mind. Man is epistemologically limited because he is hamartiologically infected.

Process theology, we may conclude, represents a potent force in contemporary philosophical theology. It involves a mysticism of the *élan vital*, which presently enjoys considerable popularity. We find no justification for scuttling the classical theism of Augustine, Anselm, and Calvin in favor of the revisionist system of Whitehead and com-

---

[60] *The Golden Treasury of Puritan Quotations* (Chicago: Moody, 1975) 297.

pany. In truth, recent evangelical theologians have and are making the kind of theological course corrections for which Pinnock in his essay in this volume pleads.[61]

We count it, then, a misfortune that many theological practitioners in our day flock to the fountains of process theology to drink of its waters. Those tempted to dip their cup in its stream would do well to heed the following caution: "The disadvantage of founding a theology upon relevance is that it may suddenly become irrelevant and die."[62]

---

[61]L. Berkhof, *Systematic Theology* (London: Banner of Truth, 1958) 41ff., 135ff. Geisler, "Process Theology," 267–81. See also, in the present volume, the essay of Gordon Lewis.

[62]K. Hamilton, *Revolt Against Heaven* (Grand Rapids: Eerdmans, 1965) 91.

3

The Need for a Scriptural, and Therefore a Neo-Classical Theism

Clark Pinnock

This paper was commissioned to explore some of the intellectual issues pertaining to classical Christian theism. It was my assignment to draw attention to certain inadequacies in classical theism and to indicate, if I could, the direction for overcoming them. It is my conviction that the form of theism received from great theologians like Augustine and Anselm is not completely faithful to Scripture and has adopted certain philosophical notions, Greek in their origin, and therefore does not stand beyond criticism from a biblically-oriented evangelical. When I call for a "neo-classical" theism, the reader is not to identify my view with process theism often called by that name, but simply to understand me to be appealing for an exposition of theism which would go *beyond* traditional theism and hence be fairly called "neo-classical" in an unprejudiced use of that term.* In fact I am *not* calling for process theism which in my opinion subverts biblical theism even more seriously than classical theism does, by allowing in its case modern monistic, philosophical ideas to mute the biblical witness. Nevertheless I do agree with much of the process critique of traditional theism and in that negative sense at least would express my admiration for it.[1]

---

*Editors' note: Pinnock thus uses "neo-classical" in a somewhat different sense than Demarest in chap. 2.

[1]David R. Griffin, for example, registers most telling criticisms in his book, *God, Power, and Evil* (Philadelphia: Westminster, 1976).

Before launching into the argument it is essential to define for the reader what is meant by "classical theism." It is that form of theistic belief which came to full flower in Augustine, according to which the deity, in addition to other perfections I will pass over, is taken to be *immutable* in the strong metaphysical sense, *timeless* in his eternity, and *impassible* in relation to the experience of any feelings. I limit myself to these three aspects of the classical model because they are of central importance and enable me to limit the scope of the paper.

THE CLASSICAL SYNTHESIS

Classical theism according to friend and foe alike was forged out of materials both biblical and philosophical. It is in fact a *synthesis* of revelational and rational elements. For that reason also it is open to criticism and correction from the side of evangelical theology which confesses the primacy of Scripture over philosophy. H. P. Owen, defender of the synthesis, writes: "So far as the Western world is concerned, theism has a double origin: the Bible and Greek philosophy."[2] Needless to say, critics of classical theism are quick to argue the same point. Brunner not only recognizes this to be the case, but contends that the resulting synthesis is a subversion of biblical faith.[3] He detects an abstract notion of God entering theology through the Fathers which is at odds with the biblical conception. Whether or not we agree with him, as I do, the fact that classical theism *is* a synthesis of the Bible and certain Greek ideas seems to me undeniable.

Let me refer now to the three perfections I listed in my earlier definition. In regard to the immutability of God, although the Scriptures plainly teach God's constancy and reliability in the moral and religious sphere, nowhere do they teach or imply immutability in the strong metaphysical sense which was adopted in the classical tradition. On the contrary there are innumerable texts in which God's responses and actions are described so as to convey real and dynamic change in him. The idea that God must be unchangeable in *every* conceivable sense is completely foreign to the Bible, while being axiomatic in Greek thought.[4] Pelikan traces the rise of this concept in early Christian theology, drawing attention especially to the difficulties which it

---

[2]H. P. Owen, *Concepts of Deity* (New York: Herder and Herder, 1971) 1.

[3]E. Brunner, *The Christian Doctrine of God* (Philadelphia: Westminster, 1950) 151–6.

[4]Cf. R. B. Edwards, "The Pagan Dogma of the Absolute Unchangeableness of God," *Religious Studies* 14 (September 1978) 305–13.

created for Christology.[5] Plato, not the apostles, taught that God was not subject to change from within or from without (*Republic,* II. 380–1).

Regarding timelessness, Augustine was the first thinker to propose in a systematic way that we should think of God as existing outside the temporal sequence altogether. He borrowed the idea, no doubt thinking it a good and useful one, from Platonic thought according to which God, if he were temporal in any way, would be *limited* on that account. Going beyond the Bible, which is satisfied to declare that God is everlasting, Augustine decided to consider him to be timeless, a negative notion deriving from Plato and defined later by Boethius, despite the fact, obvious to us, that such an idea presents no small threat to the Bible's depiction of God as an historical agent and actor.

The impassibility of God is an even clearer case of a category applied to God which is emphatically Greek and not biblical in origin. It is indeed, as Owen candidly admits, "the most questionable aspect of classical theism."[6] In each of these three cases we see an example of the synthesis which classical theism is, being the product of biblical revelation and Greek reasoning. It would therefore be quite wrong to speak as if biblical theism and classical theism were just the *same* thing, or, as if nonclassical forms of theism are automatically nonbiblical or subchristian. Classical theism is *not* a revealed model of deity beyond criticism and correction. It must stand under the light of Scripture equally along with competitive theories.

THE BASIC INADEQUACY

If it were true that classical theism borrowed from Greek sources only ideas which were compatible with scriptural theology there would be no problem. Measured by biblical revelation, Greek thought is right on some points and wrong on others, just as all human culture is. Unfortunately, some borrowing of Greek ideas foreign to Scripture and contradicted by it took place in the early period and quite serious tensions arose in each of the three categories I have selected for this paper.

Karl Barth was correct to substitute the term *constancy* for the term *immutability* in his superb treatment of the perfections of God,[7] be-

---

[5] J. Pelikan, *The Emergence of the Catholic Tradition* (Chicago: University of Chicago, 1971) 22, 52, 198, 229–31.

[6] Owen, *Concepts of Deity,* 24.

[7] K. Barth, *Church Dogmatics,* II. 1 (Edinburgh: T. & T. Clark, 1957) 491–522.

cause immutability in the strong Greek sense contradicts the Christian faith and is subevangelical. The fourth Gospel says that the Word *became* flesh in the incarnation, to mention only one example of many texts which indicate God's ability to change in his glorious freedom. How ironical for classical theism to claim that God is *unlimited, and deny that he is able to do the very things the Bible says that he can and does do! Changing is something God can* do, and more wonderfully it is something God *wills* to do for the sake of our salvation. We have to say that the Greek idea of utter unchangeableness in God is false and misleading when measured by the Scripture. Rahner is right: "If we face squarely and uncompromisingly the fact of the Incarnation which our faith in the fundamental dogma of Christianity testifies to, then we have to say plainly, God can *become* something."[8]

In response to these texts, classical theists will often declare them to be anthropomorphic and figurative speech, having no real application to how God is in himself. Scripture may *say* that God changes or repents, but they assure us it does not really *mean* that. But how then is it that they decide when the Scriptures are speaking literally and when figuratively? The criterion employed here is simply the Greek ideal of perfection. The meaning of Scripture is not then determined from within Scripture, but on the basis of a higher standard, the requirements of adopted philosophical assumptions. It is this criterion which tells them that Scripture is figurative when it ascribes change to God, and literal when a text appears to deny it. Belief in God's absolute unchangeability becomes the dogma by which Scripture is controlled and through which its teachings filtered.

As for timelessness, not only is it a platonic category, it is also one which seriously jeopardizes the reality of contingent and significant history and makes the central biblical symbol of God as personal agent very difficult to accept. It is not that we cannot think up some useful pastoral and philosophical implications stemming from the idea. The difficulty rather is that this extrabiblical notion (I see it nowhere in the Bible) casts up serious problems we would be better off without,[9] the most obvious of which is the way future contingent events are frozen into a timeless simultaneity and the way God's agency in the sphere of time is rendered so unnecessarily problematic. The negative notion of timelessness is just not rich enough to handle the requirements that future events be truly contingent, and not in name only, and that a temporal dimension be recognized within the life and being of God himself. The Bible speaks *temporally* of God, and the theologian or

---

[8]K. Rahner, *Foundations of Christian Faith* (New York: Seabury, 1978) 220.

[9]Nelson Pike has pointed out most of them. *God and Timelessness* (New York: Schocken Books, 1970).

philosopher has no right to declare such language improper or merely figurative. God's eternity according to the Bible refers to his everlasting existence without beginning and without end, but does not teach a simultaneity of past, present, and future in God all at once.

Impassibility, as we noted earlier, introduces the most serious distortion of all. For Owen to say that God cannot experience sorrow, sadness, or pain sounds incredible to the reader of the Bible. For Anselm to declare, "When Thou beholdest us in our wretchedness, we experience the effect of compassion but Thou dost not experience the feeling," our eyes blink in astonishment.[10] All our evangelical instincts cry out that it is not so. Imagine declaring that God cannot do precisely what the Bible boldly declares he can and does do! He hears the cry of his suffering people, feels their anguish along with them, and is deeply concerned (cf. Exod 2:23–25). His ability to suffer and his willingness to do so, far from being a difficulty to explain, is the glory of the gospel. As Moltmann argues with such force, the cross compels us to reject a metaphysics that does not permit God to suffer.[11] I believe he is right. The notion of impassibility is a singularly inappropriate notion to be applied to the God who reveals himself in the Bible.

Where then does the difficulty lie? It is a *doctrinal problem*. The classical synthesis does not square with the requirements of biblical revelation. There is a logic at work in the borrowed Greek notions that obscures the gospel. The problem arises from the attempt to interpret a message which is historical and personal at its core by means of metaphysical categories which are ahistorical and impersonal at their core. It cannot work because there is a basic incompatibility operating. Scripture on the one hand presents a God who is a personal agent relating dynamically to history, whereas Greek philosophy bequeaths an image of deity which is strictly changeless, locked into a timeless present, and incapable of sharing the sufferings of his creatures. The *dynamic* ontology of the Bible clashes inevitably with the *static* ontology of the Greek thinkers, so that when the two visions of reality are brought together, biblical teaching becomes warped and twisted and the resultant synthesis doctrinally objectionable.

THE NEEDED CORRECTIVE

If I am right to suppose that classical theism is a synthesis, and a synthesis not altogether wise, let me conclude by indicating the correc-

---

[10]Cf. C. Hartshorne and W. L. Reese, *Philosophers Speak of God* (Chicago: University of Chicago, 1953) 99.

[11]J. Moltmann, *The Crucified God* (London: SCM, 1974) 267–78.

tive that is needed from an evangelical standpoint. We must allow revelational norms to exercise *control* over any and all philosophical influences, and allow Scripture to create its own impression on us unhindered by outside assumptions. If, for example, Scripture uses the language not only of "being" but also of "becoming" as it does in reference to God's nature, we will gladly accept it. It is not as if we had some *more* authoritative metaphysical intuition than Scripture which declares the language of *being* acceptable and the language of *becoming* unacceptable. That would be to subject Scripture to the primacy of philosophy, and to treat philosophy as a second revelational light. God gives himself to be known in the Bible as One who becomes flesh in Christ despite Greek immutability, who suffers with us and for us despite Greek impassibility, and who enters easily into history despite platonic timelessness. He is *free* and at liberty to do all these things, and we acclaim this joyfully. We are not disappointed that he falls short of our philosophical expectations, but believe he is capable of being and doing what the Bible describes him doing and being, even things which according to Greek thought he is incapable of doing and being. It is simply a question of recognizing the "sola scriptura" principle in the realm of theism.[12]

There is a lesson to be learned from this discussion about the relation of Scripture and philosophy. Philosophical ideas have to be rigorously subordinated to scriptural revelation or else they will tend to take over in theology. The fact that this has occurred at least to some extent in Augustine, who was a biblical conservative if there ever was one, should give us pause. Obviously it is not only in liberal theology where this occurs, but among the orthodox as well. Philosophical borrowings can easily come to rival scriptural teachings and become idols that compete with God's self-disclosure. We are hearing this warning from Barth, Thielicke, Hamilton, Bloesch, and others and we ought to heed it.

This does *not* mean that philosophical tools and resources have no positive value or uses. It may well be that we shall be helped in our formulation of a neo-classical theism by modern philosophical ideas which are ripe for theological expropriation. But *if we do make use of them,* let us exercise the greatest of care not to twist the Scriptures on their behalf. Our motto ought to be, Let God be God!

---

[12]Barth is to be congratulated for understanding this most clearly and expressing it most adequately. See C. E. Gunton, *Becoming and Being. The Doctrine of God in Charles Hartshorne and Karl Barth* (Oxford: Oxford University, 1978).

Christology from Above and Christology from Below: A Study of Contrasting Methodologies

Millard J. Erickson

In the study of any area of theology, the question of methodology logically precedes and determines that of theological content. In this paper we will primarily focus upon the issue of methodology in the study of Christology.

Traditionally, the major issue in Christology was the relationship between the two natures of Christ—his humanity and his divinity— how these two could be combined in one person. It was assumed that the Scripture taught both, and the problem was simply to understand how these could co-exist. With the rise of the historical method and its application to the study of the Bible, however, this problem came to be supplanted by the problem of the two histories. Stemming from Martin Kähler's famous essay of 1892, a distinction was drawn between *Historie* and *Geschichte*.[1] The former is the mere facticity of what has occurred. The latter is significant history—the actual effect upon believers of the events of history. The former, then, is found in the chronicled history. The latter is found in the faith of the apostles, as witnessed to especially in their preaching. Consequently, two types of Christological methodologies have arisen, each concentrating upon one of these types of histories. "Christology from above" constructs its understanding of Jesus Christ primarily from the faith of the church, as found in the epistles and the sermons in the book of Acts. "Christ-

---

[1]M. Kähler, *The So-called Historical Jesus and the Historic, Biblical Christ.* (Philadelphia: Fortress, 1964).

ology from below," on the other hand, concentrates upon the historical Jesus and attempts to reconstruct the picture of the type of person the earthly Jesus was—what he actually said and did. We will examine each of these in turn, then briefly evaluate each before suggesting a third possibility.

CHRISTOLOGY FROM ABOVE

The approach of a Christology from above can only be understood correctly when seen as a reaction against the "search for the historical Jesus." In the nineteenth century, a whole series of essays was written, each attempting to get at just who and what the man Jesus was. Renan, Strauss, Harnack—these are but a few of those who were at work in this enterprise. For the most part, these searches were attempts to get back to the real Jesus, who had somehow been lost to the church. Basically, the belief was that underneath the layers of historical accretion in the Gospels was a simple Jesus, who taught about the kingdom of God, the fatherhood of God, the infinite value of the human soul, and the brotherhood of all men. On to this simple and basically human Jesus, whose message pointed to the Father and not to himself, Paul added a theologized belief. Thus Jesus came to be known as the Son of God, and this became reflected in the Gospels, which themselves are considerably later than the writings of Paul.

Theologians like Karl Barth, Emil Brunner, and Rudolf Bultmann reacted against this type of teaching for several reasons. The first was the subjectivity that rather obviously was present in these supposedly objective reconstructions of who Jesus was, what he was like, what he said and did. This was dramatically expressed in George Tyrrell's famous comment on Harnack's view of Jesus:

> The Christ that Harnack sees, looking back through nineteen centuries of Catholic darkness, is only the reflection of a Liberal Protestant face, seen at the bottom of a deep well.[2]

There was a growing suspicion that the supposed biographers of Jesus were actually creating him in their own image. Carl Braaten likens them to plastic surgeons or artists and observes: "There was, in most cases, unmistakable resemblance between their portrayal of the religion of Jesus and their own personal religious stance."[3]

---

[2]G. Tyrrell, *Christianity at the Cross-roads* (London: Longmans, Green and Co., 1918) 44.

[3]C. Braaten, *New Directions in Theology Today,* II; *History and Hermeneutics* (Philadelphia: Westminster, 1966) 55.

A second reason for abandoning the search for the historical Jesus was the apprehension that these searchers were in the process inevitably losing a vital part of the traditional orthodox belief about Jesus Christ. There seemed to be an implicit presupposition in this method excluding the deity of Christ. Albert Schweitzer had showed in his *Quest of the Historical Jesus* that the attempt to construct a picture of a simple, human, noneschatological Jesus was a failure. The Jesus who really emerged from an examination of the Gospels was a thoroughly eschatological person, who, however, in Schweitzer's estimation, was of course mistaken.[4] Similarly, those elements in the Gospels which seemed to suggest that Jesus thought of himself as deity, were treated as reflections of later theologizing. Increasingly, however, it became apparent that the conclusion was already assumed and was interpreting the data in such a way as to support the conclusion. In other words, circular reasoning was being employed.

Finally, there was a growing skepticism regarding the utility of the historical method. In particular, the rise of form criticism called into question the likelihood of getting behind the written documents on which the Gospels were based and the oral traditions which in turn underlay them to determine the nature of the real Jesus. Bultmann, for example, said that "we can now know almost nothing concerning the life and personality of Jesus."[5] In some forms, the skepticism was less radical. Thus, when Emil Brunner said, "Even the bare fact of the existence of Christ as an historical person is not assured,"[6] he was only pointing up the fact that the historical method can only give a relatively certain conclusion: "The question is only solved within the limits of historical evidence; this means, however, that the solution is not absolute."[7]

Christology from above was the basic strategy and orientation of the theology of the earliest centuries of the church. It also was, to a large extent, the Christology of orthodoxy during the precritical era when Scripture citations could be made from any portion of the Bible rather indiscriminately. In the twentieth century, it has been especially associated with the Christology of Karl Barth, Rudolf Bultmann, and of Emil Brunner in his early book, *The Mediator*. (His *Christian Doctrine of Redemption* represents a different approach.) We may take

---

[4]A. Schweitzer, *The Quest of the Historical Jesus: A Critical Study of its Progress from Reimarus to Wrede* (London: Black, 1954).

[5]R. Bultmann, *Jesus and the Word* (New York: Charles Scribner's Sons, 1958) 8.

[6]E. Brunner, *The Mediator* (London: Lutterworth, 1934) 187.

[7]Ibid.

Brunner's treatment in *The Mediator* as an example. Let us note several key features of theology from above, as illustrated in this writing.

1. The basis of the understanding of Christ is not the historical Jesus. It is much more to be found in the kerygma, the account of the church's proclamation regarding the Christ. Brunner says:

> This makes it clear why we are bound to oppose the view that the Christian faith springs out of historical observation, out of the historical picture of Jesus of Nazareth. Christendom itself has always known otherwise. Christian faith springs only out of the witness to Christ of the preached message and the written word of the Scriptures. The historical picture is indeed included in the latter (how this is treated will come up again later); but this picture itself is not the basis of knowledge.[8]

2. In constructing a Christology, there is a marked preference for the writings of Paul and the fourth Gospel over the synoptic Gospels. The former contain more explicitly theological interpretations, versus the more matter-of-fact reporting of actions and teachings of Jesus in the synoptics. This is closely tied to the first principle above.

> If once the conviction is regained that the Christian faith does not arise out of the picture of the historical Jesus, but out of the testimony to Christ as such—this includes the witness of the prophets as well as that of the Apostles—and that it is based upon this testimony, then inevitably the preference for the Synoptic Gospels and for the actual words of Jesus, which was the usual position of the last generation, will disappear.[9]

3. Faith in the Christ does not take its basis and legitimation from rational proof. It cannot be scientifically proven. The content believed lies outside the sphere of natural or historical reason and consequently cannot be conclusively proven. While historical reason may serve to remove the obstacles to belief in the deity of Jesus Christ, for example, it cannot succeed in establishing it. "Jesus taught a group of disciples beside the sea" may be probable by the techniques of historical research; "Jesus is the second person of the Trinity" is not. One accepts historical evidence by being rationally persuaded. He accepts proclamation by belief.

Brunner draws a distinction which is significant for understanding the sense in which, for him, Christology is historical and the sense in which it is not. The distinction is between the "Christ *in* the flesh" and the "Christ *after* the flesh." By "Christ in the flesh" he means that

---

[8]Ibid., 158.
[9]Ibid., 172.

Christ became incarnate, that the Word became flesh, penetrated history. The "Christ after the flesh" is the Christ known by the historiographer, the chronicler, with his methods of historical research. To know "Christ in the flesh" is to know something more than the "Christ after the flesh."

> The believer also knows Christ only as the One who has come in the flesh, as Him of whom the chronicler and the humanist historian must have something to say. But he knows this "Christ in the flesh" in a way of which they can know nothing; he knows Him therefore as someone quite different, and this is what matters. For the knowledge of others—of the chronicler and of the humanist historian—is not yet knowledge of Christ, of the "Word made flesh," but is itself "after the flesh."[10]

Brunner is careful to insist upon the Christ in the flesh. Although faith never arises out of the observation of facts, but out of the Word of God, the fact that this Word has come "into the flesh" means that it is connected with observation. While faith arises out of the witness of the church, that witness always includes the picture of Jesus.

CHRISTOLOGY FROM BELOW

With the publication of Bultmann's *Jesus and the Word*, Christology from above reached its apparent zenith. Here in effect was a statement that the faith in the kerygmatic Christ could not with certainty be established as connected with the actual earthly life of Jesus of Nazareth but that this did not really matter. The initial and increasing stream of negative reaction to Bultmann grew into an enunciation of positive methodology. Probably the most significant of these early reactions was Ernst Käsemann's "The Problem of the Historical Jesus," published in 1954.[11] Käsemann affirmed the necessity and hoped for the possibility of building belief in Jesus upon a historical search for who he was and what he did. While this was not merely a resumption of the nineteenth-century search, it deserved the title "the *new* search for the historical Jesus."

It might be said that the nineteenth-century searches scarcely were real Christologies. They perhaps better deserved to be called "Jesusologies." The Jesus who emerged from those studies was often a

---

[10]Ibid., 158.

[11]E. Käsemann, "The Problem of the Historical Jesus," *Essays on New Testament Themes* (London: SCM, 1964) 15-47.

human being and little more. It seemed to some in the "new quest" that this was a result of anti-supernatural biases within the historical method itself; in other words, of a methodological inadequacy. In some of the new quests for the historical Jesus, there is a possibility of a genuine Christology: of arriving at belief in a genuine and complete deity of Jesus Christ at the end, not the beginning, of the historical investigation.

The most instructive examples for us of a contemporary "Christology from below" is undoubtedly that of Wolfhart Pannenberg. In *Jesus—God and Man*[12] Pannenberg has done a thoroughly Christological treatment, as indicated by the title. He has carefully scrutinized and criticized the presuppositions of Christological methodology in order to assure a genuinely open method.

Pannenberg, while recognizing certain benefits in the approach of "Christology from above," indicates three basic reasons why he cannot employ this method.

1. It presupposes the divinity of Jesus. The task of Christology, however, is to offer rational support for such a confession, for it is this which is disputed in the world today.[13]

2. It tends to neglect the real significance inherent in the distinctive features of Jesus of Nazareth as a real historical man. In particular, his relationship to the Judaism of his day, as essential to understanding his life and message, becomes relatively unimportant in this approach.[14]

3. Strictly speaking, a Christology from above would only be possible from the position of God himself. This, however, is not possible for us. We are limited, earthbound human beings, and we must begin and conduct inquiry from that perspective.[15]

In distinction from the approach "from above," Pannenberg presents a positive investigation by which he hopes to construct a full Christology, including the deity, from the life of the man Jesus of Nazareth.

The positive features of Pannenberg's view are instructive for seeing the basic contour of Christology from below as contrasted with the Christology from above.

1. Historical inquiry behind the kerygma of the NT is both possible and theologically necessary. Form criticism has demonstrated that an exact chronological sequence of Jesus' life cannot be constructed. It is

---

[12]W. Pannenberg, *Jesus—God and Man* (Philadelphia: Westminster, 1968).
[13]Ibid., 34.
[14]Ibid., 34–35.
[15]Ibid., 35.

nonetheless possible to get back to the major contour of Jesus himself from the witness of the apostles. This knowledge of Jesus is necessary. If we rest our faith upon the kerygma alone, rather than the historical facts of Jesus' life, we cannot escape the suspicion and the fear that our faith is based upon that which is itself a matter of faith. To put it differently: Pannenberg would perhaps say, we may find ourselves believing, not in Jesus, but in Luke, Matthew, Paul, or someone else. Further, we can see the unity binding together the NT witnesses. The witnesses themselves give us only diversity and even antithesis. To find a unity, we must penetrate behind these varied witnesses to discern the one Jesus to whom they all refer.[16]

In the judgment of Pannenberg, it is extremely important to bring open presuppositions to the historical investigation. The problem with many nineteenth-century searches and with Bultmann's demythologizing lay in certain rather narrow conceptions of what was historically possible and what was not. Thus, the resurrection of Jesus was often excluded from belief from the very beginning of the process. Rather, it must be possible for our horizon of the present to overlap the horizon of biblical times. It is only when naturalistic or anti-supernaturalistic presuppositions are laid aside that a Christology from below can be properly constructed.[17]

2. History is unitary, not dualistic. The events involved in the life, teachings, and ministry of Jesus, including his death and resurrection, are not a unique, special type of history, distinct from history in general. There is no special realm of redemptive or sacred history, be that *Geschichte, Urgeschichte, Heilsgeschichte,* or whatever. The history of the Christ is one with the rest of world history. It cannot be separated or isolated from it. Consequently, it does not have to be known in a different way or by a different method or faculty from that used for knowing ordinary history. The same historical method used in investigating the Napoleonic wars is to be applied to the inquiry of Christology.[18]

3. It is obvious that a Christology from below can give us a fully human Jesus. Can it, however, establish the deity of Jesus? The most common avenue to establishing from below Jesus' unity with God is through his claim to authority in his proclamation and work. There is a remarkable concurrence upon this point by a large number of theologians. Werner Elert maintains that Jesus claimed to be *the* Son

---

[16]Ibid., 23-25.

[17]Ibid.

[18]W. Pannenberg, "Redemptive Event and History," *Essays on Old Testament Hermeneutics* (Atlanta: John Knox, 1964) 314-15.

of God. When he spoke of his Father, he never included the disciples. His address to them was always in terms of "your Father."[19] Similarly, Paul Althaus says that the authority claimed by Jesus presupposes nearness to God that no other man has. "What Jesus does is blasphemy unless it comes from special authority. He claims this authority for himself."[20] In their own ways, Friedrich Gogarten, Hermann Diem, Günther Bornkamm, and Hans Conzelmann all make basically the same effort. Pannenberg comments: "The basic agreement is striking. Dogmatics seems in this case to have preceded historical research."[21]

Pannenberg believes, however, that this effort to demonstrate Jesus' divinity through his claim to authority must inevitably fail. The reason for this is that Jesus' pre-Easter claim to authority is related to the future verification of his message which will take place through the future judgment. "Rather," he says, "everything depends upon the connection between Jesus' claim and its confirmation by God."[22]

This confirmation is to be found in the resurrection of Jesus. Pannenberg believes that the resurrection is a historical fact and as such can be proved, just like any other historical fact. He examines separately the evidences stemming from the appearances of the resurrected Lord and the empty tomb. The Gospel appearance accounts are so strongly legendary in character that one can scarcely find in them a historical kernel of their own. The historical question must be posed entirely in terms of Paul's report in 1 Corinthians 15:1-11. He concludes:

> Thus the resurrection of Jesus would be designated as a historical event in this sense: If the emergence of primitive Christianity, which, apart from other traditions, is also traced back by Paul to appearances of the resurrected Jesus, can be understood in spite of all critical examination of the tradition only if one examines it in the light of the eschatological hope for a resurrection from the dead, then that which is so designated is a historical event, even if we do not know anything more particular about it.[23]

---

[19]W. Elert, *Der Christliche Glaube: Grundlinien der lutherischen Dogmatik*, 3rd ed. (Hamburg: Furche, 1956) 303.

[20]P. Althaus, *Die Christliche Wahrheit*, 6th ed. (Gutersloh: C. Bertelsmann, 1962) 430.

[21]Pannenberg, *Jesus—God and Man*, 257.

[22]Ibid., 66.

[23]Ibid., 98.

Pannenberg similarly finds validity to the empty tomb accounts. He concludes that if this tradition and the appearance tradition came into existence independently of one another, then,

> by their mutually complementing each other they let the assertion of the reality of Jesus' resurrection, in the sense explained above, appear as historically very probable, and that always means in historical inquiry that it is to be presupposed until contrary evidence appears.[24]

If this were all there was to the resurrection events, however, then all we would have would be mere brute facts. The question of the meaning or interpretation of the fact would be an open one subject to possible debate and perhaps would be merely a matter of faith. Given the fact of the resurrection, there might be many possible meanings attached to it. From Pannenberg's perspective, however, this is not so. Given its place within the history of traditions and the cultural expectations, the resurrection carried with it a definite meaning. The event cannot be evaluated or understood in isolation from the traditions and expectations of the Jews. The idea of this resurrection occurring apart from the will and activity of God would be unthinkable for a Jew. This would mean that God had given his approval to the claims of Jesus and that these claims, which would be blasphemous unless Jesus really were the Son of Man, were true. Thus, not only the historical fact of mere occurrence, but also the theological truth of the deity, has been established.[25]

EVALUATION

Each of these two types of Christology has its own distinctive strengths and weaknesses, which by now have become rather well known. In some cases, the statement of one position has also constituted a criticism of the other approach.

Christology from above has the strength of recognizing that the real aim and value of the incarnation was the effect which the life of Jesus had upon those who believed in him. Thus, their testimony comes from those who most intimately knew him and were perhaps in the best position to describe him to others. Further, this approach has been committed to a genuine supernaturalism, something which has

---

[24]Ibid., 105.
[25]Ibid., 67–68.

not always been true of Christologies from below. It left open the possibility of a divine, miracle-working Jesus.

The basic problem for a Christology from above, however, is the question of the reality of the belief. Is the Christ of faith really the same person as the Jesus who walked the paths of Galilee and Judea? Is the commitment to the kerygmatic Christ based upon what really is, or is it mere unfounded faith? The problem of subjectivity in one form or another always plagues this type of Christology. If the Christ we know is the one who encountered the apostles and whom we encounter in our own experience today, how can we be sure we are knowing Jesus as he really is and not merely our own feelings? A final problem refers to the content of this faith. While it is all well to say we take this by faith, the problem is the determination of what it is we are taking by faith. Without an empirical referent, the Christ of faith is somewhat unreal and vague.

Christology from below, on the other hand, blunts the charge that at best Christian theology (and specifically the teachings about the person of Jesus) is based upon faith and at worst it may be completely vacuous. It has attempted to preserve subjectivity without subjectivism. Recognizing that there needs to be subjective involvement (or commitment) by every believer, it has attempted to avoid this being filtered through the subjectivity of another group of believers, the first disciples.

There is one persistent problem which attaches to Christologies from below, however. Especially in the form in which Pannenberg has enunciated it, Christology from below depends for its success upon establishing its historical contentions with objective certainty. This, however, proves difficult to do. If the facts of Christology are matters of genuinely objective history, then it ought to be possible to demonstrate the divinity of Jesus to any honest objective inquirer. In practice, however, this does not happen. Some who examine the evidences remain quite unconvinced. Paul Althaus has particularly criticized Pannenberg's unitary view of history, maintaining that faith here becomes a function of reason.[26] Pannenberg has responded by contending that faith is indeed a gift of the Spirit, not a product of reason. Nonetheless, the knowledge of the historical revelation is logically prior to faith, although not psychologically prior. Reason in its essential structure is sufficient to grasp God's revelation and recognize its truth. Man's reason, however, has fallen into an unnatural state and

---

[26]P. Althaus, "Offenbarung als Geschichte und Glaube: Bemerkungen zu Wolfhart Pannenbergs Begriff der Offenbarung," *TLZ* 87 (1962) 321–30.

needs to be restored. It is not a case of being supernaturalized but of being naturalized, through the aid of the kerygma and the Spirit.[27] The distinction, however, scarcely seems really helpful. Regardless of whether this is a case of needing to be supernaturalized or merely truly naturalized, the same specter of subjectivity, which this theology attempts to avoid at all costs, still seems to haunt this view. It seems as if historical reason, although logically prior to faith, is not psychologically prior. Although the Spirit employs the historical evidences to create faith, there is still the problem of whether this faith is veridical. May not someone else, on the basis of the same evidences, come to a different conclusion? Are we not again, at least to a small extent, driven back to the "Christ of faith" in the attempt to arrive at the "Jesus of history"? The real point of Christology from below has been yielded when one begins to appeal to such concepts as unnaturalized reason. Although the gap between objective historical evidences and the conclusions of faith has been narrowed a bit, it is still there.

AN ALTERNATIVE SUGGESTION

We have seen that each of these two seemingly mutually exclusive positions has certain strengths and weaknesses. Is there some way to unite Christology from above and Christology from below in such a way as to preserve the best elements of both while minimizing the problems of each? Can the two histories, the kerygmatic Christ and the historical Jesus, faith and reason, be held together? The evangelical's concern to retain both stems in part from the evangelical understanding of history. According to this view, revelation is both the historical events and the interpretation of them. These are two complementary and harmonious means by which God manifests himself. Both are therefore sources of knowledge of him. I would like to suggest a conceptual analysis and model which I think may enlighten the issue.

Since the Jesus of history is approached through historical reason and the kerygmatic Christ is seized by faith, it appears to me that we are here dealing with a case of the classic faith-reason issue. Whereas the traditional form of this was the relationship between faith and philosophical reason, here it is faith and historical reason that are involved. In each case, the question is the utility and value of reason

---

[27]Wolfhart Pannenberg, "Einsicht und Glaube: Antwort an Paul Althaus," *TLZ* 88 (1963) 81–92.

for grounding faith. In the philosophical realm there were three basic positions regarding the relative role of these two; similarly, the three options can be found here.

The Christology from above approach is basically fideistic. Particularly in the form expounded by Brunner and other existentialist theologians, it draws heavily upon the thought of Sören Kierkegaard. On this basis, the knowledge of the deity is not grounded in any historically provable knowledge of the earthly life of Jesus. It is a faith based upon the faith of the apostles as enunciated in the kerygma.

Similarly, Christology from below is primarily Thomistic. It attempts to demonstrate the supernatural character of Christ from historical evidences. Hence, this aspect of the person of Christ need not be presupposed. It is the conclusion of the process, not the starting point. The appeal is to historical reason, not to faith or authority. As faith predominates in the former model, reason does here.

There is also a third model which I believe can be applied here, namely, the Augustinian. In that model, faith precedes but does not remain permanently independent of reason. Faith provides the perspective or starting point from which reason may function. It enables one to understand what he could not otherwise.

When applied to the issue before us, it would mean beginning with the kerygma, the belief and preaching of the church about Christ. This belief, however, would serve as a hypothesis, which would be used to interpret and integrate the data supplied by inquiry into the historical Jesus. On this basis, the interpretation of or faith in the kerygmatic Christ which the church had would enable us to make better sense of these historical phenomena than would any other hypothesis. Thus, it is not the Christology from below, which without the kerygma would lead us to conundrums in attempting to understand the "mystery of Jesus," as theologians often referred to it in the nineteenth century. Similarly, it is not an unsupported Christology from above, constructed without reference to the earthly life of Jesus of Nazareth, but rather tested and supported and rendered cogent by the historically ascertainable facts of who and what Jesus was and the claims he made.

This would mean following neither faith alone nor historical reason alone, but both together, in an intertwined, mutually dependent, simultaneously progressing fashion. Increased familiarity with the kerygmatic Christ would enable us to understand and integrate more of the data of historical research. Similarly, a greater understanding of the Jesus of history will increasingly support the cogency of the apostles' interpretation of the Christ of faith.

There is biblical basis for this contention. Some of those who during

Jesus' earthly life knew his words and deeds very well did not arrive at a very accurate knowledge of him thereby. So, for example, the Pharisees observed Jesus' miraculous healings which were done by the power of the Holy Spirit (Matt 12:22–32; Mark 3:20–30; Luke 11:14–23). Although they certainly were familiar with the Jewish traditions and presumably had observed Jesus for quite some time, their appraisal was, "He casts out demons by the power of Beelzebub." Somehow they had failed to draw the right conclusion, although they possessed adequate knowledge of the facts. Even those closest to him failed to "know him" fully. Judas betrayed him. The other disciples failed to realize the significance of his crucifixion and even his resurrection. The religious authorities obviously knew the facts of the empty tomb but did not correctly interpret them.

Positively, there are indications that where a believer came to a correct perception of Jesus, it was on the basis of something more than merely natural perception. Thus, when Jesus, after hearing the apostles' recital of men's opinions about him, asked, "But who do you say that I am?" Peter replied, "You are the Christ, the Son of the living God" (Matt 16:16). Jesus' comment was: "Flesh and blood has not revealed this to you, but my Father who is in heaven" (v. 17). While we might debate at length over the exact meaning of "flesh and blood," it does appear that Jesus was contrasting some sort of direct revelation from the Father with the merely human sources, such as the opinions of others.

Another case in point, proceeding from the other side of the dialectic, is John the Baptist. In prison he began to wonder about the reality of the kerygmatic Christ. His question was: "Are you he who is to come, or shall we look for another?" (Luke 7:19). Jesus' answer was to point out the concrete historical deeds which he was doing: "The blind receive their sight, the lame walk, lepers are cleansed, and the deaf hear, the dead are raised up, the poor have the good news preached to them" (22). The historical Jesus was the confirmation of the Christ of faith.

On this model the two factors will be held in conjunction: neither the Jesus of history alone, nor the Christ of faith alone, but the kerygmatic Christ of faith as the key that unlocks the historical Jesus, and the facts of Jesus' life as supporting the message regarding the Son of God. Faith in the Christ will lead us to understanding of the Jesus of history.

5

Why Has God Incarnate Suddenly Become Mythical?

John Warwick Montgomery

Christianity has been about for quite some time now, and during its history of almost two millennia it has consistently proclaimed, in the superb phraseology of the Nicene Creed, that its Lord Jesus Christ is

> the only-begotten Son of God, begotten of his Father before all worlds, God of God, Light of Light, very God of very God, begotten, not made, being of one substance with the Father; by whom all things were made; who for us men and for our salvation came down from heaven, and was incarnate by the Holy Ghost of the Virgin Mary, and was made man; and was crucified also for us under Pontius Pilate; he suffered and was buried, and the third day he rose again according to the Scriptures; and ascended into heaven, and sitteth on the right hand of the Father; and he shall come again with glory to judge both the quick and the dead: whose kingdom shall have no end.

This confession expresses what C. S. Lewis felicitously termed "mere Christianity": that which all Christians everywhere have believed. The Eastern Orthodox, Roman Catholic, and Protestant branches of Christendom, whatever their differences, have remained united on the common teaching of the ecumenical creeds (Apostles', Nicene, and Athanasian) that for man's salvation God became incarnate in Jesus Christ. This universal confession has endeavored to mirror faithfully the testimony of those who were closest to Christ Himself:

> We have not followed cunningly devised fables [Gk., *mythoi*] when we made known unto you the power and coming of our Lord Jesus Christ, but were eyewitnesses of His majesty (II Peter 1:16).

Remarkably, however, 1977 saw the publication of an influential volume by a team of seven British theologians, one of them the chairman of the Church of England's Doctrinal Commission, expressly arguing, contra the apostolic witness, that God's incarnation in Christ is mythical. Indeed, *The Myth of God Incarnate*,[1] edited by John Hick, takes a position from within the church which differs in no material respect from that of such contemporary secular detractors of incarnational Christianity as historian Hugh Trevor-Roper.[2]

Why, we might well ask, has this sudden onslaught against incarnational Christology come about? One might expect that a radical denial of the two-millennia-old central teaching of the church militant would require at very least the discovery of new and better documentation concerning Jesus—documentation that would show the fallaciousness of the eyewitness portrait that has been the church's heritage. However, no such historical discovery preceded the advent of John Hick's book. Is the explanation simply cultural, the logical consequence of the death-of-God theologies of the sixties and the secular Christianity of the seventies, and these in turn the inevitable product of the humanistic climate of opinion of our time?[3] Occasionally, the contributors to *The Myth of God Incarnate* seem to attribute their denials of the incarnation to such factors, as in the following (typically Bultmannian) passage:

> The Christians of the early church lived in a world in which supernatural causation was accepted without question, and divine or spiritual visitants were not unexpected. Such assumptions, however, have be-

---

[1] *The Myth of God Incarnate*, ed. John Hick (Philadelphia: Westminster Press, 1977). Westminster Press is an official "agency of the United Presbyterian Church that is charged with promoting the cause of Christ through books" (*Christianity Today*, Sept. 23, 1977, p. 30); in 1966 Westminster published Thomas Altizer's *The Gospel of Christian Atheism*. The English edition of *The Myth of God Incarnate* was issued by SCM Press (the publishing house of the Student Christian Movement in Great Britain).

[2] See, for example, Hugh Trevor-Roper, "The Creation of Christ," *Intellectual Digest*, Nov., 1971, pp. 14–16 (based upon an earlier article by the author in *The Spectator*).

[3] Cf. my "Parable of the Engineers," illustrating the self-destruction of contemporary mainline theology: Montgomery, *The Suicide of Christian Theology* (Minneapolis: Bethany Fellowship, 1970), pp. 25ff. To be sure, from an historical standpoint, *The Myth of God Incarnate* stands in the tradition of radical Anglican "exploratory" volumes, beginning with *Essays and Reviews* (1860), and continuing through *Lux Mundi* (1889), *Foundations* (1912), *Essays Catholic and Critical* (1926), to *Soundings*, edited by Alec Vidler (1962).

come foreign to our situation. In the Western world, both popular culture and the culture of the intelligentsia has come to be dominated by the human and natural sciences to such an extent that supernatural causation or intervention in the affairs of this world has become, for the majority of people, simply incredible.[4]

But such an explanation—though it might have seemed adequate in the Newtonian-Humean eighteenth century, or in the technological-evolutionary-progressivistic nineteenth century—hardly suffices today. We live in an open, relativistic, Einsteinian age, whose cosmological options include antimatter, black holes, and time flips (to say nothing of close encounters of the third kind). This decade has witnessed a tremendous revival of interest in parapsychology and the occult; and not merely a willingness but a veritable passion to believe in the supernatural has displayed itself in both healthy forms (the current evangelical revival) and its very opposite (Jim Jones' Guyana cult). Our epoch is simultaneously characterized by anti-supernaturalism *and* the quest for Immanuel (God with us); the question before us is why the authors of *The Myth of God Incarnate* should have opted for the one and ignored the other.

THE INCARNATION LOSES TO DOCUMENTARY CRITICISM

The decisive factor that leads John Hick and his associates to reject historic incarnational theology is their willingness to accept the full implications of modern New Testament criticism. Historical-critical method treats the New Testament documents as incapable of yielding a reliable, objective portrait of Christ; since (in this view) the biblical picture of Jesus is essentially a product of the faith-conceptions of the early church, the modern Christian—though he has heretofore hesitated at such a radical but consistent step—has every right to develop his own revised Christology in accord with his personal needs. A humanistic, anthropocentric critical method applied to the New Testament now reveals a humanistic, anthropocentric Jesus.

The following catena of typical passages from *The Myth of God Incarnate* will show how form criticism in its twin varieties, *Redaktionsgeschichte* and *Traditionsgeschichte*, underlies the book's fundamental theme, namely, that the incarnation must be regarded not as history but as myth.

---

[4]*The Myth of God Incarnate*, p. 31 (essay by Frances Young).

There is not one christology in the New Testament, there are many. By now it has almost become common knowledge that if you look at the New Testament writings from any point nearer than a distant mountain, you can distinguish a number of different pictures of Christ. In fact you will find that each writer has his own and you may even decide that one of them, Paul, shifted his viewpoint within the writings which expose his mind to us.[5]

If we start from where we are, as Christians of our own day, we begin amidst the confusion and uncertainty which assail us when we try to speak about Jesus, the historical individual who lived in Galilee in the first third of the first century of the Christian era. For New Testament scholarship has shown how fragmentary and ambiguous are the data available to us as we try to look back across nineteen and a half centuries, and at the same time how large and variable is the contribution of the imagination to our "pictures" of Jesus.... And each of these different "pictures" can appeal to some element among the various strands of New Testament tradition.[6]

In the opening of the gospel Luke follows Matthew in a virginal conception story, and both of them are then faced with the problem of what to do with the older Davidic sonship tradition. Matthew's solution is to fabricate a bogus genealogy back to David and Abraham, with *legal* paternity only in the final link with Joseph. Luke follows him, but has it both ways by extending the line on the father's side back to God also.[7]

The *metaphysical* uniqueness of Jesus, as traditionally taught, has always been taken to have carried with it a unique *moral* perfection.... It is impossible to justify any such claim on purely historical grounds, however wide the net for evidence is cast. So far as the gospels are concerned, the material in them is too scanty, and too largely selected and organized with reference to other considerations, to provide the necessary evidence.[8]

The force of such arguments in *The Myth of God Incarnate* is quite plain: at minimum, objective historical testimony would be required to justify belief in a *de facto* incarnation; the New Testament documents—when subjected to historical-critical method—offer no such objective portrait of Jesus, but rather present diverse Christ-ologies reflecting the varied faith-experiences of the early church; the modern churchman, therefore, is not obligated to maintain a traditional incarnational Christology if his own faith-experience and contemporary orientation point in other, more personally meaningful directions.

---

[5]Ibid., p. 125 (essay by Leslie Houlden).
[6]Ibid., p. 167 (essay by John Hick).
[7]Ibid., p. 80 (essay by Michael Goulder).
[8]Ibid., pp. 194–95 (essay by Dennis Nineham).

EVANGELICALS AND FORM CRITICISM

The evangelical community is duly horrified over the collapse of historic, biblical Christology in *The Myth of God Incarnate*.[9] However, with isolated exceptions,[10] evangelicalism has not taken a decisive stand against the employment of the form critical techniques which underlie its Christological conclusions. Indeed, these techniques are being positively promoted by some evangelical scholars as an aid to faith. Institutionally, the most active promotion is being carried on by Christ Seminary—Seminex—the breakaway theological school from Concordia Seminary, St. Louis, Missouri. At Seminex, historical-critical method is advocated as part of that institution's efforts to move beyond an inerrancy view of Scripture. But even among scholars who adhere to the inerrancy of the Bible, form critical technique finds advocates. Thus Grant R. Osborne is actively encouraging evangelicals to embrace historical-critical methodologies. In my recent work, *Faith Founded on Fact*, I briefly treated Osborne's approach;[11] here I want to carry the analysis a bit further and relate it to the Christological issues under immediate discussion.

In tbe Spring, 1976, issue of the *Evangelical Theological Society Journal*, Osborne defended an evangelical use of *Redaktionsgeschichte* in his article, "Redaction Criticism and the Great Commission." There he argued that in the case of Matthew 28:19, "it seems most likely that at some point the tradition or Matthew expanded an original monadic formula." Such redaction should not surprise us, for "the evangelists did not attempt to give us *ipsissima verba* but rather sought to interpret Jesus' words for their audiences. In other words, they wished to make Jesus' teachings meaningful to their own *Sitz im Leben* rather than to present them unedited. Relevancy triumphed over verbal exactness."

A more recent article by Osborne in the *Evangelical Theological Society Journal* offers an evangelical rehabilitation of "tradition criticism"

---

[9]See such evangelical analyses of the book as those by John R. W. Stott and Harold B. Kuhn in *Christianity Today* (Nov. 4, 1977, pp. 34–35; Feb. 10, 1978, pp. 63–65), and also the semi-evangelical book-length symposium response, *The Truth of God Incarnate*, ed. Michael Green (Grand Rapids: Eerdmans, 1977).

[10]The two most prominent exceptions are the Lutheran Church–Missouri Synod (through its Commission on Theology and Church Relations) and the Melodyland School of Theology, Anaheim, California: see Montgomery, *Faith Founded on Fact* (Nashville: Thomas Nelson, 1978), pp. 223–27.

[11]Ibid., pp. 220–21.

(June, 1978: "The Evangelical and *Traditionsgeschichte*").[12] Osborne begins by critiquing what he calls "the negative criteria" for establishing the genuine underlying core of Jesus' life and teachings; he then goes on to give "a positive approach" in which virtually the same criteria appear in milder form. Thus:

> Pericopae that are not characteristic of either Judaism or the later Church may be regarded as trustworthy. Earlier we pointed out the limitations of this method, but with those in mind this still yields the most certain results from a critical standpoint.... Features that could not survive in the primitive setting unless they were genuine may well be an indication of authenticity.... If there is no satisfactory *Sitz im Leben* for an episode, it is traditional and perhaps even authentic. For example, the sayings on Jewish particularism (e.g., Matt. 10:6; 15:24) would not fit the later Church.... If given in language and containing emphases not characteristic of the author, the passage is traditional.... Aramaic or Palestinian features may well indicate an early origin.... Features that occur in more than one independent tradition may also be trustworthy.

Osborne is aware that the employment of such redaction- and tradition-criticism has cast a pall of doubt over the reliability of the portrait of Jesus in the New Testament. Nevertheless he assures his evangelical readers that this need not be the case. Why? Simply because the evangelical will regard the redaction and the formation of the tradition as guaranteed to be inerrantly true by the divine inspiration of Holy Scripture.

Others, who unlike Osborne do not adhere to the orthodox doctrine of Biblical inspiration, appeal to the Holy Spirit in an even more disquieting way. For them "the Spirit" becomes a *deus ex machina*, supporting very different Christological understandings. "The Spirit" led Thomas Altizer through the redacted New Testament documents to his "fully kenotic Christ." More important for our present purposes, the authors of *The Myth of God Incarnate* likewise appeal to spirit and experience for the new Christology they arrive at on the basis of the "assured results" of contemporary form criticism. Leslie Houlden writes:

> If we have reservations about what we have called the creedal approach, not simply because formulas of the past become obsolete but funda-

---

[12]The essay originally appeared in *The New Testament Student*, 5 (1978), edited by John H. Skilton. For an even more unfortunate example of the potential collapse of bibliology and Christology through evangelical application of form criticism, see Robert H. Gundry's "Inspiration, Imprecision, Literary Genre and Matthew," a theological postscript to his forthcoming redactional-critical commentary on Matthew (to be published by Eerdmans).

mentally because such a use of language is improper concerning God, then we may be led to formulate the christological question thus: what must I say about Jesus when as a result of him, by innumerable routes, I have been brought to that experience of God which has been my lot and privilege? The resulting answer may be far from traditional words, but it will avoid the obstruction of technicality, it will have a refreshing realism, it will reach out towards spirituality.[13]

And in the "Final Comment" to the volume, Don Cupitt declares:

I acknowledge the limitations of our critical-historical knowledge of Jesus. However, the core of a religion does not lie in the biography or personality of the founder, but in the specifically religious values to which, according to tradition, he bore witness. By these values I mean possible determinations of the human spirit whereby it relates itself to the ultimate goal of existence, such as are embodied in the injunction to "Repent, for the kingdom of God is at hand."

This cluster of "principles of Spirit" is at the center of the tradition, and I believe it to be contingently the case that Jesus proclaimed them, though it is not strictly necessary to prove it by the critical method. Precisely because they command us to die to the self, to the world which is passing away and so on, they assert the possibility of transcending relativity. As principles of transcendence they are the only non-relativistic criterion of the subsequent development of the tradition.

In history, a man proclaimed the possibility of transcending history; and we, in history also, can verify his claim in practice.[14]

THE INCOMPATIBILITY OF HIGHER CRITICISM AND HIGH CHRISTOLOGY

Claims to an "experiential" or "spiritual" stabilizing factor for form-critical conclusions necessarily leave the objective life and words of Jesus in darkness and obscurity, since one can never be sure when the text is representing Jesus Himself and when it is merely reflecting the diverse faith-experiences of early Christian communities. Redaction- and tradition-criticism open the door wide to all manner of subjectivistic reformulations of the person and work of Jesus Christ. The classic Christology of the ecumenical creeds is based upon the existence of an objectively veridical portrait of the Christ in the New Testament, and it is that very portrait which form criticism puts in doubt.

The answer to *The Myth of God Incarnate* therefore requires a fron-

---

[13]*The Myth of God Incarnate*, p. 131.
[14]Ibid., p. 205.

tal, non-compromising attack on higher critical technique. Evangelicals should not shrink from that task, for much of the groundwork
has already been laid. C. S. Lewis, literary scholar, demonstrated in
his essay, "Modern Theology and Biblical Criticism," that the assumptions of form criticism are hopelessly subjectivistic and its application
overwhelmingly dubious even in the realms of modern and contemporary literature.[15] German theologian Gerhard Maier has recently
produced a long-needed critique titled, appropriately, *The End of the
Historical-Critical Method.*[16] Of particular value is Humphrey Palmer's
study, *The Logic of Gospel Criticism,* which keenly identifies many of the
devastating flaws in form-critical reasoning. Here are some typical
examples of Palmer's conclusions:

> In the complete absence of comparative material, and the wide range
> of informed opinion about the methods of composition, its occasion and
> its purpose, a decision about what is to count as establishing a Gospel
> source is very difficult. ... In the gospels, each division produces a
> difficult grouping. Squinting through his microscope, the critic sees
> only a reflection of his eye.

> If we are ready to believe next to nothing about Jesus, but almost
> anything about the early Church, the classification into "forms" is re-
> quired only to add a spice of scholarship and variety.... Were the first
> Christians adept at thinking up stories-of-Jesus to suit a situation in
> their Church? Form-critics do not show this, but take it for granted in
> all their reasonings. These reasonings do, however, show how adept
> form-critics are at thinking up early-Church-situations to suit stories of
> Jesus.

> Guessing at traditions behind the gospels is a fascinating occupation.
> For public discussion of the subject to be profitable, reasons must be
> given why some guesses should be preferred to others. The classifica-
> tion of story-forms, though interesting in itself, has not produced any
> new reasons of this sort.

> It seems unlikely that the disciples were clever enough to invent all
> those world-shaking ideas *and* simple enough to attribute them all to
> someone else.... Nor can we proceed by listing as Jesus' all the revo-
> lutionary doctrines, and leaving the rest to be filled in by his disciples,
> for such a list may only reflect *our* idea of what is basic, seminal, or
> revolutionary.

> Jesus presumably spoke Aramaic. The gospels appear to have been
> composed in Greek. We may therefore ask, for each story or doctrine,

---

[15]C. S. Lewis, *Christian Reflections,* ed. Walter Hooper (Grand Rapids:
Eerdmans, 1967), pp. 152-66.
[16]Gerhard Maier, *The End of the Historical-Critical Method,* trans. E. W.
Leverenz and R. F. Norden (St. Louis: Concordia, 1977).

to which background it belongs. This question has turned out less simple than it looked, for there are Semitic turns of phrase in Koine Greek, and Palestine was under Greek rule until the time of the Maccabees. No one can prove that Jesus spoke no Greek. Ideas cannot, in consequence, be affiliated simply by the language in which they are expressed.

Statistical work can improve our judgments of style. They remain judgments, and so "subjective." New Testament writings are too short and specialized for judgments of style, with or without numbers, to carry much weight in decisions about authorship.[17]

In sum, evangelical theology has nothing to gain but everything to lose should it attempt to baptize historical-critical method. That method by its very nature generates unwarranted doubt concerning the objective reliability of the biblical records, and doubtful biblical records necessarily mean a doubtful Christology, for all we know of Christ comes from Scripture. If we would effectively proclaim to our age "the terrifying assertion that the same God who made the world lived in the world and passed through the grave and gate of death,"[18] we had better stick closer to Scripture. Expounding John 1:2 in the year 1537, Luther put it this way:

> We have not invented this text about the eternal Godhead of Christ. By the special grace of God it has come down to us and will, I dare say, remain despite all heretics—many of whom will yet try their prowess on it—and will continue to the end of the world.[19]

---

[17]Humphrey Palmer, *The Logic of Gospel Criticism* (London: Macmillan, 1968), pp. 172-73, 185, 188, 190, 191, 224.

[18]Dorothy Sayers, "The Dogma is the Drama," in *Christian Letters to a Post-Christian World*, ed. Roderick Jellema (Grand Rapids: Eerdmans, 1969), p. 26. Significantly, *The Myth of God Incarnate* contains not a single reference to Sayers, C. S. Lewis, Charles Williams, or J. R. R. Tolkien—those great modern English Christian writers who understood the true "deep myth" of the Gospel story; in Tolkien's words, "There is no tale ever told that men would rather find was true, and none which so many sceptical men have accepted as true on its own merits" (see Montgomery, *Myth, Allegory and Gospel* [Minneapolis: Bethany, 1974], especially pp. 116-18).

[19]*W. A.*, VII: 551 f.

6

The Holy Spirit in Christian Theology

William W. Menzies

INTRODUCTION

I would define Christian theology as the ongoing enterprise of bringing God's revelation to bear on the crucial questions men ask. Looking at the theological affirmations of a given age, or of a given theologian, permits one to appreciate what the questions were which demanded attention at that time. There is no aspect of theology in which this "shifting of the target" is truer than in regard to the theology of the Holy Spirit. If I were to append a subheading to the topic I have been asked to address, I would use "The Changing Questions: An Essay on Historical Issues."

In the brief space available for this essay, it would be virtually impossible to attempt a comprehensive study. Rather, I have arbitrarily chosen what I believe to be significant spokesmen who have had, or do now have, a role in the shaping or reflecting of American evangelical belief respecting the person and work of the Holy Spirit. Even here, some are mentioned as representative of others closely allied in spirit and emphasis, so that other equally important names may indeed appear to be conspicuous by absence.

It is my contention that the ancient church, from the second century until the ninth century, was almost totally preoccupied with questions pertaining to the identity of Jesus Christ, so that what was said of the Holy Spirit was largely an appendage to theology, and was limited largely to a consideration of ontology, the Being of God within His intertrinitarian relationships. This perception of the Holy Spirit dominated medieval theology, as well.

With the upheaval occasioned by the Reformation of the sixteenth century, more attention was given to the Holy Spirit in His relations to the world, particularly addressing attention to His role in revelation (after all, the Reformation was dealing with the question of the authority of the Word of God) and in regeneration.

It was not until the eighteenth century that the "mission" of the Spirit was given special attention. A variety of theologians sought to deal with the meaning of the presence of the Spirit in the life of the believer.

The *experience* of the Spirit became an important question. By the end of the nineteenth century, a whole range of theologies of sanctification and life in the Spirit were finding expression within the ranks of evangelical Christianity.

It has been in the twentieth century that the meaning of the Holy Spirit for the life of the corporate community, for the *ekklesia,* has come to be a subject of earnest investigation and reflection.

Now, this is not to say that what was dealt with in earlier centuries was discarded later. No, it seems that for the most part, subsequent ages of the church have built upon the work done by earlier theologians. To be sure, there continue to be sniper attacks on choice of terminology used by earlier theologians. Be that as it may, as different sets of questions have moved to center stage, much of the fruit of earlier centuries has been assumed. One is tempted to say that the practical subordinationism of the Holy Spirit in Christian theology is in *process* of being corrected.

In retrospect, then, it appears that the doctrine of the Holy Spirit has not until more recent years become a central subject for theological inquiry. It has been an appendage to other issues, particularly when it comes to the "mission" of the Spirit in the world. Perhaps it is not too much to say that we are today, more than at any other time in Christian history, at the cutting edge of the theology of the Spirit. The phenomenal production of books on the Holy Spirit in very recent years seems to support this contention.

THE ANCIENT CHURCH: ONTOLOGY OF THE SPIRIT

It was Ignatius (d. ca. 117), writing to the Magnesians, who supplied in his salutation, "Fare ye well in harmony, ye who have obtained the inseparable Spirit, in Christ Jesus, by the will of God."[1] This may be

---

[1]"The Epistle of Ignatius to the Magnesians," in *The Ante-Nicene Fathers,* A. Roberts and J. Donaldson, eds. (Grand Rapids: Eerdmans, reprinted, 1973), 1. 65.

the earliest allusion to what might be called an incipient trinitarian belief in the ancient church. More to the point, the friend of Ignatius, Polycarp (70-155), in his martyrdom speech at Smyrna, offers in his concluding prayer a doxology in which the Spirit is glorified, along with the Father and the Son.[2] However, it was Justin Martyr (100-165) who really touched off the controversy. He identified the Son and the Spirit as both being "generate," an unhappy choice of language, since the current use of that term implied that neither the Son nor the Spirit could be truly divine, since that would require "ingenerate" existence, a term Justin reserved for the Father.[3]

Irenaeus (Bishop of Lyons ca. 175-195) attempted to get around the problem created by terminology of Justin by suggesting that the Son was "eternally created." The Spirit, called "Wisdom," is incidentally drawn in, with the assumption that the Son and the Spirit bear a similar relationship to the Father.[4] This still left a question about the divinity of both Christ and the Spirit, since Irenaeus insisted on the use of "created" in speaking of Son and Spirit.

Tertullian, (160-215) contributed, among other ideas, the notion of "procession."[5] It is Tertullian who said of the intertrinitarian relationships: "These three are one essence, not one person."[6] John 15:26 (NIV) says, "When the Counselor comes, whom I will send to you from the Father, the Spirit of truth who goes out [ekporeuetai] from the Father, he will testify about me." The meaning of this verse becomes the theological battleground of the patristic period, respecting the Holy Spirit. In what sense does the Holy Spirit "proceed" from the Father and/or the Son? The assumption, of course, by virtually all the fathers, was that this verse must be understood in terms of the trinitarian interrelationships, God pictured within his own Being. It is, therefore, strictly an ontological issue. The implications, however, for the divinity of the Spirit, are enormous. It does show, however, that the battleground in the earliest centuries of the church, respecting the Holy Spirit, had to do with his essential Being.

It was Origen (185-254) who added further refinement to the issue. It is he to whom the church owes the language "eternal generation" respecting the Son, and "eternal procession," respecting the Spirit. Methodius, Bishop of Tyre, introduced the indirect generation con-

---

[2]"The Epistle Concerning the Martyrdom of Polycarp," in *The Ante-Nicene Fathers,* 1. 42.

[3]"First Apology," in *The Ante-Nicene Fathers,* 1. 174.

[4]"Against Heresies," in *The Ante-Nicene Fathers,* 1. 488.

[5]H. B. Swete, *The Holy Spirit in the Ancient Church* (London: Macmillan, 1912) 370, 371.

[6]"Against Praxeas," in *The Ante-Nicene Fathers,* 3. 621.

cept, the Holy Spirit being generated by the Father "through the Son." Until this time there does not appear to be any exponent of the double procession of Spirit from both Father and Son.

Meanwhile, the Arians had picked up the idea of "generation" and insisted on attaching a temporal significance to the term. This led to the notion that if Christ, and hence, the Holy Spirit, were "generate" or "proceeding," from the Father, they must be of another substance than the Father. From this came the Arian doctrine of subordination of Son and Spirit to the Father.[7]

To combat this interpretation of the Godhead, the three Cappadocian Fathers, Basil of Caesarea (329–379), his brother Gregory of Nyssa (330–395), and Gregory of Nazianzus (330–389), employed strictly ontological language to assert a distinction between "essence" (ousia) and the form in which it exists (hypostasis). In this way they attempted to show that in showing distinguishing features within the persons of the Godhead, they were not permitting an essential distinction. Gregory of Nyssa, in his great work, "On the Holy Trinity," pointedly declares that Father and Spirit are of one "substance," regardless of what distinctions are to be made between them.[8] This not only sealed off the possibility of an Arian style of subordinationism, but also effectively refuted the Macedonians, a group who taught that the Son was on a plane with the Father, but that the Spirit was subordinate to both of them.

Augustine (354–430), Bishop of Hippo, particularly in his work of thirty years, "On the Trinity," systematized the thinking of the church in the West and influenced generations after him. For him, the procession of the Spirit is from the Son, as well as the Father, since the Father and the Son are of one essence.[9] He developed a system of reciprocal, interpersonal relationships, securing the identity of divine persons, subsisting consubstantially. However, in his development of a clear divinity of the Spirit, and a uniqueness of personality, it came at the expense of attention to the ministry of the Holy Spirit in the world. God is defined, but in an abstract manner above the world.[10]

The consensus of the church on these issues is encapsulated in the ecumenical creeds which were generated in this period. The Apostles'

---

[7]Jones, *The Spirit and the World* (New York: Hawthorn, 1975) 117.

[8]"On the Holy Trinity," in *The Nicene and Post-Nicene Fathers,* Philip Schaff ed. (Grand Rapids: Eerdmans, reprinted, 1956), 5. 329.

[9]"On the Trinity," in *The Nicene and Post-Nicene Fathers,* Philip Schaff, ed. (Grand Rapids: Eerdmans, reprinted, 1956), 3. 226.

[10]D. Gelpi, *Pentecostalism: A Theological Viewpoint* (New York: Paulist, 1971) 111.

Creed, which probably dates from the middle of the second century, has a substantial statement about God the Father, and an even more elaborate statement about God the Son, but tucked in, along with a series of other items, is the mere assertion, "I believe in the Holy Ghost." One is tempted to wonder if this authentically reflects preoccupation with issues at that time other than the Holy Spirit, or if it is not a tacit admission of a practical subordinationism.

Between the Council of Nicea (325) and Constantinople (381) developed the form of what commonly is called the Nicene Creed. It was slightly revised yet again and reaffirmed in Chalcedon in 451. It states, "And we believe in the Holy Spirit, the Lord and giver of life, who proceedeth from the Father, and with the Father and the Son together is worshipped and glorified." Rod Williams points out that this statement does recognize the Spirit in relation to the creation, and he expresses disappointment that nothing is said here about the effusion of the Spirit, "its dimensions, its significance, its results."[11] It is the person of the Spirit, not his function, which is featured.

Both the Eastern and Western wings of the church adopted the Chalcedonian Formula of 451. However, at the Third Synod of Toledo in 589, out of zeal to counteract the tenacious Arians of Spain, the bishops quietly added the *filioque* clause to the Latin version of the creed. This was probably not done out of any intended disregard for the Greek church, although it was clearly not appropriate for such a regional synod to take liberties with a document agreed upon at a general council.[12] The *filioque* clause added the words, "and from the Son," to the statement regarding the procession of the Spirit from the Father. By the ninth century this had passed into common use in the West, and subsequently was adopted without hesitation by the various families of Protestant churches which emerged. In the East, however, this became one of the principal sources of contention which led eventually to the open schism of 1054. For evangelicals, the significance of the *filioque* clause may be seen in the establishment of a strong connection between the work of the incarnate Christ and the work of the Spirit, so that life in the Spirit would be perceived as necessarily flowing out of a relationship with Christ.[13]

---

[11]J. R. Williams, "New Theology for a New Era: God's Mighty Acts" (unpublished paper delivered on July 21, 1977, in Kansas City at the Sixth International Presbyterian Conference on the Holy Spirit).

[12]P. Schaff, *History of the Christian Church* (Grand Rapids: Eerdmans, reprinted, 1973), 4. 481.

[13]G. S. Hendry, *The Holy Spirit in Christian Theology* (Philadelphia: Westminster, 1956) 69.

In summary, from the second to the ninth centuries, the church succeeded in doing two things. Couched in the philosophical terminology of the age, the divinity and personality of the Holy Spirit within the Triune Godhead were affirmed. But, since primary attention was directed to other issues, relatively little was said of the mission of the Spirit in the world. In carefully guarded terms, one might say that this amounts to a *practical* subordinationism, if not an ontological subordinationism. In other words, all that could have been said had not yet been said!

THE REFORMATION: THE SPIRIT AND THE WORD

John 16:7 (NIV) says, "But I tell you the truth: It is for your good that I am going away. Unless I go away, the Counselor will not come to you; but if I go, *I will send him to you.*" "I will send him to you." This speaks of the mission of the Spirit in the world. The ancient church had said relatively little about the "mission" of the Spirit; its concerns lay with such trinitarian matters as "procession." Subsequently, the medieval Western church, when it addressed the matter of "mission," developed a doctrine of the Spirit in which the Spirit was considered "the soul of the church." By this is meant the Spirit endows the institutional and visible church with gifts which make it truly the extension of the incarnation of Christ.[14] Indeed, this is a doctrine of "mission," but it is at considerable variance from the views that the Reformers developed.

Luther, Calvin, and virtually all the significant voices which have shaped Protestant and evangelical thought have accepted the trinitarian formulae hammered out in the early ecumenical creeds, uncritically accepting as well the additional *filioque* clause.[15] This is not to say that there has not been a certain amount of distress at the use of archaic metaphysical language to express the intended result, namely the true divinity and separate personality of the Holy Spirit within the triune Godhead.[16] The point here, is, merely that the Reformers did not expend great effort to go over ground that had already been well plowed. Their contributions went beyond this.

Luther broke with the Catholic notion of a natural theology. For

---

[14]Ibid., 55.

[15]L. M. Starkey, *The Work of the Holy Spirit* (Nashville: Abingdon, 1962) 27.

[16]J. O. Buswell, *A Systematic Theology of the Christian Religion* (Grand Rapids: Zondervan, 1962), 1. 120.

him, it was the inbreaking of the Spirit which makes it possible for man to come into a proper relationship with Christ.[17] The means the Spirit employs to bring grace to man are the Word proclaimed and the sacrament. The Spirit does not work apart from the Word. It was out of this that he displayed sharp antagonism to the "Schwärmerei," the Enthusiasts of his day who disconnected the work of the Spirit from the Word.[18] Important as this contribution is, nonetheless, it must be acknowledged that Luther did not give much attention to the mission of the Spirit. His concerns did not center in this aspect of doctrine.

Calvin, indeed, goes much further. Of special importance is Calvin's contribution to Christian theology of "the witness of the Spirit." He rejected the Roman Catholic basis for certitude being in the church, and likewise, Calvin rejected the Enthusiasts of his day who claimed certainty for faith by direct revelation of the Spirit. Calvin likewise rejected those who felt that they could demonstrate the truthfulness of the Christian faith by purely rational evidence.[19] Calvin taught that a special persuasion, a mission to man of the Spirit, is necessary to awaken, to convince. So it is that the same Spirit who inspired the writers of the Scriptures, illuminates the hearers of Scripture, and confirms the truth of God's Word to man.[20] Of great significance is the connection in Calvin's theology between the Word and the Spirit who bears witness to the Word.

Although Calvin had a more clearly-articulated understanding of sanctification than did Luther, he and those who followed closely in his steps perceived this mission of the Spirit in Christian experience to be inevitable for the elect. It really remained for the Puritan theologian of the next century, John Owen, to articulate with some precision the doctrine of progressive sanctification of the Spirit.[21]

Sampling here some of the contributions of the Reformation era, it appears that in spite of the necessity laid upon the Reformers to address other questions than that of the work of the Spirit, nonetheless important statements appear, particularly regarding the relation of the Spirit to the Word.

---

[17]R. Prenter, *Spiritus Creator* (Philadelphia: Muhlenberg, 1953) 190.
[18]Ibid., 247–305.
[19]B. Ramm, *The Witness of the Spirit* (Grand Rapids: Eerdmans, 1959) 12.
[20]J. Calvin, *Institutes,* I. vii. 1–5.
[21]J. Owen, *The Holy Spirit: His Gifts and Power* (Grand Rapids: Kregel, reprint ed., 1954) 278–99.

EIGHTEENTH AND NINETEENTH CENTURIES: THE SPIRIT
AND CHRISTIAN EXPERIENCE

Although Luther, and to a much greater degree, Calvin and his followers, discussed the strategic role of the Spirit in creating new life in the believer, it remained for others in a later age to reflect on the implications of the ministry of the Spirit respecting the new life in Christ. Perhaps out of preoccupation with other issues, the Reformers did not dwell on the dynamics of Christian experience. In part, to be sure, it was out of reaction to experientially-oriented extremists that the Reformers tended to underscore the objective, Word-centered dimension of Christian truth.[22]

John Wesley, instrument of God for refreshing England in the middle of the eighteenth century, chose to cut new theological paths. At numerous critical points, Wesley was in full agreement with the Reformers, even in his doctrine of the Spirit. He adopted wholesale the trinitarian formula, including the double procession of the Spirit. Respecting his understanding of the divinity and personhood of the Spirit, there is nothing divergent from his predecessors.[23] However, Wesley departed significantly from the Reformed tradition in his understanding of the mission of the Spirit in the life of the believer. For him, regeneration was a work of the Spirit, but was imperfect. A second work of grace was necessary, which was to be appropriated by faith, in order to facilitate the completion of the ministry of the Spirit in the individual. Defined variously as "perfect love," or "eradication of inbred sin," or "entire sanctification," it became the cornerstone of "holiness theology," which flourished in the footsteps of Wesley, particularly in the nineteenth century.[24]

---

[22]See A. Kuyper, *The Work of the Holy Spirit* (Grand Rapids: Eerdmans, 1900). Kuyper, brilliant exponent of Reformed theology, adopts the standard progressive motif common to Reformed theology of sanctification. It should be noted that the standard Reformed (and Baptistic) systematic theologies of the nineteenth century and into this century relegate the theology of the Spirit to aspects of other theological issues. The person of the Spirit is a small section under the larger caption of "Trinity," usually. The "mission" of the Spirit is scattered in various places, usually given most significant treatment as an aspect of "application of the Atonement." An example of this handling of the theology of the Spirit can be seen in the fairly recent volume by J. O. Buswell cited above. The same is true of Louis Berkhof, *Systematic Theology,* 4th rev. ed. (Grand Rapids: Eerdmans, 1939).

[23]Starkey, *The Work of the Holy Spirit,* 27.

[24]See J. Wesley, *A Plain Account of Christian Perfection,* his classic exposition of his theology of Christian experience. Further, see for an interpretation of

Lest one limit the experiential theology of the Spirit to the Wesleyan stream, let it be remembered that in the latter part of the nineteenth century, Reformed and Anglican versions of the quest for holiness in personal experience also flourished. In 1859 W. E. Boardman, a Presbyterian, wrote a widely-distributed book entitled, *The Higher Christian Life.* Its warm response seems to reflect a yearning in the hearts of a wide spectrum of Christians in the perfection-oriented nineteenth century for a deeper experience with God, an experience understood generally to be wrought by the Holy Spirit in the believer. The popularity of the Keswick conventions, which began in England in the 1870s, attests a rather widespread seeking for a dimension of Christian experience which was not addressed to full satisfaction in the standard theological systems of the day. The Keswick theology should be pictured as a Reformed base, upon which is built a more elaborate theology of the experience of the Spirit than standard Calvinism expressed.[25] These "holiness" theologies, whether Wesleyan or Keswickian, perceived the mission of the Spirit to the individual in terms of sanctification, of development of moral excellence, or manifesting of the Spirit.

"Oberlin theology" promoted principally by the colleague of Charles Finney, Asa Mahan, assisted in introducing to theological terminology the concept of "baptism in the Holy Spirit."[26] A. J. Gordon taught a doctrine of "fullness of the Spirit," by which he meant an anointing for service.[27] By the end of the century, a fair proportion of evangelical revivalists used such expressions as "baptism in the Spirit," or "fullness of the Spirit," by which was meant either an experience of sanctification or an anointing for service. Pentecostals, who arrived on the scene near the beginning of the twentieth century, should be understood to be theologically the children of the concern

---

Wesley's theology, M. B. Wynkoop, *A Theology of Love* (Kansas City: Beacon Hill Press, 1972), and Starkey, *The Work of the Holy Spirit.* A classic is R. N. Flew, *The Idea of Perfection in Christian Theology* (New York: Humanities, 1968) 313-41.

[25]See S. Barabas, *So Great Salvation* (Westwood, NJ: Revell, n.d.), for an excellent interpretation of Keswick theology.

[26]Donald W. Dayton, "From Christian Perfection to the Baptism in the Holy Ghost," in Vinson Synan, *Aspects of Pentecostal-Charismatic Origins* (Plainfield, NJ: Logos, 1975) 39-44.

[27]A. J. Gordon, *The Ministry of the Spirit* (Philadelphia: Judson, reprinted, 1949) 93. See also R. A. Torrey, *The Holy Spirit* (New York: Revell, 1927). An entire chapter is devoted to "The Baptism of the Holy Spirit," reflecting a popular evangelical theology current at the beginning of the century.

for a "higher Christian life," widely-manifested in the late-nineteenth century.[28] Typical Pentecostal theology articulates the ministry of the Spirit in the life of the believer in two forms: sanctification (sometimes defined in Wesleyan terms, but most commonly in non-Wesleyan terms) and an anointing of the Spirit for service. This latter is called "baptism in the Spirit." These two categories may be described as the "interior" ministry of the Spirit and the "expressive" ministry of the Spirit for believers.

THE CONTEMPORARY ISSUE: THE HOLY SPIRIT IN THE COMMUNITY OF FAITH

A genuine trinitarian concern which has surfaced afresh in recent days has to do with the *reciprocal* missions of Christ and the Spirit. Indeed, John reports clearly for us that when the Spirit of truth comes, he will not speak on his own, but will speak those things which will bring glory to the Son (John 16:13, 14). A mission of the Spirit, properly emphasized by virtually all evangelical theologies, is that the Spirit will bear witness to Christ. However, there are other passages which report that a mission of Christ in the world, upon the completion of His assignment in effecting atonement for sin, will be to pour out the Spirit. John 20:22 has been the object of considerable exegetical speculation, "Receive ye the Holy Spirit." Certainly this much is clear: just as the Spirit bears witness to Christ, so Christ is pictured as pouring out the Spirit. The significance of this for individual experience was a primary theological concern in the late-nineteenth and early-twentieth centuries. In the charismatic renewal, considerable theologizing continues in a variety of quarters to address the question of individual expectations with respect to the "pouring out of the Spirit" for the contemporary Christian believer.[29] However, at least since the 1950s, a recurring theme can be heard in the theological symphony, occurring in sufficient force to warrant mentioning in this essay. It has to do with the nature of the church.

---

[28]See E. L. Waldvogel. "The 'Overcoming' Life: A Study in the Reformed Evangelical Contribution to Pentecostalism." (Unpublished Ph.D. dissertation, Harvard University, 1977). A standard expression of contemporary Keswick-type Pentecostal theology is S. Horton, *What the Bible Says About the Holy Spirit* (Springfield, MO: Gospel Publishing, 1976).

[29]See the author's unpublished address, given November 30, 1978, at the annual meeting of the Society for Pentecostal Studies, entitled: "A Taxonomy of Pentecostal-Charismatic Theologies."

The question of the meaning of the church in systematic theologies is almost inevitably linked to the Holy Spirit, since it is universally recognized that the church is a creation of the Holy Spirit.[30] Few would doubt the "mystical" presence of Christ, through the Spirit, in the life of the church. However, there is much more diversity of opinion when it comes to the "manifest presence" of God in the church of today. Specifically, the question devolved to this: in what way are the manifestations, or charisms, of the Spirit, available for the church of today? A commonly-held view in contemporary evangelical theology is that set forth by B. B. Warfield in 1918 in his book, *Counterfeit Miracles*. In this view, the role of apostolic miracles was specifically understood to bear witness to the authority of the messengers of the gospel, until the completion of the NT canon of Scripture. Augustine, and later, Calvin adopted this point of view.[31] The implication of this, of course, is quite clear: the gifts of the Spirit should not be expected in the contemporary church.

Scofieldian dispensationalism, from a somewhat different vantage point, likewise contributed to a propensity within modern evangelicalism to rule out the value, even the possibility of, manifestations of the Spirit, such as are described as occurring in the apostolic church.[32]

This is a question which has to do with the meaning of the church itself. What indeed should the church be like, if it is to be authentically biblical, and, further, to be effective in an increasingly pagan world? Is it possible that important and useful theologians of the past, who contributed much to our understanding of God's will for us in this world, were conditioned historically in such fashion that this important question about the Spirit in the corporate body, the church, was not really adequately addressed?

In 1953, Emil Brunner wrote his thought-provoking volume, *The Misunderstanding of the Church*. This grew out of a recognition that the failure of the ecumenical movement lay principally in its failure to understand *what* it was they were seeking to unify. In this little volume he proposed that the real church is a spiritual fellowship, a fellowship generated by the presence of the Spirit.[33] Shortly afterward, Lesslie

---

[30]G. W. Forell, *The Protestant Faith* (Englewood Cliffs, NJ: Prentice-Hall, 1960) 204.

[31]Calvin, *Institutes,* I. ix. 3. F. D. Bruner, *A Theology of the Holy Spirit* (Grand Rapids: Eerdmans, 1970), is a current exponent of this historic position.

[32]See, for example, M. F. Unger, *New Testament Teaching on Tongues* (Grand Rapids: Kregel, 1971).

[33]E. Brunner, *The Misunderstanding of the Church* (Philadelphia: Westminster, 1953) 50.

Newbigin, bishop of the Church of South India, added further fuel to this fire, with his book, *The Household of God.* His earnest plea was that the church invite the Holy Spirit to flow in a manner like that described of the apostolic community, without making rationalizations why this was not to be.[34] To voices like these in the 1950s must be credited the beginning of a stirring which today is commonly called the "charismatic renewal." The significant point is that the question which produced the ferment was the role of the Spirit in the church.

Closer to traditional evangelical circles, one should cite the important contribution to this question by men like George Eldon Ladd. His perception of the trinitarian issue is clear. He sees the inauguration of the church as an eschatological fulfillment, long awaited. The advent of the church, at Pentecost, was the inbreaking of the eschaton, the beginning of the "last days." For this reason, Peter, when he said "This is that," (Acts 2:16), was holding the hands of the OT prophet Joel and the hands of all who belong to the age of the church. The pouring out of the Spirit was a logical consequence of the coming of Messiah! In fact, these are theologically inseparable missions of Spirit and Son![35] I would not venture to say that Ladd expects personally the reappearance of apostolic manifestations of the Spirit, but surely his profound theological insight opens the door wide to such an expectation!

I am impressed, further, with the writings of others, who seem to perceive the yearning of many in our day for a fresh understanding of life in the spiritual community. James Jones, in *The Spirit and the World,* addresses the question squarely. It is his contention that apart from the full range of gifts of the Spirit, the church is impoverished.[36] Even more surprising is the provocative volume, *The Problem of Wineskins,* written by a Holiness missionary, Howard Snyder. Snyder makes virtually the same plea.[37] And, even more recently, Charles Hummel has probed the matter in his thoughtful book, *Fire in the Fireplace.*[38] The common denominator in each of these books is a humble cry, a passionate desire for the people of God, that the Holy Spirit be given a place of proper honor in the body of believers.

---

[34] L. Newbigin, *The Household of God* (London: SCM, 1957) 88ff.

[35] G. E. Ladd, *A Theology of the New Testament* (Grand Rapids: Eerdmans, 1974) 342–56.

[36] Jones, *The Spirit and the World,* 78–106.

[37] H. Snyder, *The Problem of Wineskins* (Downers Grove: InterVarsity, 1975) 129–38.

[38] C. Hummel, *Fire in the Fireplace* (Downers Grove: InterVarsity, 1978) 163–75.

CONCLUSION

I have sought to journey over a great span of time, attempting to capture what appears to me to be the significant contributions of various ages in the Christian church with respect to the theology of the Holy Spirit. I have attempted to display the fact that each era cited had something to contribute, but that even up to this time, fresh questions regarding the Holy Spirit are surfacing, and these are deserving of courageous, fresh, and biblical response! Let him, whose mission has been to testify about our Savior, be given a place of full honor in our midst!

7

Predestination: A Calvinistic Note

Fred H. Klooster

The assignment for this paper calls for a survey of the changes that have recently taken place within Calvinistic circles with respect to the doctrine of predestination. The tensions and doctrinal changes that I am most aware of have occurred within churches that subscribe to the Belgic Confession, the Heidelberg Catechism, and the Canons of Dort. Criticism of the Reformed doctrine of predestination has usually come from outside of the Reformed churches; recently criticisms have mushroomed from within. Behind most of the criticism, concentrating on the Canons of Dort, looms the large shadow of Karl Barth.

Doctrinal changes concerning predestination occurred first in the Dutch Reformed Church (Nederlandse Hervormde Kerk). Then they began to occur within the Reformed Churches of the Netherlands (Gereformeerde Kerken van Nederland) with G. C. Berkouwer at center stage. Gradually the echoes of these discussions were heard in other Reformed churches throughout the world which maintain close ties to the Dutch churches. I am not aware of any significant parallel development in churches of the Westminster tradition during the last quarter century. The changes in the larger Presbyterian denominations occurred earlier.

THE CANONS ON PREDESTINATION

Recent discussion of predestination within Calvinistic circles has concentrated on criticism of the Canons of Dort. The Canons consider predestination in the First Head of Doctrine. The starting-point is the confession of the blameworthiness of the entire human race fallen in Adam and its desert of eternal death. Then the Canons speak of God's love in sending Jesus Christ so that everyone who believes in him may have eternal life. To that end God mercifully sends heralds of the cross to preach the good news of the gospel and to call all to repentance and faith. This preaching of the gospel has a twofold result—forgiveness and eternal life for those who truly believe, but the continuing wrath of God for those who do not believe this gospel (I. 4). The Canons then state that the cause or blame for this unbelief as well as for all other sins is man; the "cause or blame" for sin and unbelief is "by no means to be found in God" (I. 5). On the other hand, according to the Canons, "faith in Jesus Christ . . . and salvation through Him, is a gracious gift of God . . ."[1] Only at this point and in this context do the Canons refer to the eternal decree of predestination: "that some in time are given faith by God and that others are not given faith proceeds from His eternal decree" (I. 6).

According to the Canons, then, some are given faith and some are not given faith. There is a sovereign "discrimination" by God, but this "discrimination" concerns people who are "equally worthy of condemnation because of their sin" (I. 6; also 1. 7, 15). Those who are not elected, those who are not given faith, are left by God "in their own wickedness and hardness by a just judgment" (I. 6). This perspective is crucial for a right understanding of the Canons. The fall and sin are the perspective from which God views the race in his eternal predestination. Recent criticisms of the Canons rarely do justice to this basic perspective.

The remaining articles of the First Head of Doctrine (I. 7-18) explain election and reprobation. Here one finds the main features of the doctrine of predestination that are under attack today from within the Reformed churches. I shall summarize these main features under seven headings.

The major features of I. 7-18 of the Canons of Dort are the following:
1. God's decree of predestination, including both election and reprobation, is a sovereign, eternal decree—but it is not arbitrary.

---

[1] The text of the Canons is quoted from "A New English Translation of the Canons of Dort" by A. A. Hoekema, *Calvin Theological Journal*, 3.2 (November 1968) 133-61. It is available in booklet form as part of the "Monograph Series" issued by Calvin Theological Seminary. The Christian Reformed Church has a committee at work to prepare an official, new translation in English.

2. The presupposition of God's eternal decree of predestination is that the human race is viewed as fallen and human (ir)responsibility is emphasized for all sin.

3. Election and reprobation are seen as "equally ultimate" in that both are included in the sovereign, eternal decree of God, but they are certainly not "in all respects parallel."

4. Election involves rescue from sin and gracious giving of the gifts of salvation; God's election is election in Christ, and Christ is both the foundation of election and the foundation of salvation (I. 7).

5. Reprobation is viewed as a sovereign and just leaving of some "in their own wickedness and hardness" (I. 6), a passing by "in the eternal election of God" whereby he "has decreed to leave [them] in the common misery into which they have by their own fault plunged themselves, and not to give them saving faith and the grace of conversion" (I. 15). The decree of reprobation includes preterition and condemnation.

6. Both election and reprobation are viewed as individual, personal, specific, particular. I. 7 refers to "a certain number of specific men" as elect; I. 15 states that "not all men are elect but that certain ones have not been elected" but passed by in God's decree.

7. The eternal decree of God is effectuated in history through the use of means which call for genuine human responsibility. The gospel must be preached to all with urgency; decisions in history are meaningful and God's agency in history is also meaningful. In election there is a direct divine agency which involves the giving of gifts and blessings of salvation. Unbelief involves human irresponsibility and is not linked to divine causality.

These seven points of summary of the Canons I. 7–18 are the main issues in recent discussion and criticism of the Reformed doctrine of predestination from within certain Reformed churches. Before expanding on the precise criticism, I shall survey the main participants in this discussion and then return to the seven points.

THE MAIN PARTICIPANTS IN RECENT CRITICISM OF PREDESTINATION

1. Karl Barth (1868–1968)

The huge shadow of Karl Barth cuts across all recent criticism of the Reformed doctrine of predestination. In 1942 Barth published that part of the *Church Dogmatics* which sets forth his view of election.[2]

---

[2] K. Barth, *Church Dogmatics,* II/2 (Edinburgh: T. & T. Clark, 1957) 3–506.

He acknowledged in the preface that he had experienced "greater anxiety" in producing this volume than he had experienced earlier. He admits that he "would have preferred to follow Calvin's doctrine of predestination much more closely, instead of departing from it so radically."[3]

Barth constructs a radically new doctrine of election; all seven summarizing points of the Canons are rejected or radically modified by Barth. For him election is the sum of the whole gospel, and election is intimately linked to preaching. But election does not concern an eternal, sovereign decree of God; such a *decretum absolutum* would be in conflict with the freedom of God. Barth historicizes and actualizes election. According to Barth Jesus Christ is both electing God and elected man; at the same time he is both elect and the only real reprobate. The three main parts of Barth's discussion concern the election of Jesus Christ, the election of the Community (Israel and the church), and the election of the Individual. Election is universal. The implications of Barth's theology are clearly universalistic throughout, yet he refused to affirm or deny universal salvation.[4]

2. The Nederlandse Hervormde Kerk (Dutch Reformed Church)

The greatest impact of Barth's theology was experienced at an early stage by the Hervormde Kerk of the Netherlands. The developments in this church were paralleled a bit later in the Gereformeerde Kerken as G. C. Berkouwer indicates in *A Half Century of Theology*.[5]

a. An article on "Predestination" by O. Noordmans in 1930 set the stage. Berkouwer indicates that he was attracted to that article when it was published. Looking back on that article in 1974 he states: "Prior to Barth, Noordmans pleaded for an understanding of 'election in Christ' so that election could be freed from the shackles of logical deduction. . . . Noordmans was ahead of his time with respect to understanding what the heart of the church [*cor ecclesiae*] involved."[6]

---

[3]Ibid., x. For an overview of Calvin's view see F. H. Klooster, *Calvin's Doctrine of Predestination*, Second Edition (Grand Rapids: Baker, 1977).

[4]For a survey of Barth's view of election see F. H. Klooster, *The Significance of Barth's Theology: An Appraisal with Special Reference to Election and Reconciliation* (Grand Rapids: Baker, 1961) 39-74.

[5]G. C. Berkouwer, *A Half Century of Theology* (Grand Rapids: Eerdmans, 1977; Dutch edition 1974) 75-106. Cf. also K. Runia, "Recent Reformed Criticisms of the Canons" in *Crisis in the Reformed Churches: Essays in Commemoration of the Great Synod of Dort, 1618-1619*, ed. P. Y. De Jong (Grand Rapids: Reformed Fellowship, 1968) 161-80.

[6]Berkouwer, *A Half Century*, 93.

b. In 1951 J. G. Woelderink published a booklet, *The Election,* criticizing the Canons' emphasis on the decree. Woelderink called this "causality," and favored election as an act of God in time. Reprobation as an eternal decree was entirely rejected.[7]

c. By 1953 a *gravamen* against the Canons of Dort was submitted by Reverend A. Duetz to the synod of the Hervormde Kerk. Entitled *The Heart of God, the Heart of the Church,* this *gravamen* was directed against the first of the five canons. Rev. Duetz objected to the Canons' appeal to Scripture, to certain deterministic tendencies in the Canons, and to the division of the human race into two groups of elect and reprobate.[8]

d. In 1961 the Synod of the Hervormde Kerk issued a *Pastoral Letter* as a response to the *gravamen* of 1953. Berkouwer summarizes this way:

> The guidelines dealt critically with the Canons' appeal to Scripture and with abstract theories of divine sovereignty; this was accompanied by an accent on election in Jesus Christ, in a gesture toward Calvin's insight into Christ as the "manifestation of election." The publication of the guidelines provoked a renewed consideration of the deepest intentions of the Arminians of the seventeenth century: their fear of the thought that God would be the author of sin and their fear of determinism.[9]

3. The Gereformeerde Kerken van Nederland (Reformed Churches of the Netherlands)

The criticism of the classic Reformed doctrine of predestination and of the Canons in particular followed a similar course in these churches. G. C. Berkouwer was the leading spokesman. Yet the criticism in these churches never went quite as far as it did in the Hervormde Kerk, and the ties to the confessions were usually stronger in connection with predestination.

a. G. C. Berkouwer moved from a critical stance over against K. Barth to one of increasing congeniality. This is evident in the change from his *Karl Barth* of 1936[10] to *The Triumph of Grace in the Theology of Karl Barth* in 1954.[11] His criticism of Barth's view of infant baptism

[7]Runia, "Recent Reformed Criticisms," 165–6.

[8]Berkouwer, *A Half Century,* 104; Runia, "Recent Reformed Criticisms," 166–7.

[9]Berkouwer, *A Half Century,* 104; Runia, "Recent Reformed Criticisms," 166–8.

[10]G. C. Berkouwer, *Karl Barth* (Kampen: J. H. Kok, 1936).

[11]G. C. Berkouwer, *The Triumph of Grace in the Theology of Karl Barth* (Kampen: J. H. Kok, 1954; E. T. Grand Rapids: Eerdmans, 1956).

appeared in 1947.[12] In 1955 Berkouwer published his book on *Divine Election*,[13] although he has recently informed us that its publication was "not without hesitation and persistent questions."[14] Berkouwer gradually overcame these hesitations and was more openly critical of the Canons in a 1963 article dealing with questions relating to the confessions.[15] In his 1974 publication, *A Half Century of Theology*, this criticism of the Canons was even sharper.[16] Now absolute decree, causality, numbers are all words of criticism and even caricature. Reprobation has fallen away. Yet he wishes to maintain the intention of the Canons while disagreeing with its framework. Election and preaching, election and comfort, election as the heart of the church—these are the positive emphases of the Canons and an authentic biblical echo. We must add that this gradually growing critique by Berkouwer is not only linked to his changing evaluation of Barth's theology and the developments in the Hervormde Kerk. There is also a strong negative reaction to the views of Reverend Herman Hoeksema.

Berkouwer met Hoeksema in 1952 during a lecture visit to the United States. Berkouwer reflected upon Hoeksema's views in his recent publication: "I have seldom met a theologian who reasoned through so consistently from his original standpoint; he never wavered from his starting point. He was one of the few who dared draw implications from reprobation for the task of preaching the gospel to all men."[17] Hoeksema was once a Christian Reformed minister. This church saw him as a hyper-Calvinist, a strong supralapsarian, a logicistic thinker, a denier of common grace and of a well-meant gospel proclamation to all. Berkouwer apparently saw things differently: "I do not believe that he came to his excessive formulations by way of his special supralapsarianism. I think they resulted from his

---

[12]G. C. Berkouwer, *Karl Barth en de Kinderdoop* (Kampen: J. H. Kok, 1947).

[13]G. C. Berkouwer, *Divine Election* (Grand Rapids: Eerdmans, 1960; Dutch edition 1955).

[14]Berkouwer, *A Half Century*, 100.

[15]"Vragen Rondom De Belijdenis," *Gereformeerd Theologisch Tijdschrift*, Feb. 1963, 1–41. Cf. Runia, 171.

[16]Berkouwer, *A Half Century*, 75–106. A beginning of this autobiographical account of his development with respect to Barth and predestination is present in Berkouwer's contribution to the C. Van Til *Festschrift, Jerusalem and Athens: Critical Discussions on the Philosophy and Apologetics of Cornelius Van Til*. E. R. Green, editor (Nutley, NJ: Presbyterian and Reformed, 1971) 197–204. Cf. also Runia, 168–73; and A. L. Baker, *A Critical Evaluation of G. C. Berkouwer's Doctrine of Election* (Dissertation, 1976) 331.

[17]Berkouwer, *A Half Century*, 98.

having set his thought processes within his vision of double predestination."[18] Herman Hoeksema's shadow also cuts across recent criticisms of the Canons of Dort. Both in the Gereformeerde Kerken and in the Christian Reformed church today, one gets the impression that such critics as Berkouwer, J. Daane, and H. Boer regard Hoeksema's interpretation of the Canons as the legitimate one. But this is to distort the teaching of the Canons of Dort.[19]

b. Berkouwer's development in criticism of the Canons was somewhat paralleled by Herman Ridderbos who published a monograph on *Israel in the New Testament, According to Romans 9–11* in 1955,[20] somewhat earlier than Berkouwer's *Divine Election* of the same year. "Before my book appeared," Berkouwer reports, "I enjoyed some probing theological conversations with Herman Ridderbos." Berkouwer saw "his own questions multiply before him," but "here, in the Bible's radical and open character, I found a way of speaking that is not defined by some darksome eternal background, but by the way of history that led Paul to his remarkable doxologies."[21]

Although Berkouwer does not want to identify Ridderbos's view with that of Barth, he does observe "a congeniality with the way Barth began his doctrine of election, at least on one point, 'The doctrine of election is the sum of the gospel.' "[22] At a ministers' conference Ridderbos once submitted the thesis that "the New Testament does not recognize a *problem* of predestination: it has only a predestination *gospel*."[23]

c. A. D. R. Polman, retired professor of systematic theology in the Reformed Seminary at Kampen (Gereformeerde), also agrees with Berkouwer on predestination. "In his earlier publications he [Polman] fully upheld the views of the Canons, but gradually, mainly under the influence of Barth and Berkouwer, he has changed his mind," to use K. Runia's summary.[24]

d. A *gravamen* was submitted to the synod of the Gereformeerde Kerken in 1966. B. J. Brouwer, a physician, had difficulties in signing the formula of subscription as an elder in the church. His main diffi-

---

[18]Ibid., 99.

[19]See F. H. Klooster, "The Doctrinal Deliverances of Dort" in *Crisis in the Reformed Churches*, 52–94. Cf. n. 5 above.

[20]Berkouwer, *A Half Century*, 100.

[21]Ibid.

[22]Ibid., 101.

[23]Ibid.

[24]Runia, "Recent Reformed Criticisms," 172. Cf. A. D. R. Polman, "De leer der verwerping van eeuwigheid op de Haagse conferentie van 1611" in *Ex Auditu Verbi* (Kampen: J. H. Kok, 1965) 176–93.

culty was with the teaching of the Canons on reprobation, which he considered blasphemous. Berkouwer reports that the synod was unanimous in understanding that the central thrust of the Canons was "the unmerited sovereign grace of God." But in 1970, on the basis of a study report from a committee charged with considering the *gravamen* of Brouwer, the synod of the Gereformeerde Kerken did remove the binding character of the Canons with respect to reprobation.[25]

e. Berkouwer indicates his basic agreement with this "far-reaching decision" which involved a "profound shift within the confessional life of the Reformed (Gereformeerde) churches."[26] Berkouwer concludes his 1974 review of these matters by reference to what he judges to be "the growing theological (and exegetical) consensus on this point." In his judgment "the content and motives of this consensus have led many of us to think that the freedom of God in his works is recognized and honored only in terms of grace" and this opens the way to the doxology of Romans 11.[27]

4. The Christian Reformed Church

Echoes of these developments in the Netherlands were heard in the Christian Reformed Church and in other churches throughout the world with close ties to the Netherlands. The majority of the reactions in these churches has been critical of the Dutch developments. Articles critical of the Canons of Dort and favorable to the Dutch developments have come mainly from James Daane and Harry Boer.

a. James Daane's writings culminated in his 1973 publication, *The Freedom of God: A Study of Election and Pulpit.*[28] Daane's is a radical critique of the Canons which shows remarkable affinity with Barth's doctrine of election. Daane's first chapter is called "the sum and substance of the Gospel." Three successive chapters are entitled "The Election of Israel," "The Election of Jesus Christ," and "The Election of the Church." The book is a frontal attack upon "decretal theology," and it is not free from caricature and historical misunderstanding, as M. E. Osterhaven of Western Theological Seminary has ably shown in his review of the book.[29] Daane radically historicizes divine election and appears to read the Canons entirely in the way of Hoeksema.

---

[25]Berkouwer, *A Half Century,* 105.
[26]Ibid.
[27]Ibid., 105f.
[28]J. Daane, *The Freedom of God* (Grand Rapids: Eerdmans, 1973).
[29]M. E. Osterhaven, *Reformed Review,* 27,3:151–4.

b. Harry Boer has also participated for a long time in critical discussions of the Canons and predestination. After numerous detours in the discussion, he has finally submitted a "confessional revision *gravamen*" to the synod of the Christian Reformed Church, in which he questions the biblical support for the doctrine of reprobation. It did not reach the Christian Reformed Synod in the form of a *gravamen* until 1977 so that it is now in the hands of a study committee which is expected to report to synod in 1980.[30] Boer's criticism is not as far reaching as that of J. Daane since the present focus is simply upon the biblical support for the articles on reprobation. Yet the issue is raised in the context of the Dutch developments and, at least in part, is an echo of those developments. Is reprobation required by scriptural teaching or is it simply a logical deduction from the doctrine of election? And if reprobation is not a biblical doctrine, what happens to the doctrine of election in the Canons? Such questions are now before the Christian Reformed Church.

CRITICISMS OF THE CANONS ON PREDESTINATION

Now I shall return to my seven-point summary of the Canons of Dort and indicate the criticisms that have been voiced with respect to these issues in recent discussions. I shall first present a summary of what I understand the Canons to teach and then reflect upon the criticisms that are made on each of these issues.

1. Absolute Decree

a. *The Canons*

God's decree of predestination, including both election and reprobation, is a sovereign, eternal decree—but it is not arbitrary! Notice how the Conclusion rejects arbitrariness.

b. *Recent Criticism*

All the recent critics of the Canons on predestination, from Barth through Berkouwer to Boer, sharply attack the Canons as setting forth a *decretum absolutum,* an arbitrary decree. The sharpest attack appears in J. Daane's *The Freedom of God,* in which he attacks what he calls "decretal theology." While A. Kuyper spoke of election as the "cardinal confession of the Reformed Church," Berkouwer says, "for

---

[30] *Acts of Synod,* 1977, 132–3, 664–79.

many it was only a sign pointing to a dark, hidden, mysterious, and arbitary decision 'behind the scenes' of the history of every child of man, a decision that was extremely difficult to rhyme with a gospel of love comforting to the heart."[31] "By arbitrariness we have in mind," says Berkouwer, "the 'once-for-all' decision made in eternity that seals the lot of all people forever."[32] On this score all the recent critics use only pejorative words and caricatures as they speak of "hidden decree," "barren and abstract concepts of sovereignty," and "a prioristic double decree," "arbitrariness," "causality," "decretal theology," *decretum absolutum.*

2. Sin the Presupposition of God's Decree

a. *The Canons*

The presupposition of God's eternal decree of predestination in the Canons is that the human race is viewed as fallen. Human irresponsibility is emphasized for all sin. If this perspective is meant when the Canons are said to be "infralapsarian," the designation may be appropriate; yet there is no speculation in the Canons about a logical order of the divine decrees. This perspective on sin as the presupposition of God's decree of election and reprobation is absolutely basic for a right interpretation of the Canons on reprobation as preterition.

b. *Recent Criticism*

To my amazement all recent critics ignore this fundamental perspective in interpreting the Canons. While it must be granted that this perspective involves complexity in understanding the eternal decree of God, it is basic to the questions of "causality," reprobation and unbelief, and the charge of "arbitrariness." The result is that most critics read the Canons in a supralapsarian manner. Berkouwer, Daane, and Boer seem to take Herman Hoeksema's supralapsarian reading of the Canons as normative. In my judgment this has thrown the entire discussion and the criticisms offered into hopeless confusion.

3. Equal Ultimacy

a. *The Canons*

Election and reprobation are viewed as "equally ultimate" in that both are included in the sovereign, eternal decree of God, but they

---

[31]Berkouwer, *A Half Century,* 79.
[32]Ibid., 82f.

are certainly not "in all respects parallel." This is clear, not only in the Canons themselves, but it is also emphasized in the Conclusion. The Conclusion states that "the Reformed Churches not only do not acknowledge, but even detest with their whole soul" the following among several issues:

1) that the same doctrine teaches that God, by a mere arbitrary act of his will, without the least respect or view to any sin, has predestinated the greatest part of the world to eternal damnation, and has created them for this very purpose;

2) that in the same manner (*eodem modo*) in which the election is the fountain and cause of faith and good works, reprobation is the cause of unbelief and impiety.[33]

b. *Recent Criticism*

Recent critics fail to distinguish between the terms "equal ultimacy" and "in all respects parallel." They employ the two statements from the Conclusion to object to or to revise statements within the Canons themselves. They usually employ the phrase "*non eodem modo*" ("not in the same manner") as a hermeneutical key even while rejecting reprobation because of causality thought to attach to a *decretum absolutum*.[34] In other words, "not in all respects parallel" in the Conclusion is used to reject the sovereignty (equal ultimacy) of the decree, at least in respect to reprobation. Again, the failure to make this important distinction leads to confusion in interpreting the Canons, and the Reformed doctrine in general.[35]

4. Election

a. *The Canons*

Election involves rescue from sin and the gracious giving of the gifts of salvation; it is election in Christ—Christ is both the *foundation of election* and the *foundation of salvation* (I. 7). The direct agency of God is involved in granting faith and all the gifts of salvation.

b. *Recent Criticism*

This is the part of the Canons apparently most immune to recent criticism. Yet most critics do not think that "election in Christ" goes

---

[33]P. Schaff, *The Creeds of Christendom* (New York: Harper & Brothers, 1919), 3. 596. A. Hoekema's new translation (cf. n. 1) does not include the Conclusion.

[34]Runia, "Recent Reformed Criticisms," 169.

[35]Cf. my discussion of this issue in the debates between C. Van Til and J. Daane in *Calvin's Doctrine of Predestination*, 71–9.

far enough in the Canons. The involvement of election in the eternal decree provides difficulty for those who historicize or actualize election. The divine agency obviously involved in the biblical doctrine of election is strangely not discussed by the critics in terms of "causality." While Barth has entirely and radically recast the doctrine of election, the other critics spend most of their time in criticizing other features of the Canons and do not really make clear the kind of doctrine of election that remains in the face of their other criticisms.

5. Reprobation

a. *The Canons*

Reprobation is viewed as a sovereign and just leaving of some "in their own wickedness and hardness" (I. 6), a passing by "in the eternal election of God" whereby he "has decreed to leave [them] in the common misery into which they have by their own fault plunged themselves, and not to give them saving faith and the grace of conversion" (I. 15). Thus God's decree not to give them faith, not to elect them, is *not* the cause of their unbelief. I. 5 specifically states that "the cause or blame for this unbelief . . . is . . . man." Furthermore, "God has decreed finally to condemn and punish [them] eternally, not only on account of their unbelief but also on account of all their other sins, as a declaration of His justice" (I. 15).

b. *Recent Criticism*

This perspective and the presupposition of sin in connection with divine preterition is mainly ignored in current discussions. Reprobation is said to be the cause of unbelief and the Canons are thought to be dangerously close to "blasphemy" on this score.[36] Ignoring this perspective in the Canons has contributed to the caricatures of the Canons. The result has been that all the critics either openly reject or seriously call into question the doctrine of reprobation. This doctrine is generally said to be the result of logical deduction from the doctrine of election. Interestingly, Romans 9:6–13 rarely comes under close exegetical scrutiny by the critics of the doctrine of reprobation.

6. The Numbers Question

a. *The Canons*

Both election and reprobation are viewed as individual, personal, specific. I. 7 refers to "a certain number of specific men" as elect; I. 15

---

[36]Berkouwer, *A Half Century*, 104f.

states that "not all men are elect but that certain ones have not been elected, or have been passed by in the eternal election of God." Election and reprobation are very concrete, specific, personal; yet the intention is not "individualistic," for the elect are brought into fellowship with Christ. One must admit that the Canons do not emphasize the communal, but the Heidelberg Catechism and the Belgic Confession do, and the Canons are a defense of these creeds.

b. *Recent Criticism*

Recent criticism of the Canons tends to deny personal reprobation except as judgment upon unbelief in history. Although personal election is not excluded, the tendency is rather to stress corporate election in ways that echo Barth's theology. Yet none of the recent critics moves into the universalistic tendencies inherent in Barth's theology. Strangely, the rejection of what is called absolute and abstract sovereignty has eliminated the concreteness and personalness of predestination and ended with a rather abstract election. The "numbers question" is usually treated in a pejorative manner. It is difficult to see how the concreteness of individual persons in election can be eliminated when the recent critics are so interested in emphasizing the comfort of election and the importance of preaching election.

7. Decree and History

a. *The Canons*

The eternal decree of God is effectuated in history through the use of means which call for genuine human responsibility. The gospel must be preached to all with urgency. Human history is meaningful history within the sovereignty of God. It is not meaningless replay. In election there is a direct divine agency but the elect are drawn into Christ's fellowship "through His Word and Spirit" (I. 7). Those not elected or passed by are left "in the common misery into which they have by their own fault plunged themselves" and are not given "saving faith and the grace of conversion" (I. 15). But this passing by and "not giving" is not the cause of their sin and unbelief; they fall "by their own fault" and reject the gospel preached to them.

b. *Recent Criticism*

The relation of eternal decree and history is usually criticized as "causality." The reprobation part is thus rejected. The election side is not discussed in great detail in terms of divine agency in effectuating God's decree of election. The general tendency is to historicize election. The larger questions concerning the nature of God and his relation to history in effectuating salvation are not discussed in the detail which the criticism of the Canons really requires.

CONCLUDING REMARKS

I cannot deny that the doctrine of predestination has sometimes been approached in rationalistic, logicistic ways. I must admit that preaching has tended to avoid this doctrine; comfort and assurance have not always emerged in ways that echo the biblical doctrine. Yet I do not find myself in sympathy with the criticism of the Canons surveyed above. Not only is injustice done to the Reformed doctrine but to the biblical foundations of that doctrine as set forth in the Reformed confessions.

Recent criticism of the Canons, as well as the other Reformed confessions, calls for renewed examination of biblical teaching along with careful exegesis proceeding from a hermeneutic perspective that is faithful to Scripture itself. Romans 8–11 must be reexamined and the bearing of 9:6–13 on election and reprobation (Jacob and Esau) may not be ignored. Preaching may not ignore the doctrine of God's predestination, but the criterion for preaching must be all that Scripture teaches, nothing less. And such a biblical doctrine must indeed issue in comfort and assurance even while the decisions made in history are to be seen as meaningful and urgent. In and through all of this we shall see increasingly that one's entire view of God and his relation to history will call for deeper reflection. And through it all, let us hope and pray that we shall not end with a God who is less than God, the living God of Abraham, Isaac, and Jacob!

8

A Wesleyan Note on Election

Wilber T. Dayton

Here we are primarily examining the Wesleyan viewpoint of election and only secondarily the soteriological context in which it is considered. It may come as a shock to some that Wesley and the Wesleyans have almost nothing of a positive nature to say about election. Most that they say is aimed rather at refutation of concepts of election that were, to their minds, destructive of evangelism and of obedience to the gospel.

Under these circumstances, it will be difficult indeed to be true to the historical facts without saying a number of unpleasant things. The purpose, however, will not be to spread malice but to examine viewpoints in the search for truth. I would like to acknowledge my great affection for and great debt to many true Christian brethren who do not agree with the views that are about to be expressed.

WHY NO ELABORATE WESLEYAN SYSTEM?

The only system on election, if one could call it such, that Wesley built has two affirmations. The first meaning of election, to him, is "a divine appointment of some particular men to do some particular work in the world."[1] The second is "a divine appointment of some men to eternal happiness."[2] But Wesley hastens to say, "But I believe

---

[1] "Predestination Calmly Considered," *Works of John Wesley,* 10. 210.
[2] Ibid.

this election to be conditional, as well as the reprobation opposite thereto. I believe the eternal decree concerning both is expressed in these words: 'He that believeth shall be saved; he that believeth not shall be damned.'"[3] Wesley does use the words "election" and "decree," but in any soteriological reference his viewpoint is more of a denial than an affirmation of election as generally taught. In other words, Wesley understands the decree to be of conditional rather than unconditional election. God elects those who meet the conditions.

Once the issue of conditionality is settled, the need for a doctrine of election is decreased almost to the vanishing point. Instead of constructing theories or doctrines about God's purpose in salvation, one quite naturally searches the Scriptures to see for whom Christ died, to whom the gospel should be preached, on what terms forgiveness and salvation are offered, and just how one is to be assured that he has met the conditions and is saved.

Wesleyans believe firmly in the holiness, justice, love, and grace of God. They are not restricted in their universal proclamation by hard-to-explain decrees. They believe that salvation is only in Christ. And they insist that Christ died for all, according to the Scriptures. If God commands repentance and faith of all men, they believe that God, by prevenient grace, makes the response possible. If the gospel is to be preached to all, the Wesleyans believe that it is not God's will that any should perish (2 Peter 3:9). The gospel call is not mockery. It is a genuine offer of salvation. Those who believe can know that they have eternal life (1 John 5:13). And victorious, Spirit-filled living, conformed to the image of Christ, is required and possible by grace in this life (Rom 8).

To Wesleyans, this is both orthodox and dynamic. The gospel offer of eternal salvation does not build around a doctrine of election. In fact, any doctrine that modifies or contradicts the clear revelation in Scripture is that far in error. And it was exactly on this basis that Wesley found fault with unconditional election. He was so sure of God's free offer of full salvation to all men that he could see nothing but error in a doctrine of election that was unconditional and for only some people. He went so far as to say,

> That it is an error, I know; because, if this were true, the whole Scripture must be false. But it is not for this—because it is an error—that I so earnestly oppose it, but because it is an error of so pernicious conse-

---

[3]Ibid., and quoting Mark 16:16.

quence to the souls of men; because it so naturally tends to hinder the inward work of God in every stage of it.[4]

It is this unconditionality that Wesley believed to be in error. God does indeed choose or elect to save whoever will respond in repentance and faith. And God has a plan of salvation whereby He will bless those elect with all spiritual blessings. God has even revealed the goal and nature of that plan—to make us conformed to the image of His Son (Rom 8:29). For Wesleyans, that is the sum-total of both election and predestination. Election is God's universal offer of salvation, and predestination is God's wonderful plan of achieving salvation for all who will respond. Wesley apparently saw no further need for a doctrine of election.

AN ALTERNATE SYSTEM

Wesley did have a system, though not of election. It was of holiness. His system was intensely practical. It concerned the holy life. While Calvinists emphasized justification, Wesley was more concerned about regeneration and sanctification. Calvinists, in keeping with election, were more interested in one's standing before God. Wesley was equally concerned with one's state or condition. To him it was inconceivable that one should be justified before God if he was not righteous and holy before men. Transformation, holy living, a walk with God, perfect love, a kind of Christian perfection, fulness of the Spirit—these are the marks of the Christian. Wesley's concern, as always, was with the practical. As opposed to the logical sequence of unconditional election, justification of sinners by decree, and inevitable perseverance, Wesley posited a know-so salvation here and now, attested by a clear witness of the Spirit and bearing the fruit of the Spirit unto everlasting life. This is the offer that God elected to give and this is the plan that God offered for all whom he called. To Wesley, salvation was neither a logical syllogism nor a decree; it was a vital, know-so experience. How, in any case, could it be by unconditional decree and also by faith? Wesleyans had not tarried for the answer.

So Wesley began early to search the Scriptures, seeking holiness. He found that one must be justified before he can be sanctified, but still holiness was his goal. Finally, God thrust him out to raise up a holy

---

[4]Ibid., 10. 256.

people. As election was the lodestone of the Calvinist emphasis, holiness was the controlling factor of redemption for Wesley. Christ died to make men holy. Accordingly, Wesley drew from the Sermon on the Mount and the whole Bible the elements of a system on the circumcision of the heart, scriptural Christianity, the way to the kingdom, the witness of the Spirit, Christian perfection, original sin, free grace, and various themes on the ethical content of Christian living. He was a specialist in holiness but not in election. Others have been specialists in election but not in holiness. The differences are logical but not absolute. Fortunately, all Christians meet at the foot of the cross. He who has the Son has life (1 John 5:12). Even so, the traditions flow in different channels. We are not surprised that Wesley has no full system on election nor Calvin on holiness.

IMPLICATIONS OF THE WESLEYAN VIEWPOINT

Some have exaggerated the points of harmony between Wesley and the Calvinists and have made it seem that the differences between them were only two letters of one word: the difference between unconditional and conditional election and predestination. In a sense the statement is true. But the two letters push the positions to opposite poles. They negate each other in the whole soteriological process. If there are five basic affirmations of Calvinism, the non-Calvinists must say the opposite at each point. If God works by unconditional decrees, the whole application of salvation to man will be quite different than if the divine government is a moral government turning on human response. If election to blessedness or damnation is relevant at all, it is central to the whole system of soteriology. If it is not central, it is suspect, in need of proof, and perhaps subversive. One must watch that it not be allowed to destroy the moral basis of God's work with man.

Historically, this was Wesley's problem. The passion of his life was evangelism. He told his preachers that they had no business but to save souls. Though he himself wrote, translated, edited, or produced some four hundred books and other items for publication, carried on a massive correspondence, and was deeply involved in a varied ministry, John Wesley was primarily an evangelist. His theology left him no alternative. And his evangelism demanded his theology for a rationale. To him the very gist of the gospel was to call sinners to repentance and faith. Everything else must be understood in this light and not vice versa. As A. Skevington Wood says, "Wesley's theology was practical and occasional rather than theoretical and systematic."[5] It had to be preachable. And unless grace is free for all as well as free in all, he did not feel that there was an effective gospel to preach. Anything else he considered "damning grace,"[6] "such love as makes your blood run cold."[7] Wesley simply could not absorb any part of a doctrine of election that limited the gospel of free grace.

Yet Wesley disliked controversy. He felt that contention and hot disputes were subversive to religion.[8] When predestination had to be considered, it should be done calmly, even if it took ninety devastating propositions to make his point.[9] On this principle and because of his regard for a godly colleague, he did not begin to edit the *Arminian Magazine* until after the death of Whitefield. To avoid confusion and controversy, he turned down repeated invitations to fill certain pulpits.

But to clear the air for evangelism and for the assurance of the gospel, Wesley did express his position and viewpoint with candor in his sermon on "Free Grace" and in "Predestination Calmly Considered." Grace is free in all and for all. It depends on God alone, who freely gave His own Son for us all. In the sermon much emphasis is given to the destructive effect of the doctrine of unconditional election upon preaching, holiness, happiness, good works, and revelation. In the larger treatise, reasoning and Scripture references are joined to remove all doubt of the universal offer and the conditionality of saving grace. He concludes that unconditional election is an error and he attacks the alleged error in order to preach the truth with greater power. Even so, he ended his long treatise with the conciliatory note that "if we serve God, our agreement is far greater than our difference."[10]

Generally speaking, then, Wesley's followers consider election to be simply God's love for all and His provision for the salvation of all who believe (John 3:16). Predestination, then, is simply God's plan of salvation. The plan includes not only the method and the conditionality of salvation but its purposes—"to be conformed to the image of His Son" (Rom 8:29) as well as all the spiritual blessings in Christ (Eph 1:3).

---

[5]A. Wood, "The Contribution of John Wesley to the Theology of Grace," *Grace Unlimited*, C. H. Pinnock, ed. (Minneapolis: Bethany, 1975) 210.

[6]*Works of Wesley*, 10. 229.

[7]Ibid.

[8]Ibid., 12. 240.

[9]Ibid., "Predestination Calmly Considered," 10. 204–59.

[10]Ibid., 259.

ATTEMPTS AT SYSTEM

A few attempts have been made both before and after Wesley to state the Arminian position in a way that is readily compared with the Five Points of Calvinism and with the other statements on election and predestination. Schaff quotes the Five Arminian Articles produced by the Remonstrants in A.D. 1610.[11] For accuracy and completeness, these are in the three languages (Dutch, Latin, and English). In substance they are in agreement with Wesley's viewpoint and with the more extended treatments in *The Writings of James Arminius* (3 vol). Dr. George E. Failing briefly summarizes these articles and proposes an acrostic of his own:

A tonement for all,
B elievers alone are elected,
C onvicting grace
D eliverance from sin
E ndurance of believers[12]

The obvious intent was to place the acrostic over against the TULIP of Five Point Calvinism:

T otal depravity
U nconditional election
L imited atonement
I rresistible grace
P erseverance of the saints

Arminius himself presented his own sentiments in four articles which he called absolute decrees and to which he appended twenty notes.[13] Under terms of decrees and predestination, he describes free grace for all and claims the approval of the great majority of professing Christians of all times. Later he added an article on perseverance of the saints that could be called a fifth.[14] As usual, he was impressed with the conditionality of grace but he left the question of final perseverance more open than the other points.

But, as has been said, Wesley and Wesleyan Arminians have not emphasized creedal statements. They have been content to preach the

---

[11]P. Schaff, *Creeds of Christendom,* 3. 545–9.

[12]G. E. Failing: *For Whom Did Christ Die? or Five Points of Arminianism* (Reprint, George E. Failing, PO Box 2000, Marion, IN) 6–12.

[13]*The Writings of James Arminius,* 1. 247–51.

[14]Ibid., 254.

Word in confidence that God puts both initial and final salvation within the reach of every man who will respond in repentance and faith. And from a negative standpoint they have doubted anything and everything that might obscure the gospel of free grace and full salvation for all. With this viewpoint, they built no towers of scholarly arguments for their position on election. Their emphasis was on holiness, love, and fulness of grace. In this area Wesleyan literature often has excelled. But it has not always been a matter of surprise that Calvinists have not been the best customers for the purchase of the "holiness classics" that present this Wesleyan approach.

What has amazed some people both inside and outside the Wesleyan tradition is the recurring interest in the Wesleys, in the Wesleyan revival, and in the concepts on which that revival was based. As the original evangelical revival went way beyond the Wesleyan societies, so have various American awakenings. And after Watergate and other disheartening events, some have mentioned the quickened interest in Wesleyan thought. A few have gone so far as to predict that the next great revival will stress holiness much as the earlier Wesleyan revival. Human attempts to lift society have not been noticeably successful, at least in moral realms. It may well be that our generation will not be satisfied with anything less than a dynamic call to repentance and faith that lays hold on the power of God and the moral force of an awakened conscience and a pure heart. For such a revival we pray. And we think the Wesleyan approach could again be an instrument of God to that end.

RECENT DEVELOPMENTS

However that may be, there is a new thing happening or at least it is happening in a new way in our day. Whereas a generation ago doubts were being expressed about "double election" (i.e. both election and reprobation) in what had been assumed to be Calvinistic territory, today volumes are coming out which blast unconditional election in as strong terms as ever Wesley or the Arminians have used. It is all the more striking that Robert Shank, in the preface to his *Life in the Son*, calls his book "the testimony of one whose study of the Scriptures led him to abandon a definition of doctrine he once cherished."[15] The sheer weight of his exegesis in this and the sequel volume[16] is to deny

---

[15]R. Shank, *Life in the Son* (Springfield, MO: Westcott Publishers, 1960) vii.

[16]R. Shank, *Elect in the Son* (Springfield, MO: Westcott Publishers, 1970).

unconditional election and unconditional perseverance and to draw serious attention to unlimited but conditional grace. His conclusions remind one of both Wesley and Arminius. And one is also reminded that Arminius himself was once a most competent and trusted Calvinistic theologian in Leyden. Likewise, John Fletcher, the theologian of Methodism, grew up in the shadow of Geneva.

Note the almost Wesleyan character of Shank's exegesis on the election of grace.[17] It is the expansion of three propositions:

I. The Election Comprehends All Men Potentially
II. The Election Comprehends No Man Unconditionally
III. The Election of Grace Comprehends the Israel of God Efficiently

He is at great pains throughout to show that these propositions are the only proper understanding of the great body of Scripture. Shank is thoroughly convinced of these perfectly Wesleyan conclusions and is convincing in the more than six hundred pages of his two books. Yet, like Wesley, he does not present a positive system of particular election to salvation or to damnation. He simply denies such a doctrine in the interest of the gospel of free grace to all who believe and abide in Christ.

In some respects there is a still more amazing volume under a 1975 copyright. It is *Grace Unlimited,* a symposium edited by Clark H. Pinnock.[18] The ten contributors are all men of stature in institutions in the United States, Canada, and England, most of whom would be expected on the basis of training and association to be of the Calvinistic viewpoint. But they have one thing in common in the case they present. Each affirms that Christ died for all men, and makes His offer of salvation to all. This again is not a rival doctrinal construct on election. It is rather an emphatic denial of limited atonement and of particular unconditional election or reprobation. All of this is done in the interest of unleashing the universal gospel call with unlimited grace provided for all men.

Pinnock's introduction furnishes adequate illustrations of the thrust of the book. He speaks of the "dreadful doctrine of double predestination."[19] Again, "If Scripture speaks of the universal salvific will of God, as it does repeatedly, the matter is settled. We need hardly give any theology that limits the gospel a second look."[20] Again, "The

---

[17]Ibid., 89–158.
[18]C. Pinnock, *Grace Unlimited* (Minneapolis: Bethany, 1975).
[19]Ibid., 12.
[20]Ibid., 13.

contributors to this volume are all convinced that belief in a limited election is mistaken, and does not represent fairly the biblical doctrine."[21] He refers to the innovation in Augustine of limited election as opposed to the earlier and biblical view of universal grace.[22] Again he says, "Although grace is certainly prevenient, it is not coercive."[23] He refers to "a smothering determinism," "fatalism," inconsistent with human freedom and undermining the reality of history and man's moral responsibility, making God the author of sin.[24] These statements and the thesis of the book remind one of Wesley's treatises on free grace and predestination. With Wesley, we wish there were a kinder way to say it. But this is still the Wesleyan understanding of soteriology in general and of election in particular. We try to say it in love and without rancor because we do appreciate our evangelical brethren with whom we agree more than we disagree.

---

[21]Ibid.
[22]Ibid., 14.
[23]Ibid., 15.
[24]Ibid., 16–17.

9

The Doctrine of Election: A Lutheran Note

David P. Scaer

Several months ago a colleague remarked in a chapel sermon that in his memory he had been the only one who had ever preached a sermon on the doctrine of election. With all due respect for his position and perhaps with less respect for his memory and analytical abilities, I was slightly taken aback by his assertion. First of all it is questionable whether sermons can ever be merely popular styled discussions of isolated doctrines. Secondly the discussion of any one doctrine is always done in conjunction with other doctrines comprising the Christian doctrinal corpus. Doctrines never have autonomous existences strung out like beads on a necklace, lying side by side in Nestorian isolation, whose only unifying theme is the string that runs through their center holding them together. Christian doctrines are more like pieces of cake, all made and baked from the same dough, though their places on the circumference of the plate are different and distinct. Whether a sermon deals with God,[1] Christ, salvation, atonement, or eschatology, it will also be a sermon on the election, even though the explicit word may not be used. The doctrine of election is

[1]The concept of God in Calvinism differs from that of Lutheranism. Typical of traditionally oriented Calvinistic dogmatics is the discussion of God's sovereignty in a prominent place. In his anticipated four-volume popular dogmatics James Montgomery Boice entitles the first volume *The Sovereign God,* Foundations of the Christian Faith (Downers Grove: InterVarsity, 1978). The discussion of God's sovereignty takes up as many pages (149–59) as does his triune essence (137–47). Robert D. Preus in his discussion of doctrine of

a divisive doctrine among conservative evangelical Christians. It has been notably divisive among Reformed Protestants, i.e., those who are not professing Lutherans. Nevertheless it was the doctrine of election in the last century that split Lutherans in the United States right down the middle and it more than any other doctrine is responsible for the manifold divisions in Lutheranism in America that last to this day.[2] This splintered division remains, though the causes for it have changed.

Among non-Lutherans there are clearly recognizable opposing views on election, without denying that there are variations within these views. Simply put, one sees God as the sole or major determinative factor both in salvation and damnation and the other sees man as decisive, at least in the sense of making some type of contribution. On the drawing board Lutheran theology occupies the halfway house holding that God alone is responsible for the salvation of the redeemed and that each man alone is responsible for his own damnation. This view may be described as single predestination, though this terminology is not common. If this is indeed a mediating position within Protestantism, it is purely accidental without any deliberate premeditation or the slightest desire to occupy a politically comfortable position in order to reconcile opposing views. For some it appears as philosophically the most unsatisfactory. Lutherans come to their view because it best satisfies the biblical data and it finds a firm basis in the great Reformation principles which recognizes the total depravity of man and more especially the magnificence of God's grace in the salvation of man, the *sola gratia*. The doctrines of the total depravity and the *sola gratia* stand in such a delicate juxtaposition that the slightest imbalance can introduce fatalism or synergism. While Lutherans in the *Formula of Concord,* the last of the historic Lutheran Confessions, set forth the biblical support for their doctrine of election, they had indeed set their position forth in the *Augsburg Confession* in the articles on original sin and justification.[3] Man is so perverse

---

God in the 16th- and 17th-century Lutheran dogmaticians lists fourteen attributes for God and makes no mention of sovereignty. *The Theology of Post-Reformation Lutheranism* (St. Louis: Concordia, 1972), 2. 5–6. There is no discussion of sovereignty in Francis Pieper's *Christian Dogmatics* (St. Louis: Concordia, 1953), probably most widely used doctrinal theology among conservative English-speaking Lutherans.

[2]F. Meuser, *The Formation of the American Lutheran Church* (Columbus, OH: Wartburg, 1958) 62–72.

[3]*Augustana* II. "That is, all men are full of evil lust and inclinations from their mothers' wombs and are unable by nature to have true fear of God and true faith in God."

Augustana IV. "It is also taught among us that we cannot obtain forgiveness

that left to his own desires he despises the things of God. Only a divine act of grace can rescue man from continued and final exclusion from salvation. What man sees as grace working in his life bringing him to faith is from God's viewpoint a deliberate choice and decision made in eternity. Election is only the side of the coin from grace. What is viewed as grace in time is viewed as election from the perspective of eternity. Therefore to preach grace alone is to preach the election.[4]

The doctrine of election can only be known through the special revelation now contained in the Holy Scriptures, and to inquire about it outside of this revelation is wrong. The personal knowledge of individual election is proclaimed to the believer in any sermon proclaiming God's universal love for sinners on account of Jesus Christ.

The Protestant Reformation principle is *sola gratia* with the *sola* underlined and italicized for ineradicable permanency. Without the *sola,* the *gratia* is no longer *gratia.* Even the *sola fide* principle only reinforces the *sola gratia* and can only be regarded a description of man's passive nature in coming to salvation. Faith cannot be regarded as a contributory factor. Knowledge of the doctrine of election is intended only for those who have already come to faith and should not be proclaimed to unbelievers.[5] The doctrine of election belongs at the end and not the beginning of spectrum.[6] The sinner who has come to faith in Christ eventually may become aware of certain factors in his life and a definite progression. No matter how hard the personal struggle was by which he resisted the Holy Spirit, he realizes that it was by grace and grace alone that he was saved. He can never say that he chose God. It was not really his decision, but a decision of the triune God. The Father of the Lord Jesus Christ by his Holy Spirit working through baptism and the preached word has brought that sinner to faith. At that moment he can say with St. Paul: "No man can

---

of sin and righteousness before God by our own merits, works, or satisfactions, but that we receive forgiveness of sin and become righteous before God by grace, for Christ's sake, through faith. . . . " All translations of the Lutheran Confessions are taken from *The Book of Concord,* ed. T. Tappert (Philadelphia: Fortress, 1959), hence referred to as Tappert.

[4]Francis Pieper, perhaps the most influential dogmatician of The Lutheran Church—Missouri Synod, speaks in a similar way, calling the doctrine of election a confirmation of the *sola gratia. Dogmatics,* 492–3.

[5]Ibid., 490–1.

[6]It is debatable where the doctrine of election should be discussed in connection with the doctrine of God. In traditional Reformed theology the subject is discussed in connection with God or his divine decrees. Cf. L. Berkhof, *Systematic Theology* (Grand Rapids: Eerdmans, Fourth Revised and Enlarged Edition, 1965) 109–25. Lutheran theology places it with grace, soteriology, and church. Pieper, *Dogmatics,* 473.

say that Jesus is the Lord but by the Holy Ghost."[7] Or he can say with Luther: "I believe that I cannot by my own reason or strength believe in Jesus Christ, my Lord, or come to Him, but the Holy Ghost has called me by the Gospel, enlightened me with His gifts and kept me in the one true faith."[8] There is nothing in the Christian's life which cannot be credited solely to God's grace revealed by the Holy Spirit in the Word and sacraments. God by a deliberate act of election in Christ is responsible for the awakening from the death of sin to a new life in Christ just as he is responsible for the glorification of our dead bodies on the day of resurrection.[9] The doctrine of election takes grace back one step before our conception and birth and states that the initiation for grace in the life of the Christian rests with God in eternity.[10] Any suggestion that the initiative rests with man within time detracts from God's glory, robs the cross of its power, and finally embezzles from grace that one quality that makes it grace—the initiative and the completion rest with God alone.[11]

From a historical perspective it is not difficult to see how Luther came to accept an extreme and radical understanding of grace in his own personal life and then later in his theology. His long and anxious search for salvation by works was only resolved by his discovery that the gospel was the free offer of salvation in Jesus Christ. God's grace was seen as all-embrace in the Christian's life from election in eternity to resurrection. Even the suggestion of the slightest human contribution, especially in the area of the human will, could only be considered a relapse into the synergism and semi-Pelagianism in the Church of Rome from which Luther extricated himself. At the beginning of the Reformation Luther set forth his position in *The Bondage*

---

[7] 1 Cor 12:3.

[8] Martin Luther, *Small Catechism*, "Explanation to the Apostles' Creed," Tappert, 345.

[9] "Without doubt God also knows and has determined for each person the time and hour of his call and conversion. But since he has not revealed this to us, we must obey his command and operate constantly with the Word, while we leave the time and hour to God" (Acts 1:7). "Formula of Concord" (FC), "Solid Declaration" (SD), XI, 56, Tappert, 625. See also 623–4.

[10] "If we stay with this and hold ourselves thereto, it is indeed a useful, salutary, and comforting doctrine, for it mightily substantiates the article that we are justified and saved without our works and merit, purely by grace and solely for Christ's sake." Ibid., 623.

[11] The Lutheran doctrine is deliberately anti-synergistic. "It is therefore false and wrong when men teach that the cause of our election is not only the mercy of God and the most holy merit of Christ, but that there is also within us a cause of God's election on account of which God has elected us to eternal life." Ibid., 631.

of Will against Erasmus's *The Freedom of the Will*.[12] After Luther had died, his co-worker Philipp Melanchthon, who belonged at least in part to the humanistic tradition of Erasmus, suggested that the human will was a type of contributory factor in personal salvation. Melanchthon was the first of many who claimed the name Lutheran for themselves, but who were not fully committed to the doctrines of grace and election as set forth by Luther and the officially recognized Lutheran Confessions.[13]

Formula of Concord, XI, both in the "Epitome" and "Solid Declaration" sets forth the classical Lutheran understanding of the election. It is unique in that it is the only article which does not speak to a specific controversy within the Lutheran Church at that time,[14] though Melanchthon's synergism and Calvin's double predestination teaching were clearly regarded as dangers. The authors of the *Formula* with near prophetic vision saw the doctrine on election as a bone of contention in the future because of certain apparent internal complexity. God alone was recognized as the sole cause of salvation, but without in any way being responsible for sin and evil.[15] The doctrine of election also was set forth along with Lutheran understandings of the Word and sacraments, justification, and sin. Yes, the redeemed are chosen and elected by a special decision of God, but this election is revealed only in the gospel whether that gospel is preached or tied down to sacramental action.[16] It is wrong to pry into God's mysteries at this point. It is also wrong to suggest that the elect have performed some-

---

[12]For a discussion of Luther's position on predestination, see Harry Buis, *Historic Protestantism and Predestination* (Philadelphia: Presbyterian and Reformed, 1958) 28-61. Buis is convinced that "Martin Luther held to the doctrine of predestination as strongly as did Calvin" (p. 2). Buis is convinced that Luther held to a double predestination (p. 48). Buis was writing to show that Calvin's concepts have had wide acceptance in Christianity. The citation brought up to demonstrate that Luther held to double predestination speaks of God's eternal love and hatred. This is not the same as God's predestination and causing evil.

[13]Philipp Melanchthon, co-worker of Luther and author of three of the historic Lutheran Confessions—Augsburg Confession, Apology, and the Treatise—offered a position on the Lord's Supper which Calvin could accept. Though he is often considered as one of the founders of the Reformed faith especially for his 1541 edition of the Augsburg Confession, his final position was synergistic as even Buis admits. Ibid., 81.

[14]Tappert, 616.

[15]"The source and cause of evil is not God's foreknowledge (since God neither creates nor works evil, nor does he help it along or promote it). . . ." Tappert, 617.

[16]Ibid., 622-3.

thing meritorious to earn God's special favor[17] or that they are less sinless than others or even to suggest that God loves those who are eventually damned less than He loves those who are redeemed.[18] It may not be said that the will of the damned is more obstinate. When the doctrine of election is sundered from the question of the sinner's justification before God, we are no longer dealing with the Christian doctrine of the election but with the arbitrary and capricious decisions of a deity whose greatest delight is to make a show of His omnipotence even if it is at the expense of hapless, helpless, hopeless sinners. The doctrine of election is revealed not because God needs more glory, but rather that the troubled sinner may know that his salvation does not depend upon his own whimsical choice which today may accept Jesus but tomorrow may reject him. The assurance of salvation rests not with the individual but with God's choice in eternity.[19]

Formula of Concord, XI, brings a wide range of biblical data into the presentation of election. Ephesians 1:4, 5 is cited to demonstrate that election applies only to the redeemed and not the damned. "On the other hand, the eternal election of God or God's predestination to salvation does not extend over both the godly and the ungodly, but only over the children of God, who have been elected and predestined to eternal life 'before the foundation of the world was laid,' as St. Paul says 'Even as he chose us in him, he destined us in love to be his sons through Jesus Christ' (Eph. 1:4, 5)."[20] The *Formula* holds that personal knowledge of one's own election comes through the gospel proclamation. Within the context of the word and faith, Christian certainty of election exists. "This is revealed to us, however, as Paul says, 'Those whom God has foreknown, elected and decreed, he has also called.' "[21]

In setting forth the doctrine of election to salvation, the *Formula* specifically rejects the idea "that God does not desire to save everyone"[22] or that "God has predestined certain people to damnation so that they cannot be saved."

Alongside of the *sola gratia* principle is the equally important *gratia*

---

[17]See n. 11.

[18]"Hence if we want to consider our eternal election to salvation profitably, we must by all means cling rigidly and firmly to the fact that as the proclamation of repentance extends over all men (Luke 24:47), so also does the Gospel promise." Tappert, 620.

[19]See n. 10.

[20]Tappert, 617.

[21]Ibid., 620.

[22]Ibid., 497.

universalis principle. Just as grace has its cause in God alone, so also God intends that all men should benefit from his grace. Grace is as universal as is sin; this is the message of Romans 8:28ff. Lutheran theology finds it impossible for several reasons to posit an evil will in God. There is the problem of whether two opposing wills can exist side by side in God. If Satan's house falls because it is divided against itself, certainly a schizophrenic deity would also suffer from this malfunctioning. Secondly, the God who conquers evil through the atoning death of his Son cannot be the cause of sin, damnation, or any other evil without finally being found to be in a miserable, pitiable contradiction with himself. Why should God destroy with the death of his Son that for which he alone is responsible? The *Formula* explicitly says, "The source and cause of evil is not God's foreknowledge (since God neither creates nor works evil, nor does he help it along and promote it), but rather the wicked and perverse will of the devil and of men, as it is written, 'Israel, thou hast plunged thyself into misfortune, but in me alone is thy salvation' (Hos 13:9)."[23]

The explicit Lutheran rejection of a predestination to damnation means that Lutheran theology is firmly committed to the concept of *gratia universalis* and a universal atonement. For these views the *Formula* finds wide biblical support: John 3:16, "For God so loved the world"; John 1:29, "Behold the Lamb of God that taketh away the sin of the world"; John 1:7 and 2:22 where the blood of Jesus is described as "the propitiation for the sins of the world."[24]

Behind the doctrine of universal salvation and universal atonement is the doctrine of the incarnation itself. We confess with St. Paul that "God was in Christ reconciling the world to himself." Christ's death has an infinite worth not because of a decree of the Father, but rather because his human nature was thoroughly and completely permeated by the divine nature.[25] The death of Christ was the death of God. His death placed in the scales of justice placed the entire world in a favorable position, tipping those scales in the favor of every man. Now this atonement has made it possible for God to be gracious to everyone. There is more forgiveness than there is sin.[26] The *Formula* cites Romans 11:32, "God has included all men under disobedience so that he

---

[23]Ibid., 617.

[24]Ibid., 620.

[25]David P. Scaer, "The Nature and Extent of the Atonement in Lutheran Theology," *BETS*, X (4) 179–87.

[26]Lutheran and Reformed Christologies significantly differ. The Formula of Concord quotes Luther to the end that the divinity of the God-Man Jesus Christ tips the balances of justice in man's favor. Tappert, 599.

might have mercy on all," and 2 Peter 3:9, "The Lord is not willing that any should perish, but that all should turn to repentance."[27]

In maintaining the doctrine of the election of the redeemed to salvation, the *Formula* is absolutely adamant in opposing any suggestion that God's universal message of salvation is not sincerely intended.[28]

> The reason why "many are called and few are chosen" is not that in his call, which takes place through the Word, God intended to say, "Externally I do indeed through the Word call all of you, to whom I give my Word, into My kingdom, but down in My heart I am not thinking of all, but only of a certain few. . . ." In this it would be taught that God, who is eternal Truth, contradicts himself. Yet God himself punishes men for such wickedness when they say one thing and think and intend something different in their hearts (Ps 5:10, 11; 12:3, 4).

If the *Formula,* XI, the article on election in the Lutheran Confessions is a tribute to *sola gratia,* it is at the same time a firm testimony to *gratia universalis.* The invitation to salvation is sincere. The parable of the invitation to the wedding of the king's son is cited. The refusal to accept the invitation does not rest with God but with men. "The majority despise the Word and refuse to come to the wedding." Here the *Formula* must be cited as its own witness.[29]

> The reason for such contempt of the Word is not God's foreknowledge but man's own perverse will, which rejects or perverts the means and instrument of the Holy Spirit which God offers to him through the calls and resists the Holy Spirit who wills to be efficaciously active through the Word, as Christ says, "How often would I have gathered you together and you would not!" (Matt 23:37).

In more specific theological language St. Paul says that the atonement is universal in stating that Christ "gave himself as a ransom for all (*antilutron huper panton*)" (1 Tim 2:6) and that God desires the salvation of all in stating that "God will have all men to be saved (*hos pantas anthropous thelei sothenai*)" (1 Tim 2:4).[30] This gracious will of God to save all men even includes those who are eventually damned and not the elect only. Even those who build roads to hell for others

---

[27]Ibid., 620–1.

[28]Ibid., 622.

[29]Ibid., 623.

[30]Though there have been attempts to mitigate Calvin's concept of a double predestination, the concept of a universal atonement is still not accepted. Scriptural references to "all" are reinterpreted to fit this concept of limited atonement.

are embraced by the atonement and universal salvation. The false prophets who are described as the bearers of destructive heresies are said to deny "the Master who bought them, bringing upon themselves swift destruction" (2 Peter 2:1). The Epistle to the Romans which stands with Ephesians as the great manifesto on the election speaks of God enduring with much patience those who will eventually be damned (Rom 9:22, 23).

In Lutheran theology the *sola gratia* and *gratia universalis* stand in tension. It recognizes that God is the only cause of the salvation of the redeemed and that this divine cause has its origin in eternity and is called election. At the same time God embraces all men in his redeeming love and desires their salvation. Those who are eventually damned have only themselves to blame. Lutheran theology does not recognize any theory of God's bypassing the damned. But this in no way permits or suggests that those who are elected are morally or intellectually superior to those who are finally damned. The dilemma, if it is indeed a dilemma, is summarized in a short Latin phrase of four words: *Cur alii alii non?* "Why some and not others?" Paraphrased it would read, "Why are some chosen and others not?" This is the mystery which Lutheran theology chooses to believe, but not resolve.[31] The failure to resolve is not because it fears such ventures, but the two other alternatives require a negation of significant portions of the divine revelation. The anguish over the question of predestination and universal grace is comparable to Paul's anguish over God's rejection of the Jews and the acceptance of the Gentiles. He would even give himself over to wrath if his fellow countrymen could be saved. But he stops at the door of the mystery and refuses to enter. God's riches, wisdom, and knowledge are too deep for human comprehension (Rom 11:29–36).

Christians can only marvel at the mysteries but cannot explain

---

[31]For a discussion of this see Pieper, *Dogmatics*, 501–3. Two other Latin phrases also express the dilemma: *Cur non omnes?* (Why are not all saved?) and *Cur alii prae aliis?* (Why are some saved before others?) Buis is disturbed that the *Formula* does not resolve the dilemma in favor of the double predestination of the Reformed, stating that even though *Formula* explicitly denies synergism, the synergistic position of Melanchthon is really the one which the confession endorses. "For example, the Formula of Concord (1580) [sic!] was contradictory on this point. It supposedly opposed the teachings of Melanchthon and denied synergism. Yet it denied irresistible grace and affirmed the universality of the offer of the Gospel. The position of the Formula of Concord amounted to conditional predestination which became the accepted Lutheran doctrine in the seventeenth century. It stated that predestination is the will of God that all who believe are saved. It said that the foreknowledge

them. With the doctrine of election we have to face the questions of redemption and damnation. The problem cannot be better summarized than in the theologically accurate words of Jesus: "O Jerusalem, O Jerusalem, thou that killest the prophets, and stonest them which are sent unto thee, how often would I (*ethelesa*) have gathered thy children together, even as a hen gathereth her chickens under her wings and ye would not (*ouk ethelesata*)?" (Matt 23:37). God is the cause and the only cause of salvation and man is the sole cause of his own damnation.

In Lutheran theology the doctrine of election is never that prominent, but its principles are derived from its doctrine of God, Christ, Word, sacraments, salvation, and church. It attempts to steer a difficult but clear course through the dangers of synergism and double predestination. It refuses to understand the atonement in light of election as do the Calvinists and refuses to understand the election in light of the atonement as do the Wesleyans. For Lutherans the election is limited to those who are eventually saved, and the atonement embraces all men.

Perhaps the doctrine of election can best be described graphically. It is only for the Christian who here in time through his faith focuses back past through time into eternity and recognizes that in one eternal moment God destined him for salvation. Beyond this it is better for the Christian not to ask and if he asks, then realize that God has here a mystery whose solution has not been revealed.

When a Lutheran goes to church, he has no trouble singing hymns praising God's universal redemption and his predestination. He can sing John Wesley's translation of Zinzendorf's "Jesus Thy Blood and Righteousness" where in the fifth verse are these words:

> Lord, I believe were sinners more
> Than sands upon the ocean shore,

---

deals with the good and the evil, but that predestination deals only with salvation. Thus the large wing of the Protestant Church which is composed of the various bodies of Lutherans came to hold a position denying absolute predestination in spite of the fact that their great leader, Martin Luther had been a strong advocate of such predestination." Buis, *Historic Protestantism*, 82. Buis is correct in seeing that the Lutheran dogmaticians, perhaps unawaringly, did introduce a concept of conditional election with their concept of *intuitu fide*, i.e., God chose those who would believe, and that this view infiltrated Lutheranism. He is wrong in his assessment that the *Formula* does not hold an absolute election of the redeemed. His few words indicate that the real source of his problem lies elsewhere, i.e., in his denial of the doctrines of universal grace and the ability of man to reject the gospel as it comes through Word and sacraments.

> Thou hast for all a ransom paid,
> For all a full atonement made.

The Lutheran can also sing with the Congregationalist Calvinist Josiah Conder:

> Lord, 'tis not that I did choose Thee;
> That, I know, could never be;
> For this heart would still refuse Thee
> Had Thy grace not chosen me.

Martin Luther himself catches the authentic Lutheran spirit which sees the doctrine of election from a personal, individualistic, and almost existential spirit.

> But God beheld my wretched state
> Before the world's foundation
> And, mindful of His mercies great,
> He planned my soul's salvation.
> A father's heart He turned to me,
> Sought my redemption fervently;
> He gave His dearest treasure.[32]

Within the cross and only within the cross does the doctrine of election have its foundation and its goal.

---

[32]These translations are taken from *The Lutheran Hymnal* (St. Louis: Concordia, 1941), Hymn Nos. 37, 371, 377.

10

An Evangelical Theology of Liberation

Ronald J. Sider

The emergence of theologies of liberation—whether black, feminist, or Latin American—is probably the most significant theological development of our decade. At the heart of liberation theology is the attempt fundamentally to rethink theology from the standpoint of the poor and oppressed. The central theological foundation of this approach is the thesis that God is on the side of the poor and oppressed.

It is that basic thesis that I want to probe. Space here is too limited to develop a comprehensive evangelical theology of liberation, so instead I want to answer two questions. How biblical is the view that God is on the side of the poor and the oppressed? Second, in light of the answer to this first question, how biblical is evangelical theology?

I want to argue that one of the central biblical doctrines is that God is on the side of the poor and the oppressed. Tragically, evangelical theology has largely ignored this central biblical doctrine and thus our theology has been unbiblical—indeed even heretical—at this important point.

Before I develop this double thesis, however, I want to outline some things I do *not* mean when I say that God is on the side of the poor and oppressed.

I do not mean that material poverty is a biblical ideal. This glorious creation is a wonderful gift from our Creator. He wants us to revel in its glory and splendor.

Second, I do not mean that the poor and oppressed are, because they are poor and oppressed, to be idealized or automatically in-

cluded in the church. The poor sinfully disobey God in the same way
that we wretched middle-class sinners do and they therefore need to
enter into a living personal relationship with Jesus Christ. Only then
do they become a part of the church. One of the serious weaknesses in
much of liberation theology is an inadequate ecclesiology, especially
the tendency to blur the distinction between the church and the
world. And one can understand why. It is understandable that black
and Latin American theologians would be impressed by the double
fact that whereas most of the organized church regularly ignores the
injustice which causes poverty and oppression, those who do care
enough to risk their lives for improved conditions are often people
who explicitly reject Christianity. Hence one can understand why
someone like Hugo Assmann would conclude that

> the true Church is "the conscious emergence and the more explicit
> enacting of the one meaning of the one history," in other words, a
> revolutionary consciousness and commitment. The explicit reference to
> Jesus Christ becomes in this view gratuitous in the original sense of the
> word—something which is not demanded by or needed for the struggle
> [of socio-economic liberation].... The reference to Jesus Christ does
> not add an "extra" to the historical struggle but is totally and without
> rest identified with it.[1]

In spite of deep appreciation for the factors which lead to an identification of the church with the poor and oppressed or the revolutionary
minority that seeks liberation for them, one must insist that such a
view is fundamentally unbiblical.

Third, when I say that God is on the side of the poor and oppressed, I do not mean that God cares more about the salvation of the
poor than the salvation of the rich or that the poor have a special
claim to the gospel. It is sheer nonsense to say with Enzo Gatti:

> The human areas that are poorest in every way are the most qualified
> for receiving the Saving Word. They are the ones that have the best
> right to that Word; they are the privileged recipients of the Gospel.[2]

God cares equally about the salvation of the rich and the poor. To be
sure, at the psychological level, Gatti is partly correct. Church growth
theorists have discovered what Jesus alluded to long ago in his comment on the camel going through the eye of the needle. It *is* ex-

---

[1]J. M. Bonino, *Doing Theology in a Revolutionary Situation* (Philadelphia:
Fortress, 1975), 161-2.
[2]E. Gatti, *Rich Church—Poor Church* (Maryknoll: Orbis, 1974) 43.

tremely difficult for rich persons to enter the kingdom. The poor *are* generally more ready to accept the gospel than the rich.[3] But that does not mean that God desires the salvation of the poor more than the salvation of the rich.

Fourth, to say that God is on the side of the poor is not to say that knowing God is nothing more than seeking justice for the poor and oppressed. Some—although certainly not most—liberation theologians do jump to this radical conclusion. José Miranda says bluntly, "To know Jaweh is to achieve justice for the poor."[4] "The God who does not allow himself to be objectified, because only in the immediate command of conscience is he God, clearly specifies that he is knowable *exclusively* in the cry of the poor and the weak who seek justice."[5] Tragically it is precisely Miranda's kind of one-sided, reductionist approach that offers comfortable North Americans a plausible excuse for ignoring the radical biblical Word that seeking justice for the poor is inseparable from—even though it is not identical with—knowing Jahweh.

Finally, when I say that God is on the side of the poor, I do not mean that hermeneutically we must start with some ideologically interpreted context of oppression (for instance a Marxist definition of the poor and their oppressed situation) and then reinterpret Scripture from that ideological perspective. Black theologian James H. Cone's developing thought is interesting at this point. In 1969, in *Black Theology and Black Power* he wrote,

"The fact that I am Black is my ultimate reality." My identity with *blackness,* and what it means for millions living in a white world, controls the investigation. It is impossible for me to surrender this basic reality for a "higher more universal reality."[6]

By the time Cone wrote *God of the Oppressed,* however, he realized that such a view would relativize all theological claims including his own critique of white racist theology.

How do we distinguish our words about God from God's Word...? Unless this question is answered satisfactorily, black theologians' distinction between white theology and Black Theology is vulnerable to the

---

[3]See Samuel Escobar's summary of Donald McGavran in S. Escobar and J. Driver, *Christian Mission and Social Justice* (Scottsdale: Herald, 1978) 45-7.
[4]J. Miranda, *Marx and the Bible* (Maryknoll: Orbis, 1974) 44.
[5]Ibid., 48.
[6]J. H. Cone, *Black Theology and Black Power* (New York: Seabury, 1969) 32-3. But see a conflicting, more biblical emphasis on 34, 51.

white contention that the latter is merely the ideological justification of radical black polities.[7]

To be sure, Cone believes as strongly as other liberation theologians that the hermeneutical key to Scripture is God's saving action to liberate the oppressed. But how does he know that?

> In God's revelation in Scripture we come to the recognition that the divine liberation of the oppressed is not determined by our perceptions but by the God of the Exodus, the prophets, and Jesus Christ who calls the oppressed into a liberated existence. Divine revelation *alone* is the test of the validity of this starting point. And if it can be shown that God as witnessed in the Scriptures is not the liberator of the oppressed, then Black Theology would have either to drop the "Christian" designation or to choose another starting point.[8]

One can only wish that all liberation theologians agreed with Cone!

When then I say that God is on the side of the poor, I do not mean that poverty is the ideal; that the poor and oppressed, *qua* poor and oppressed, are the church or have a special right to hear the gospel; that seeking justice for the oppressed is identical with knowing Jahweh; or that hermeneutically one should begin with some ideologically interpreted context of oppression and then reinterpret Scripture from that perspective.

In what sense then *is* God on the side of the poor and oppressed? I want to develop three points:[9]

1. At the central points of revelation history, God also acted to liberate the poor and oppressed.

2. God acts in history to exalt the poor and oppressed and to cast down the rich and oppressive.

3. God's people, if they are truly God's people, are also on the side of the poor and oppressed.

First, I want to look briefly at three central points of revelation history—the exodus, the destruction of Israel and Judah, and the Incarnation. At the central moments when God displayed his mighty acts in history to reveal his nature and will, God also intervened to liberate the poor and oppressed.

God displayed his power at the exodus in order to free oppressed

---

[7]J. H. Cone, *God of the Oppressed* (New York: Seabury, 1975) 84.
[8]Ibid., 82; Cone's italics.
[9]The following section relies heavily on chapter three of my *Rich Christians in an Age of Hunger* (Downers Grove: InterVarsity, 1977).

slaves! When God called Moses at the burning bush, he informed Moses that his intention was to end suffering and injustice: "I have seen the affliction of my people who are in Egypt, and have heard their cry because of their taskmasters; I know their sufferings, and I have come down to deliver them out of the hand of the Egyptians" (Exod 3:7-8). Each year at the harvest festival, the Israelites repeated a liturgical confession celebrating the way God had acted to free a poor, oppressed people.

> A wandering Aramean was my father; and he went down into Egypt and sojourned there.... And the Egyptians treated us harshly and afflicted us, and laid upon us hard bondage. Then we cried to the Lord, the God of our fathers, and the Lord heard our voice, and saw our affliction, our toil, and our oppression; and the Lord brought us out of Egypt with a mighty hand ... (Deut 26:5ff).

Unfortunately some liberation theologians see in the exodus only God's liberation of an oppressed people and miss the fact that God also acted to fulfill his promises to Abraham, to reveal his will and to call out a special people. Certainly God acted at the exodus to call a special people so that through them he could reveal his will and bring salvation to all people. But his will included the fact, as he revealed ever more clearly to his covenant people, that his people should follow him and side with the poor and oppressed. The fact that Yahweh did not liberate all poor Egyptians at the exodus does not mean that he was not concerned for the poor everywhere any more than the fact that he did not give the Ten Commandments to everyone in the Near East means that he did not intend them to have universal significance. Because God chose to reveal himself in history, he disclosed to particular people at particular points in time what he willed for all people everywhere.

At the exodus, God acted to demonstrate that he is opposed to oppression. We distort the biblical interpretation of the momentous event of the exodus unless we see that at this pivotal point, the Lord of the universe was at work correcting oppression and liberating the poor.

The prophets' explanation for the destruction of Israel and then Judah underlines the same point. The explosive message of the prophets is that God destroyed Israel, not just because of idolatry (although certainly because of that), but also because of economic exploitation and mistreatment of the poor!

The middle of the eighth century B.C. was a time of political success and economic prosperity unknown since the days of Solomon. But it was precisely at this moment that God sent his prophet Amos to announce the unwelcome news that the northern kingdom would be destroyed. Why? Penetrating beneath the facade of current prosperity and fantastic economic growth, Amos saw terrible oppression of the poor. He saw the rich "trample the head of the poor into the dust of the earth" (2:7). He saw that the affluent lifestyle of the rich was built on oppression of the poor (6:1-7). Even in the courts the poor had no hope because the rich bribed the judges (5:10-15).

God's word through Amos was that the northern kingdom would be destroyed and the people taken into exile (7:11, 17). Only a very few years after Amos spoke, it happened just as God had said. Because of their mistreatment of the poor, God destroyed the northern kingdom. If there were room, it would be easy to document the same point with reference to the destruction of the southern kingdom (eg., Jer 5:26-29; 34:3-17). The cataclysmic catastrophe of national destruction and captivity reveals the God of the exodus still at work correcting the oppression of the poor.

When God acted to reveal himself most completely in the Incarnation, he continued to demonstrate his special concern for the poor and oppressed. St. Luke used the programmatic account of Jesus in the synagogue at Nazareth to define Jesus' mission. The words which Jesus read from the prophet Isaiah are familiar to us all:

> The Spirit of the Lord is upon me,
> because he has anointed me to preach good news to the poor.
> He has sent me to proclaim release to the captives
> and recovery of sight to the blind,
> to set at liberty those who are oppressed,
> to proclaim the acceptable year of the Lord (Luke 4:18-19).

After reading these words, he informed the audience that this Scripture was now fulfilled in himself. The mission of the Incarnate One was to preach the good news to the poor and free the oppressed.

Many people spiritualize these words either by simplistically assuming that he was talking about healing blinded hearts in captivity to sin or by appealing to the later OT and intertestamental idea of "the poor of Jahweh" (the *'anawim*). It is true that the latter Psalms and the intertestamental literature use the terms for the poor (especially *'anawim*) to refer to pious, humble, devout Israelites who place all their trust in Jahweh.[10] But that does not mean that his usage had no

---

[10]See R. Batey, *Jesus and the Poor: the Poverty Program of the First Christians* (New York: Harper, 1972) 83-97; A. Gelin, *The Poor of Yahweh* (Collegeville, MN: Liturgical Press, 1964). See too C. Schultz, "*'Ani* and *'Anaw* in Psalms" (Unpublished Ph.D. Dissertation, Brandeis University, 1973); P. D. Miscall, "The Concept of the Poor in the Old Testament" (Unpublished Ph.D. Dissertation, Harvard University, 1972).

connection with socio-economic poverty. Indeed, it was precisely the fact that the economically poor and oppressed were the faithful remnant that trusted in Jahweh that led to the new usage where the words for the poor designated the pious faithful.

The Hebrew words for the poor were *'ani, 'anaw, 'ebyon, dal,* and *raš. 'Ani* (and *'anaw,* which originally had approximately the same basic meaning) denotes one who is "wrongfully impoverished or dispossessed."[11] *'Ebyon* refers to a beggar imploring charity. *Dal* connotes a thin, weakly person, e.g., an impoverished, deprived peasant.[12] Unlike the others, *raš* is an essentially neutral term. In their persistent polemic against the oppression of the poor, the prophets used the terms *'ebyon, 'ani,* and *dal.*

Later these same words (especially *'anawim*) were used to designate the faithful remnant, the "pious poor" who trust solely in Jahweh.[13] But that does not mean that the older socio-economic connotations were lost. Richard Batey puts it this way:

> Beginning with the experience that the poor were often oppressed by the wicked rich, the poor were considered to be the special objects of Yahweh's protection and deliverance (Pss. 9:18, 19:1–8 . . .). Therefore the poor looked to Yahweh as the source of deliverance from their enemies and oppressors. This attitude of trust and dependence exemplified that piety that should have characterized every Israelite. In this way the concept of the "pious poor" developed.[14]

Zondervan's *New International Dictionary of the New Testament* makes the same point:

> Only in the setting of this historical situation can we understand the meaning in the Psalm of "poor" and "needy." The poor man is the one who suffers injustice; he is poor because others have despised God's law. He therefore turns, helpless and humble, to God in prayer. . . .-
> Through the self-identification, generation after generation, of those who prayed with the poor in psalms of individual lamentation and thanksgiving . . . there gradually developed the specific connotation of "poor" as meaning all those who turn to God in great need and seek his help. God is praised as the protector of the poor (eg. Pss. 72:2, 4, 12f; 132:15), who procures justice for them against their oppressors.[15]

This same usage is common in inter-testamental literature. When Greece and then Rome conquered Palestine, Hellenistic culture and

---

[11]*TDNT,* 6. 888.

[12]Gelin, *The Poor of Yahweh,* 19–20.

[13]Ibid., 50.

[14]R. Batey, *Jesus and the Poor,* 92.

[15]*The New International Dictionary of New Testament Theology.* ed. Colin Brown (3 vols.; Grand Rapids: Zondervan, 1976), 2. 822-3.

values were foisted upon the Jews. Those who remained faithful to
Yahweh often suffered financially. Thus the term *poor* was, as J. A.
Ziesler says, "virtually equivalent to pious, God-fearing, and godly
and reflects a situation where the rich were mainly those who had sold
out to the incoming culture and had allowed their religious devotion
to become corrupted by the new ways. If the poor were the pious, the
faithful and largely oppressed, the rich were the powerful, ungodly,
worldly, even apostate."[16] Thus the faithful remnant at Qumran
called themselves "the poor" (*'ebyon*).[17] And they and other first century Jews yearned eagerly for the new age when the Messiah would
come to fulfill the messianic promises (e.g. Isa 11:4) and bring justice
to the poor.[18]

Thus when Jesus read from Isaiah 61 in the synagogue at Nazareth
and proclaimed good news to the poor, he was announcing to the
faithful remnant who trusted in Jahweh and therefore were also poor
socio-economically that the messianic age of justice for the poor had
arrived.

This is confirmed by the growing evidence, developed most convincingly in a recent dissertation at the University of Basel by Robert
Sloan,[19] that in citing Isaiah 61:1, Jesus intended to proclaim the
eschatological Jubilee. Sloan cites a Qumran document that comes
from roughly the same time as Jesus. This text links the Jubilee passage of Leviticus 25 and the Sabbatical release of debts of
Deuteronomy 15 with Isaiah 61:1. Furthermore, it gives the Isaiah
passage a specific Jubilee interpretation. Equally important, all three
texts are placed in an eschatological perspective. Thus the Qumran
text expects the economic and social reordering described in Leviticus
25, Deuteronomy 15, and Isaiah 61 to occur when the Messiah ushers
in the new age. In fact, Sloan has discovered that in Jewish literature,
the Jubilee text is almost always placed in an eschatological context. A
similar interpretation would seem to be appropriate for Luke 4:16ff.
This means that at the heart of Jesus' message was the announcement
that the messianic age of eschatological expectation was beginning in
his life and ministry ("Today this scripture has been fulfilled in your
hearing," v. 21). At the very core of Jesus' conception of the new
messianic age, then, was the economic reordering, the special concern
for the poor, the release of captives and liberation of the oppressed

---

[16]J. A. Ziesler, *Christian Asceticism* (Grand Rapids: Eerdmans, 1973) 52.
[17]*TDNT*, 6. 896–9.
[18]Batey, *Jesus and the Poor,* 93; *TDNT,* 6. 895.
[19]R. Sloan, *The Acceptable Year of the Lord* (Austin: Schola, 1977).

called for in the Jubilee. The new age which he saw himself inaugurating had specific economic and social content.

Other aspects of Jesus' teaching support this interpretation. The Lucan beatitudes promise blessing to the poor and hungry. The messianic kingdom in which the pious, but therefore also socioeconomically, poor will receive justice is now coming in the person of Jesus. Nor does Matthew represent a spiritualized version of the beatitudes.[20] The poor "in spirit" are the pious poor who are also socio-economically deprived. And they hunger and thirst for righteousness—i.e., justice! As Herman Ridderbos rightly insists, the word *righteousness* here "must not be understood in the Pauline forensic sense of imputed forensic righteousness, but as the kingly justice which will be brought to light one day for the salvation of the oppressed and the outcasts, and which will be executed especially by the Messiah. . . . It is *this* justice to which the 'poor in spirit' and 'the meek' look forward in the Sermon on the Mount."[21]

Now I do not in any way want to imply that Jesus' message was limited to proclaiming the eschatological Jubilee or that his mission focused exclusively on socio-economic concerns. His message included a central concern for forgiving sinners and he came to die on the cross for our sins. But it simply will not do to spiritualize Jesus' message and overlook the fact that right at the heart of the mission of the Incarnate One was a concern for justice for the poor and oppressed. His strong warning that those who do not feed the hungry, clothe the naked, and visit the prisoners will experience eternal damnation (Matt 25:31ff) does not represent a peripheral concern. It represents a central focus of his messianic mission.

At the supreme moment of history when God himself took on human flesh, we see the God of Israel still at work liberating the poor and oppressed and summoning his people to do the same.

The second aspect of the biblical teaching that God is on the side of the poor and oppressed is that God works in history to cast down the rich and exalt the poor.

Mary's Magnificat puts it simply and bluntly:

> My soul magnifies the Lord. . . .
> He has put down the mighty from their thrones
> and exalted those of low degree;
> he has filled the hungry with good things,
> and the rich he has sent empty away (Luke 1:46–53).

---

[20]See *TDNT*, 6. 904, n. 175.

[21]H. Ridderbos, *The Coming of the Kingdom* (Philadelphia: Presbyterian and Reformed, 1962), 190.

James 5:1, "Come now, you rich, weep and howl for the miseries that are coming upon you," is a constant theme of biblical revelation.

Why does Scripture declare that God regularly reverses the good fortunes of the rich? Is God engaged in class warfare? Actually our texts never say that God loves the poor more than the rich. But they do constantly assert that God lifts up the poor and disadvantaged. And they persistently insist that God casts down the wealthy and powerful. Why? Precisely because, according to Scripture, the rich often become wealthy by oppressing the poor and because they fail to feed the hungry.

Why did James warn the rich to weep and howl because of impending misery? Because they had cheated their workers: "You have laid up treasures for the last days. Behold, the wages of the laborers who mowed your fields, which you kept back by fraud, cry out; and the cries of the harvesters have reached the ears of the Lord of hosts. You have lived on the earth in luxury and in pleasure; you have fattened your hearts in a day of slaughter" (5:35). God does not have class enemies. But he hates and punishes injustice and neglect of the poor. And the rich, if we accept the repeated warnings of Scripture, are frequently guilty of both.

Long before the days of James, Jeremiah knew that the rich were often rich because of oppression.

> Wicked men are found among my people;
>   they lurk like fowlers lying in wait.
> They set a trap;
>   they catch men.
> Like a basket full of birds,
>   their houses are full of treachery;
> *therefore they have become great and rich,*
>   *they have grown fat and sleek.*
> They know no bounds in deeds of wickedness;
>   they judge not with justice
> the cause of the fatherless, to make it prosper,
>   and they do not defend the rights of the needy.
> Shall I not punish them for these things?
>   says the Lord (Jer 5:26-29, RSV).

Hosea and Micah made similar charges:

> A trader in whose hand are false balances,
>   he loves to oppress.
> Ephraim has said, "Ah, but I am rich,

I have gained wealth for myself";
but all his riches can never offset
     the guilt he has incurred (Hos 12:7-8, RSV).

The voice of the Lord cries to the city . . .
Can I forget the treasures of wickedness
     in the house of the wicked,
and the scant measure that is accursed?
Shall I acquit the men with wicked scales
     and with a bag of deceitful weights?
Your rich men are full of violence (Mic 6:9-12, RSV).

Job 24:1-12, Psalm 73:2-12, Ezekiel 22:23-29, and Amos 8:4-8—to
cite just a few more texts—all repeat the same point.

One more example from Isaiah is important. Through his prophet
Isaiah, God declared that the rulers of Judah were rich because they
had cheated the poor. Surfeited with affluence, the wealthy women
had indulged in self-centered wantonness, oblivious to the suffering
of the oppressed. The result, God said, would be devastating destruction.

The Lord enters into judgment
     with the elders and princes of his people:
"It is you who have devoured the vineyard,
     The spoil of the poor is in your houses.
What do you mean by crushing my people,
     by grinding the face of the poor?"
says the Lord of hosts (Isa 3:14ff., RSV).

Because the rich oppress the poor and weak, the Lord of history is at
work pulling down their houses and kingdoms.

Sometimes Scripture does not charge the rich with direct oppression of the poor. It simply accuses them of failure to share with the
needy. But the result is the same.

The biblical explanation of Sodom's destruction provides one illustration of this terrible truth. If asked why Sodom was destroyed,
virtually all Christians would point to the city's gross sexual perversity.
But that is a one-sided recollection of what Scripture actually teaches.
Ezekiel shows that one important reason God destroyed Sodom was
because she stubbornly refused to share with the poor!

Behold, this was the guilt of your sister Sodom: she and her daughters
had pride, *surfeit of food, and prosperous ease, but did not aid the poor and
needy.* They were haughty, and did abominable things before me; therefore I removed them when I saw it (Ezek 16:49-50, RSV).

The text does not say that they oppressed the poor (although they probably did). It simply accuses them of failing to assist the needy.

The third aspect of the biblical teaching that God is on the side of the poor and oppressed is that the people of God, if they are really the people of God, are also on the side of the poor and oppressed. Those who neglect the poor and the oppressed are not really God's people at all—no matter how frequent their religious rituals or how orthodox their creeds and confessions. The prophets sometimes made this point by insisting that knowledge of God and seeking justice for the oppressed are inseparable. At other times they condemned the religious rituals of the oppressors who tried to worship God and still continue to oppress the poor.

Jeremiah announced God's harsh message that King Jehoiachim did not know Jahweh and would be destroyed because of his injustice:

> Woe to him who builds his house by unrighteousness,
>   and his upper rooms by injustice;
>   who makes his neighbor serve him for nothing,
>   and does not give him his wages; . . .
> Did not your father eat and drink
>   and do justice and righteousness?
>   Then it was well with him.
> He judged the cause of the poor and needy;
>   then it was well.
> Is not this to know me?
>   says the Lord (Jer 22:13-16, RSV).

Knowing God necessarily involves seeking justice for the poor and needy (cf. also Hos 2:19-20).

The same correlation between seeking justice for the poor and knowledge of God is equally clear in the messianic passage of Isaiah 11:1-9. Of the shoot of the stump of Jesse, the prophet says: "With righteousness he shall judge the poor and decide with equity for the meek of the earth" (v. 4, RSV). In this ultimate messianic shalom, "the earth shall be full of the knowledge of the Lord as the waters cover the sea" (v. 9, RSV).

The prophets also announced God's outrage against worship in the context of mistreatment of the poor and disadvantaged. Isaiah denounced Israel (he called her Sodom and Gomorrah!) because she tried to worship Jahweh and oppress the weak at the same time (1:10-17).

> "Why have we fasted, and thou seest it not?
> Why have we humbled ourselves,
>   and thou takest no knowledge of it?"

Behold, in the day of your fast you seek your own pleasure,
   and oppress all your workers . . .
Is not this the fast that I choose:
   to loose the bonds of wickedness,
   to undo the thongs of the yoke,
to let the oppressed go free,
   and to break every yoke?
Is it not to share your bread with the hungry,
   and bring the homeless poor into your house? (Isa 58:3–7; likewise
      Isa 1:10–17, RSV).

God's words through the prophet Amos are also harsh:

I hate, I despise your feasts,
and I take no delight in your solemn assemblies.
Even though you offer me your burnt offerings
and cereal offerings, I will not accept them . . .
But let justice roll down like waters,
and righteousness like an overflowing stream (Amos 5:21–24, RSV).

Earlier in the chapter, Amos had condemned the rich and powerful
for oppressing the poor. They even bribed judges to prevent redress
in the courts. God wants justice, not mere religious rituals, from such
people. Their worship is a mockery and abomination to the God of
the poor.

Nor has God changed. Jesus repeated the same theme. He warned
the people about scribes who secretly oppress widows while making a
public display of their piety. Their pious-looking garments and frequent visits to the synagogue are a sham. Woe to religious hypocrites
"who devour widows' houses and for a pretense make long prayers"
(Mark 12:38–40). Like Amos and Isaiah, Jesus announced God's outrage against those who try to mix pious practices and mistreatment of
the poor.

The prophetic word against religious hypocrites raises an extremely
difficult question. Are the people of God truly God's people if they
oppress the poor? Is the church really the church if it does not work to
free the oppressed?

We have seen how God declared through the prophet Isaiah that
the people of Israel were really Sodom and Gomorrah rather than the
people of God (1:10). God simply could not tolerate their idolatry and
their exploitation of the poor and disadvantaged any longer. Jesus
was even more blunt and sharp. To those who do not feed the hungry, clothe the naked, and visit the prisoners, he will speak a terrifying
word at the final judgment: "Depart from me, you cursed, into the
eternal fire prepared for the devil and his angels" (Matt 25:41). The

meaning is clear and unambiguous. Jesus intends his disciples to imitate his own special concern for the poor and needy. Those who disobey will experience eternal damnation.

But perhaps we have misinterpreted Matthew 25. Some people think that "the least of these" (v. 45) and "the least of these my brethren" (v. 40) refer only to Christians. This exegesis is not certain. But even if the primary reference of these words is to poor believers, other aspects of Jesus' teaching not only permit but require us to extend the meaning of Matthew 25 to both believers and unbelievers who are poor and oppressed. The story of the good Samaritan (Luke 10:29ff.) teaches that anybody in need is our neighbor. Matthew 5:43ff. (RSV) is even more explicit:

> You have heard that it was said, "You shall love your neighbor and hate your enemy." But I say to you, love your enemies and pray for those who persecute you, so that you may be sons of your Father who is in heaven; for he makes his sun rise on the evil and on the good, and sends rain on the just and on the unjust.

The ideal in the Qumran community (known to us through the Dead Sea Scrolls) was indeed to "love all the sons of light" and "hate all the sons of darkness" (I QS 1:9-10). Even in the OT, Israelites were commanded to love the neighbor who was the son of their own people and ordered not to seek the prosperity of Ammonites and Moabites (Lev 19:17-18; Deut 23:3-6). But Jesus explicitly forbids his followers to limit their loving concern to the neighbor who is a member of their own ethnic or religious group. He explicitly commands his followers to imitate God who does good for all people everywhere.

As George Ladd has said, "Jesus redefines the meaning of love for neighbor; it means love for any man in need."[22] In light of the parable of the Good Samaritan and the clear teaching of Matthew 5:43ff., one is compelled to say that part of the full teaching of Matthew 25 is that those who fail to aid the poor and oppressed (whether they are believers or not) are simply not the people of God.

Lest we forget the warning, God repeats it in 1 John. "But if any one has the world's goods and sees his brother in need, yet closes his heart against him, how does God's love abide in him? Little children, let us not love in word or speech but in deed and truth" (3:17-18, RSV; cf. also, James 2:14-17). Again, the words are plain. What do they mean for Western Christians who demand increasing affluence

---

[22]G. E. Ladd, *A Theology of the New Testament* (Grand Rapids: Eerdmans, 1974) 133.

each year while people in the Third World suffer malnutrition, deformed bodies and brains, even starvation? The text clearly says that if we fail to aid the needy, we do not have God's love—no matter what we may say. The text demands deeds, not pious phrases and saintly speeches. Regardless of what we do or say at 11:00 a.m. Sunday morning, those who neglect the poor and oppressed are not the people of God.

But still the question persists. Are professing believers no longer Christians because of continuing sin? Obviously not. The Christian knows that sinful selfishness continues to plague even the most saintly. We are members of the people of God not because of our own righteousness but solely because of Christ's death for us.

That response is extremely important and very true. But it is also inadequate. All the texts from both testaments which we have just surveyed surely mean more than that the people of God are disobedient (but still justified all the same) when they neglect the poor. These verses pointedly assert that some people so disobey God that they are not his people at all in spite of their pious profession. Neglect of the poor is one of the oft-repeated biblical signs of such disobedience. Certainly none of us would claim that we fulfill Matthew 25 perfectly. And we cling to the hope of forgiveness. But there comes a point—and, thank God, He alone knows where!—when neglect of the poor is no longer forgiven. It is punished. Eternally.

In light of this clear biblical teaching, how biblical is our evangelical theology? Certainly there have been some great moments of faithfulness. Wesley, Wilberforce, and Charles Finney's evangelical abolitionists stood solidly in the biblical tradition in their search for justice for the poor and oppressed of their time. But twentieth-century evangelicals have not, by and large, followed their example. I think we must confess that the evangelical community is largely on the side of the rich oppressors rather than the oppressed poor. Imagine what would happen if all our evangelical institutions—our youth organizations, our publications, our colleges and seminaries, our congregations and denominational headquarters—would all dare to undertake a comprehensive two-year examination of their total program and activity to answer this question: Is there the same balance and emphasis on justice for the poor and oppressed in our programs as there is in Scripture? I am willing to predict that if we did that with an unconditional readiness to change whatever did not correspond with the scriptural revelation of God's special concern for the poor and oppressed we would unleash a new movement of biblical social concern that would change the course of modern history.

But our problem is not primarily one of ethics. It is not that we have

failed to live what our teachers have taught. Our theology itself has
been unbiblical and therefore heretical. I think James Cone is right
when he says:

> When church theologians, from the time of Constantine to the present,
> failed to see the ethical impact of the biblical God for the liberation of
> the oppressed, that failure occurred because of defective theology. To
> understand correctly the church's ethical mistake, we must see it in
> connection with a prior theological mistake. . . . *Theologians of the Chris-*
> *tian Church have not interpreted Christian ethics as an act for the liberation of*
> *the oppressed because their views of divine revelation were defined by philosophy*
> *and other cultural values rather than by the biblical theme of God as the liberator*
> *of the oppressed.* . . . We cannot say that Luther, Calvin, Wesley, and other
> prominent representatives of the church's traditions were limited by
> their time, as if their ethical judgments on oppression did not affect the
> essential truth of their theologies. They were wrong ethically because
> they were wrong *theologically.* They were wrong theologically because
> they failed to listen to the Bible.[23]

By largely ignoring the central biblical teaching that God is on the side
of the poor, evangelical theology has been profoundly unorthodox.
The Bible has just as much to say about this doctrine as it does about
Jesus' resurrection. And yet we evangelicals insist on the resurrection
as a criterion of orthodoxy and largely ignore the equally prominent
biblical teaching that God is on the side of the poor and the oppressed.

Now please do not misunderstand me at this point. I am not saying
that the resurrection is unimportant. The bodily resurrection of Jesus
of Nazareth is absolutely central to Christian faith and anyone who
denies it or says it is unimportant has fallen into heresy. But if centrality in Scripture is any criterion of doctrinal importance, then the
biblical teaching that God is on the side of the poor ought to be an
extremely important doctrine for evangelicals.

I am afraid evangelicals have fallen into theological liberalism. Of
course we usually think of theological liberalism in terms of classical
nineteenth-century liberals who denied the deity, the atonement, and
the bodily resurrection of Jesus our Lord. And that is correct. People
who abandon those central biblical doctrines have fallen into terrible
heresy. But notice what the essence of theological liberalism is—it is
allowing our thinking and living to be shaped by surrounding society's
views and values rather than by biblical revelation. Liberal theologians
thought that belief in the deity of Jesus Christ and his bodily resurrec-

---

[23]Cone, *God of the Oppressed,* 199–200; Cone's italics.

tion was incompatible with a modern scientific world view. So they followed surrounding scientific society rather than Scripture.

Evangelicals rightly called attention to this heresy—and then tragically made exactly the same move in another area. We have allowed the values of our affluent materialistic society to shape our thinking and acting toward the poor. It is much easier in evangelical circles today to insist on an orthodox Christology than to insist on the biblical teaching that God is on the side of the poor. We have allowed our theology to be shaped by the economic preferences of our materialistic contemporaries rather than by Scripture. And that is to fall into theological liberalism. We have not been nearly as orthodox as we have claimed.

Past failure, however, is no reason for despair. I think we mean it when we sing, "I'd rather have Jesus than houses or lands." I think we mean it when we write and affirm doctrinal statements that boldly declare that we will not only believe but also live whatever Scripture teaches. But if we do mean it, then we must teach and live, in a world full of injustice and starvation, the important biblical doctrine that God and his faithful people are on the side of the poor and oppressed. Unless we drastically reshape both our theology and our entire institutional church life so that the fact that God is on the side of the poor and oppressed becomes as central to evangelical theology and evangelical institutional programs as it is in Scripture, we will demonstrate to the world that our verbal commitment to *sola scriptura* is a dishonest ideological support for an unjust, materialistic status quo. But I hope and believe that in the next decade millions of evangelicals will allow the biblical teaching that God is on the side of the poor and oppressed to fundamentally reshape our culturally conditioned theology and our unbiblically onesided programs and institutions. If that happens, we will forge a new, truly evangelical theology of liberation that will change the course of modern history.

11

True and False Liberation in the Light of Scripture

Harold O. J. Brown

INTRODUCTION

Like other human beings, evangelicals frequently demonstrate a follow-the-leader pattern of behavior. Unfortunately, being in all things most conservative, we are often so far behind the pace- and style-setters that we may seem to be the spearhead of an entirely different movement, unrelated to the one that we think we have joined. During the early 1970s I was frequently asked by college and other Christian groups to address the topic of evangelical social concern. I have been peripherally related to the organization called Evangelicals for Social Concern. I am deeply interested in social, economic, and political structures and am fully convinced that the Christian has not merely a word to say but also a role to play in their maintenance and transformation. Nevertheless I have had to observe that just at the moment when we as evangelicals thought that we were finally responding to the social dimension of the gospel in a way that would gain the interest and appreciation of the socially-interested liberal churches as well as of the general community, we discovered that on a large scale general interest had shifted from the horizontal dimension of interpersonal relationships and human social structures to the vertical dimension of man's relationship to God. As a consequence we could actually observe an evangelical group on a college campus sponsoring lectures on social concern at the same time that the liberal group they were imitating was holding meetings on the spiritual life. At the present time, we evangelicals are awakening in

increasing numbers to the supposedly worldwide interest in liberation, specifically in liberation as a dimension of the Christian doctrine
of salvation. And yet we may find much of the rest of the world
turning away from liberation as the ultimate goal of revolution and
dictatorship to dictatorship as a permanent condition, simply as one
of the facts of life to be endured, while man's spiritual energy and
interest is directed towards fulfillment in other, nonpolitical endeavors. Nevertheless, although troubled by the uneasy suspicion that
even at the moment that I, a conservative, agree to participate in the
"vanguard" which may turn out to be once again the "rear guard," I
shall endeavor to grapple with the concept and phenomenon of "liberation" both as it is popularly understood and as it appears to be in
reality.

TWO PROBLEMS IN DEALING WITH LIBERATION

The concept and phenomenon of liberation presents the evangelical Christian today with two different temptations which, if yielded to,
will confront him with two different kinds of problems. In the first
case, there may be adoption of language that conveys something the
evangelical has not meant to convey, and thus is misleading. In the
second, there is the danger that the uncritical adoption of certain
slogans may lead to a change in one's own orientation—a change that
has not been deliberately decided upon, nor supported with biblical
authority, nor examined as to its probable consequences.

1. Language that Conveys Something Unmeant

Until relatively recently, the borrowing of religious terms for their
possible effect was more common among liberal Protestants than
among conservatives. We are all familiar with the very loose use made
of terms such as *evangelical* and *born again*. If the Emperor Constantine the Great inaugurated, doubtless without wishing to do so, the
age of nominal Christianity, there is reason to suspect that U.S. President Jimmy Carter may some day be seen to have inaugurated an age
of nominal evangelicalism. This less than ethical borrowing is paralleled and even exceeded by the fraudulent appropriation of traditional theological language such as "inspiration," "redemption,"
"atonement," "newness of life," and even of the sacred names of God
and of the Persons of the Holy Trinity for investment with an entirely
unbiblical, unchristian meaning. We are all familiar with the use to

which words such as "regeneration," "resurrection," and "salvation" are put, despite the fact that biblically, theologically, and historically they can be rather precisely defined.

An entire if short-lived theological school, the so-called "death-of-God" movement, offers an example of appropriation for distinctly nonchristian content of fundamental Christian concepts and doctrines. This school, incidentally, furnishes us with a helpful illustration of something that is also, happening with the theology of liberation. Combining the orthodox doctrine of the incarnation (God becoming man) with that of the substitutionary atonement (the death of Christ), Thomas J. J. Altizer asserted that God, having become man and died, had ceased to be; indeed, he called this the true meaning of the gospel, which he entitled *The Gospel of Christian Atheism,* ignoring that the doctrines he used to derive the view that God is dead, namely that God became man in Jesus Christ and that Jesus died on the cross, came from the same text that tells us that Jesus Christ is risen, ascended, glorified, and coming again with power to judge the quick and the dead. Although what Altizer meant by the death of God was certainly incompatible with biblical Christianity, his or similar language of the death of God was sometimes used by more orthodox voices to mean something rather different, something not altogether incompatible with biblical doctrine, namely that modern man acts as though there were no God, and that hence for him "God is dead."

The difficulty with such borrowing back from a school of thought like Altizer's is this: the language is a very poor and extremely misleading way to communicate a valid point. In general we may expect it to confuse more than it communicates. In fact, this new idiom was so strange and so difficult to use to communicate an evangelical content that few if any evangelicals have made any attempt to utilize it. If one who believes in the living God should succumb to the fashionable practice of saying "God is dead to modern man" to mean "modern man is deadened to the reality of God," the risk of communicating the idea that there is no God is so high that one may justly be reproached with irresponsible witnessing. Admittedly the language of the death of God is extreme and hardly popular among evangelicals; perhaps for this reason reference to it may help to illuminate what is happening with other, less provocative but nevertheless by no means harmless borrowings. I have reference, of course, to the language of "revolution" and of "liberation."

In 1969 no less reliable a witness to biblical Christianity than Leighton Ford found himself saying of the message of the early Christians: "Here was a *revolutionary* God, releasing *revolutionary* power through a *revolutionary* community, in *revolutionary* action."[1] In terms of the literal meaning of the word revolutionary, Mr. Ford was speaking truly. Yet surely most of our contemporaries who use the terms "revolutionary power" and "revolutionary action" mean something different from what he had in mind. I think that Mr. Ford's position is clear enough to all of us to enable us to realize that he was in effect saying: "You seek a radical transformation overcoming existing evil, which you call revolution, but you are looking to the wrong kind of revolution, a social and political revolution. The real radical transformation is that which comes through the power of God as exemplified in Jesus Christ and the New Testament church." In context, Mr. Ford was very explicit. Yet taken out of context, the assertion that God releases "revolutionary power" through "revolutionary action" is certainly capable of conveying something that he did not intend. And yet—and here lies the temptation and the danger—I think that he did intend just a little bit of secular revolution. For—like almost all the rest of us who are in any degree sensitive to the evil inhering in the structures of our fallen world—Leighton Ford too rejects a good deal of what is, of the status quo of late twentieth-century Christendom, and would like to see it overthrown. My contention is that the use of terminology such as "revolutionary power" and "revolutionary action" by a Christian to express this desire is very likely to be misleading and to communicate something that no Christian may responsibly assert.

2. Slogans that Change One's Convictions

The late General Charles de Gaulle was a realist when it came to dealing with the power structures of this world; France recognized Communist China shortly after its successful assumption of power, but De Gaulle never hesitated to refer to it as "la Chine rouge," *Red* China. American presidents, though tardy in recognition of China, are obsequiously punctilious in always referring to it as "the People's Republic of China." Although Russians claim that the U.S.S.R. is a union of autonomous, brotherly republics, De Gaulle was not too shy to refer to the Soviet ambassador in France as "l'ambassadeur russe," the *Russian* ambassador. Another eloquent francophone, Pierre Trudeau, ex-Prime Minister of Canada, referring to the killing of a minis-

---

[1] L. Ford, "Evangelism in a Day of Revolution," *Christianity Today* (October 24, 1969) 64.

ter of the Québec provincial government, refused to use the criminals' term "execution," and stated that it could be called nothing but "un lâche assassinat," a cowardly murder. As the former United States Ambassador to the United Nations, Daniel Patrick Moynihan, now a senator from New York, has pointed out, American politicians and media have almost totally capitulated to the slogans of despotism: a dictatorship becomes a "people's republic," even a "democratic republic," and commentators who cannot be bothered to pronounce a whole word, such as "information," but limit themselves to supplying "info," somehow manage to enunciate every syllable of the People's Republic of China. While "un lâche assassinat" becomes an "execution" in the American media, "unnatural vice" has become homosexuality and homosexuality an "alternative lifestyle," even in the language of the Evangelical Theological Society.* Now no one who participates regularly in the academic liturgy known as a faculty meeting can fail to realize that many formalities are mere formalities without significant content, and that many titles and designations are purely conventional. Nevertheless, words do gradually influence beliefs. It is easier to "terminate a pregnancy" than to "abort a fetus," and even that is easier than "killing a baby." Disposing of the "product of conception" as of "life devoid of value" is perhaps easiest of all. Use of harmless-sounding or even attractive words tends to familiarize us with and habituate us to the most dreadful reality, rather as in those states that have sought to remove the dreadful aura of capital punishment by requiring that it be administered by a "lethal injection."

The danger, then, in an evangelical adoption of nonbiblical language, such as the terminology of revolution, or of biblical language in a nonbiblical sense, such as that of liberation, is not merely the possibility of misleading one's hearers. It includes the real possibility of gradually blurring one's own original convictions in the area, not by discovery of new biblical evidence, nor even by persuasion, but simply by continual repetition of an unanalyzed slogan with an unrecognized content. Those of you who are aware of the extent to which a realistic understanding of the abortion problem, even in evangelical circles, has been impeded by the widespread currency of the abortionists' own Newspeak terminology, will understand that this is no idle speculation when applied to the language of revolution and liberation in Christian proclamation, where what is at stake is not merely the right to life, but the right to become children of God.

---

*Editors' note: Dr. Brown refers to the title of a paper incorporating that phrase read at the Thirtieth Annual Meeting.

3. The Attractiveness of the Language of Liberation

With respect to the terminology of liberation, different things are happening as it is adopted and popularized in different circles and with different goals in mind. For some, *liberation* is merely a term—and a biblical one—for what Jesus Christ does for sinners (Heb 2:15). Its chief attractiveness lies in the fact that it is a fashionable term, not one that might be immediately disdained as obsolete in secular circles, such as *salvation*. For others, the term is a happy one because it implies something that they believe, namely that the transformation of sinners through the redeeming power of Jesus Christ implies and will lead, in ways not necessarily specified in advance, to the transformation of society. For a third group, the word *liberation* is chosen because it is their intention to substitute a this-worldly, politically messianic *bouleversement* for what they conceive to be the limited, other-worldly, pie in the sky hope of bliss beyond the grave, a Beautiful Island of Nowhere. Used in this way, liberation is not an aspect of Christian salvation, but an alternative, and a very bad one.

4. A Caveat

The most dangerous alternatives to biblical Christianity are those which contain attractive elements of biblical truth, especially when those elements appeal to the secular mind or to the spirit of the age. This was recognized by Martin Luther in his vehement rejection of the uprising known as the Peasants' War, the ferocity of which has delighted Marxist and other anti-religious propagandists and embarrassed Christians almost as much as the Crusades. Without attempting to justify Luther's vigorous if ineffectual endorsement of violent repression, I suggest that we should recognize the correctness of what Luther was trying to do: he was trying to defend the evangelical, biblical sense of the *Freiheit eines Christenmenschen,* the freedom of a Christian man, against the perverted view that Christian liberty consisted in, or at least involved, the repudiation of medieval social and economic structures. When we recall that he showed a similarly vehement indignation at Carlstadt and others whose understanding of spiritual liberty led them into a total spiritualization of the substantial reality of the Lord's Supper, we can discern the Scylla and Charybdis between which Luther was seeking to pilot the evangelical ark: off the one bow, a politicalization that turns the spiritual content of the gospel into a political platform, off the other, a spiritualization that reduces the gospel to nothing but a new form of self-awareness with no real consequences whatsoever.

As Karl Barth pointed out in *Protestant Theology in the Nineteenth Century,* the moralization and politicalization of the gospel goes back to the Age of the Enlightenment—which was also the age of pietism. Pietists fell into it as well as deists. Since all of us, both by profession of faith and probably by devotional habit as well, have much in common with eighteenth-century pietists, we should be warned by the fact that their warm-hearted devotion to Jesus did not prevent them from falling into an error similar to that of the rationalistic deists.[2] At the same time, discerning the danger of reducing the gospel to a system of this-worldly edification and melioration, Barth himself has been accused of stepping into the alternate trap, and providing, in company with his opponent Rudolf Bultmann, an example of what Dr. Klaus Bockmuehl calls "the unreality of God in theology."[3] In the first case, we have at the very best not merely an anonymous Christianity but an anonymous God who does *not* make his light to shine nor his glory to rise upon us—for how can it be the glory of God where his name is nowhere known or honored. In the second, we have a God who is no more than the invisible gardener of Anthony Flew's famous parable,[4] a willful interpretation of reality adaptable to harmonization with any and all observable facts.

In short, what is at stake in the understanding of the language of liberation and of its domestication in the evangelical household is the second stage of the conflict, the first stage of which has reached a gratifyingly favorable conclusion in the firming up of the evangelical line of biblical inerrancy. An inerrant Bible will be little more than a doxological formula with no practical significance unless we can have a substantial measure of consensus as to what its message means, a reliable way of understanding it. If the language of liberation, as ecumenically used, is presented as an acceptable understanding of the Bible, then it may be as inerrant as one likes; it will be no more determinative of faith or practice than the Rosetta Stone. If the language of liberation in its evangelical dialect is to be accepted as a legitimate medium for communicating the content of Scripture, then it must be with careful attention, so that the unchangeable content will determine the language, not the fashionable language the content communicated.

---

[2] Karl Barth discusses this tendency in *Protestant Theology in the Nineteenth Century* (Valley Forge: Judson, 1973), especially chap. 3.

[3] K. Bockmuehl, *Atheismus in der Christenheit?* (Giessen: Brunnen, 1972), subtitle.

[4] A. Flew, "Theology and Falsification" (i) A, in A. Flew and A. MacIntyre, eds., *New Essays in Philosophical Theology* (London: SCM, 1955) 96-8.

5. Conclusion Concerning the Problems

At the risk of sounding repetitious I shall warn again, as clearly as I can, of the two dangers *for* and *from* evangelicals who use the language of the theology of liberation: the first, that they leave themselves so open to misunderstanding that they may even be guilty of deception, with the possible consequence of causing those who trust them to involve themselves in unjustifiable activities; the second, that by the adoption of the language, they may gradually accustom themselves to thinking in terms that render essential Christian convictions less and less relevant and less and less believable. Henri Blocher has pointed to the fact that once one agrees to consider the religious question from the perspective of what Bultmann considers the only valid point of departure for modern man, the existentialist analysis of existence, the gospel in the received sense becomes unbelievable and irrelevant. Something similar may be said of the effort to consider the question of man's need from the perspective of a humanistic or even specifically Marxist analysis that understands this need to result not from bondage to sin and death—which only redemption can break— but from bondage to unjust social structures, from enslavement by an oppressor class, from alienation from one's true self as a result of the conditions of labor, and the like—all of which may be remedied by "liberation," although they may persist despite individual redemption, conversion, and the assurance of salvation. If we embrace the language of liberation as an acceptable or even necessary concomitant of the salvation obtained for us by Jesus Christ, we run the strong risk of recruiting Christians for programs of organized injustice. There are situations in which we as ministers and teachers of the Word of God ought to call upon our fellow-Christians to take firm action with regard to injustice, both unjust deeds and unjust structures. But we ought to attempt to discern such situations with clarity, understand why we believe that they call for action and decide what action is called for in the light of biblical mandates and principles— not allow them to be suggested to us and eventually pressed upon us by a gradual transformation first of our language, then of our realm of discourse, and finally of our beliefs and deeds.

THE DEVELOPMENT OF LIBERATION VIEWS

Although theories and theologies of liberation are numerous and varied in Christian circles, it seems to me that they can be grouped together as a class of ideas that take their origin more directly in social circumstances than in the direct teaching of Scripture. To avoid a pejorative interpretation of what has just been said, let me say that while they claim to be and in some cases actually may be a valid interpretation of Scripture, the reflection that led to them was in general *not* stimulated by reflection on Scripture alone, but by certain pressing circumstances in the world for which a scriptural explanation and response is sought.

1. Social Factors Leading to the Development of Liberation Theologies

I think that it is possible to discern at least four major factors in recent history that clearly have contributed to the transfer of interest from an other-worldly salvation to a more this-worldly liberation. The first three of these factors are not peculiar to our present historical situation, but have appeared together at other times and other places in world history; the fourth would appear to be relatively new. When the first three factors *have* appeared together in the past, the Christian community has sometimes responded with a new orientation or program that bears certain formal similarities to theologies and programs of liberation—and more than once with one that we might find it hard to endorse today. These factors are:

a. A waning of Christian vitality in society. Perhaps we might better call the phenomenon a fading of the substance of Christendom or Christian civilization, for in some cases the waning of which I speak is accompanied by evangelical revivals or spiritual reform movements. When the structures of a society called *Christian* no longer seem to meet the real needs of people, there is a spontaneous tendency to turn away from strictly "religious" solutions and prescriptions to answers that seem to offer more realistic possibilities of true improvement.

b. A strong and growing presence of an overtly anti-Christian religious or philosophical world view. In a society where Christianity clearly dominates in the intellectual forum, pressures for social melioration, however radical they may be in the long run, seem to take shape within rather than in conflict with Christian thought: examples are abolition in the United States and the rise of the labor movement and Labor Party in Britain. In both American and British society of the time, Christianity held the intellectual reins, and although there were some nonchristian elements in both abolition and the labor movement, neither necessarily or substantially challenged Christianity, but rather drew upon it and claimed to be representing it. Today, of course, it is Marxism in its various forms, and also the liberal secular humanism that seems the only constitutionally kosher alternative to Marxism, that hold the intellectual reins. And it is from these ideologies, particularly from Marxism, that liberation thought arises as what is intended to be a Christian response.

c. Undeniable and well-known injustice on a massive scale. Slavery existed for several millennia in the world without provoking an abolition *movement*. The rise of anti-slavery conviction in Britain and later in the United States, and its growth into a mass movement, was certainly due in part to the influence of modern development and the industrial revolution on communication—rapid transportation and communication and the growth of the press. People in Britain and in New England, for example, could not be expected to agitate, much less take up arms, against slavery in Africa, overseas colonies, or the American South unless the grim reality of slavery had impressed itself firmly on their consciousness. People today likewise become concerned about injustice only to the extent that they are aware of its existence and its extent.

d. A fourth factor is the ideology of development. It was Pope Paul VI who said, "Il sviluppo e il novo nome della pace," "Development is the new name of peace." Un- or underdevelopment might then be called the new name for war. In time of war, no Christian questions the need to seek peace; calling development peace means that in time of underdevelopment hardly a Christian will be found who is not willing to seek *development*. When development is hindered or appears to be hindered by existing structures, even when they appear to have a Christian coloration, nothing is more logical than for the Christian to oppose those structures—just as for most Christians today nothing would appear more logical than for Christians to oppose, at least in retrospect, for purposes of maintaining a theoretical purity, the Christian structures that organized the Crusades. And this brings us to an interesting phenomenon:

2. Parallels to Liberation Perspectives

The fact that similar social conditions in the past have produced movements formally similar to liberation theology in our own day does not in itself discredit liberation theology. Nevertheless, the fact that at least some of these movements appear to us in retrospect as reprehensible ought to give us the incentive to examine the naturalness with which many may be tempted to accept the popularity of liberation themes.

a. The Crusades. I have already referred to the Crusades. In a forthcoming InterVarsity Press book edited by Professor Robert Clouse, I have been bold enough to argue that a crusade may be at least as good as any other war. But let us for the moment accept the generally-held Christian view of our day that the Crusades were a very bad thing. We should note that they were a Christian social response to three of the four factors mentioned above: a waning of the internal strength of Christendom, the threat of a powerful anti-Christian ideology, and widely perceived injustice. Christians of the Crusade era may have been misinformed as to the lot of Christians in the Holy Land—but then Christians of the nineteenth century may have been misinformed in some respects concerning the lot of slaves.

b. A second movement that represents a Christian or at least an ecclesiastical reaction to Christian weakness, the strength of an anti-Christian ideology, and to generally perceived injustices crying out for a remedy is the movement known as German Christianity, that of the so-called *Deutsche Christen* of the Hitler era. I suppose that even those who may find some justification for the Crusades will find it hard to do anything but condemn the National Socialist German Workers' Party movement, i.e., the Nazi movement, and pity and excoriate those nominal Christians who thought that der Führer was somehow God's man for the hour. As Jacques Ellul pointed out, the Nazis have lost, and so their political, philosophical, and metaphysical vision is no longer considered *diskussionsfähig*—we can no longer discuss it seriously. Marxism won, and the Marxist vision is not merely *diskussionsfähig*, but almost obligatory in many intellectual circles. At the very least it "must be taken seriously as a deeply earnest quest for social justice and the humanization of man." Now the interesting thing about this comparison lies in the fact that the language used by Harvey Cox in the *Secular City*, advocating Marxist progress as exemplified in Nowy Huty near Kraków, Poland, is very similar to the language of the German Christians, who likewise hailed an outspokenly anti-Christian leader and movement as somehow the fulfillment of God's plan for the world. The movement of the *Deutsche Christen*, like the radical chic of Harvey Cox and other Marxophile nominal Christians, is an attempt on the part of the church to discern where God is active in the world and to align the church with rather than against the "wave of the future." That in retrospect it looks so diabolically perverse should not blind us to the fact that learned, earnest, sincere, and sometimes even pious people at the time took it seriously and thought that it was not merely the right but the necessary direction for Christians to take. While the example of the *Deutsche Christen* by no means suggests that Christians should forswear attempting to discern the *locus* or *loci* of God's regenerating activity in the world, it should certainly warn us against any uncritical baptism of unbelieving movements and giving them recognition as anonymously Christian.

c. Post-Constantinian triumphalism. After two examples from recent and more distant history, I would like to turn to the term chosen to express the view, particularly in Roman Catholic circles, that Christian faith ought to transform society and that Christian institutions should rule—triumphalism. Triumphalism has been used to malign the view that in the structures of society the church should somehow appear to be triumphantly on top.

Triumphalism was the logical final development of the great Constantinian enterprise, the Christianization of empire. The term did not come into vogue, of course, until Constantine's donations, so to speak, had been largely withdrawn, or, to use Robert Nisbet's phrase, sterilized to the extent that they did not come under the centralizing organization of the state.[5] The introduction of the terminology of triumphalism signaled a turning away from the claim of the church to shepherd society as well as the souls of individual men and women. This turning away was frequently justified as a biblically-motivated, spiritually sensitive reevaluation of the proper role of the church and its redirection to that of a suffering, martyr church teaching not a *theologia gloriae* but a *theologia crucis*. Unfortunately for the credibility of such a critical reevaluation, it appeared on the scene only after the church had largely been driven from her previous position of leadership in society, and so smacks rather more of sour grapes than of humility gained through reflection on Scripture.

The anti-triumphalistic phase has turned out to be rather brief, however. Although humility is a Christian virtue, it comes no more spontaneously to the Christian than generosity does to the rich. Can any theologian, any church, be happy in a society where Christians really have nothing to say? If we cannot prescribe what people shall do, at least we may describe what they are doing, and, once we have gotten over the initial shock of their intractability towards our previous good advice, we may say that they are really doing just what we would have wanted, and hence showing that they in their own way are acknowledging the validity of our views.

The theology of liberation is to the Christian society rather as the views of Rudolf Bultmann are to the resurrection: it reduces what was meant to be seen as a historic space-time reality to a mere interpretation. Making society Christian is reduced to explaining how, despite all appearances and the prejudices of fundamentalists, triumphalists and other theological reactionaries, society really is Christian and accomplishing the purposes of God. This analysis will appear, to some I feel certain, a caricature. Yet there are caricatures which, while not being photographically accurate, not to say flattering, do expose something of importance about the subject. I do ask you to take seriously the possibility that the theology of liberation today may reflect

---

[5]R. Nisbet, *The Quest for Community* (New York: Oxford, 1953) 255.

still another crusading, secularizing, or triumphalistic mentality, merely under the facade of anonymity.

3. The Question of Anonymity

We have been favored in recent years—increasingly since Vatican II—with a discussion and advocacy of the concept of anonymous Christianity. Individuals can in effect be Christian without saying it, in fact even without realizing it. Liberation themes stressing the unidentified action of God in history seem to be presenting us with an anonymous divinity. Can this possibly be legitimate in the context of biblical faith? Is not the God of Scripture precisely the God who does not remain without a name, who reveals his covenant name to Moses in commissioning him to lead the Hebrews out of Egypt? Is not the Messiah witnessed to in Scripture precisely the one who has a name, date and place of birth, and even, in the Apostles' Creed, the first-century equivalent of a Social Security number: "crucified under Pontius Pilate"? In Scripture the liberating work of God—most characteristically seen in the exodus from Egypt—is both proclaimed and evidently demonstrated to be the work of God, who "by a mighty hand and an outstretched arm brought you forth." Even the Logos-concept in Christian understanding must yield place to one who is not a concept but an historic person with a name, a place, and even friends and relations: which our eyes have seen and our hands have handled, the Word of Life.

CRITICISM

Mention of the theme of anonymity, which seems to me to be implicit in the redefinition of salvation by the name of Jesus to include liberation in many names or no name at all, certainly enables us to glide almost imperceptibly from the analytical part of the presentation to the critical. Imperceptibly, perhaps, but I am sure that I reveal nothing hidden from you if I admit the possibility that the whole presentation is critical. But now we may be openly critical. My substantial criticism of the use of themes or theologies of liberation by evangelical Christians is the same as my initial formal observation: to the extent that liberation theologies detach salvation, whether or not renamed or subsumed under the name of liberation, from the name of Jesus Christ, they are either inadequate and hence misleading, or positively false and hence deceiving. To the extent that they persuade Christians to keep not the commandments of Jesus Christ, which though strict are "not burdensome," but the counsels of apostasy and atheism, they are destructive.

1. Elements of Truth and Legitimate Concern

There are, as we have already admitted, substantial elements of truth in the concept that salvation in the biblical sense is more than "mere" liberation from sin and death. (As an aside, I should add that I hate the use of the word *mere* in connection with liberation from the two great tyrants of our race, sin and death. It is rather like saying, "The gift of God is mere eternal life.") Admittedly we should proclaim that transformation of human beings inevitably involves the transformation of society. But to suggest that the transformation of society, no matter how benevolent its motives or how Utopian its end product, *is* the transformation of human beings in the only sense that is ultimately and finally significant, freedom from the bondage of sin and death, is to engage in malicious deception. There must be a better, clearer, and less ambiguous way of proclaiming the full biblical truth, the whole counsel of God, than the adoption of a terminology that drags with it both positive and negative implications that are altogether unacceptable—the positive implications that "liberation" or "revolution" is somehow truly liberating, though it leaves individuals in and of the world and prisoners of the god of this world, and the negative implication that "mere" salvation is so insignificant that to proclaim it alone is to preach the trivial and to hide the essential.

I believe that I have devoted enough of my life, energy, and treasure in recent years to telling evangelicals and others that the gospel message cannot be limited to "mere"—horrible word—individual salvation and personal sanctification to evade suspicion of a covert design merely to protect the pietistic status quo. Indeed, I believe that we dare not exclude from our preaching the kind of concern that is reflected in the evangelical terminology of liberation. But liberation alone, without labels, would at best be letting others see our good works and glorify us. At worst—and this is no idle observation—it would be the fleeing of present evils to fix on mankind, in the late Charles de Gaulle's words, "la plus odieuse des tyrannies jamais connue par l'homme"—the most odious of tyrannies ever known to man.

2. A Counterproposal

To the extent that the language of liberation is still appealing, despite all that critics such as I may say, I must make the same kind of plea that I have had to make in the context of the introduction of the concept of homophobia into the discussion of homosexuality. Some Christians warn others of homophobia—dislike or hatred for homosexuals, which I suppose really ought to be called homomisy— and give the impression that it is perhaps even worse than the practice of homosexuality. Homophobia, or homomisy, is without doubt a serious fault, but it is not in fact a fault condemned *expressis verbis* in Scripture, and it certainly is not on the same level as the active practice of what Scripture condemns as abomination. One ought to be able to warn against the fault of homomisy without appearing to countenance the practice of homosexuality. Practically, given the intellectual climate of our day, this means that if one wishes to criticize and to warn against homomisy, one must be very careful to state that one is not thereby suggesting approval of or even tolerance of homosexual practice. Likewise, if one must use the terminology of liberation to cover legitimate biblical truths and Christian concerns, one must be careful to make it abundantly plain that the freedom that is in Christ is by no means the same as that which comes through political power, whether expressed by ballot or by bullet. Thus my counterproposal to those who would use this language is to make it abundantly clear what they mean by it and what they do not mean, being precise even to the point of pedantry if necessary to avoid misunderstanding.

And to those—whom experience leads me to suppose make up the majority of evangelicals and·therefore probably the majority of my audience—who are critical of themes and theologies of liberation without having been seriously moved by the evils those themes and theologies seek to combat, let me say this: if you refuse it—as you can see I do—then provide a visible demonstration that your concern for the salvation of men and women is not limited to providing them with a new self-understanding in terms of pie in the sky by and by. No one can do everything, and no soldier can fight every battle in every place. But each one can do something. If you point out that Christian liberation from sin and death is not equivalent to or subsumed within political liberation, you speak truly. But unless you, by life, witness and ministry to some extent and in some way indicate that you understand salvation to mean *more* than just a new self-understanding, completely independent of the real conditions of human life, then you also speak hollowly, as sounding brass. To proclaim that Christ, not Marx or Mao, is the true liberator is essential. But to proclaim it without seeking to show that where his servants are involved Christ also liberates in tangible ways from present suffering, injustice, and oppression is unacceptable. We are critical of Constantine. He is if anything less fashionable today than the Crusaders. (After all, the Crusaders lost, while Constantine won.) But Constantine was a man who, having embraced the gospel, thought that he should do what was in his power to bring its benefits to others. As it turned out, a great deal was in his power. Less power has been entrusted to us. Yet it was the servant with the single talent who did worst and was rebuked.

Let me return from these historical lucubrations to the present. If there is more to salvation than a new self-understanding—and there is—then there is more to discipleship than mere declaration. If in fact we are disciples of Christ, let us not attempt to salve what Carl F. H. Henry called the uneasy conscience of the fundamentalist by agreeing with efforts to impose one of the "plus odieuse des tyrannies." Let us make an active effort to bring in many practical dimensions of "the liberty wherewith Christ has set you free." Not every one of us will be called to work in the same way. But if we are called to nothing but contemplation, then it is unlikely that we are called to be saints in the New Testament sense. Our brother Richard Lovelace has been called to invest not merely his time and energy but to some extent his reputation and possibly his future social acceptability to declare the biblical truth in the area of homosexuality. Jack Davis and Jack Cotrell have found themselves called to activity in the struggle to prevent the destruction of developing human lives. They have probably discovered, as I have, that their investments of time, person, and treasure bring a measure of weariness, frustration, and grief—and sadly, sometimes all too scant appreciation from evangelical brethren—but they are in fact demonstrating their conviction that biblical salvation, while not necessarily political in the sense of Barth's criticism of liberal religion, does extend into the tangible and corporeal dimensions of human life.

When I submitted what I had intended to be the final draft of my thesis to George Williams, he told me, "You cannot end a Harvard thesis with an altar call." And so it was removed. I am not going to end an ETS paper with an altar call, but I am going to end it with a question: if you reject as false secular visions of liberation as substitutes for salvation—as I do—what are you doing to show that the salvation of the God in whom you believe is more than just a new self-understanding? What are you doing to show that the freedom with which Christ has made you free is, to conflate—but I hope not illegitimately—freedom indeed?

12

Black Christology in Historical Perspective*

Morris Inch

Black theology is one of the few theological innovations credited to American ingenuity. It is still a relatively new phenomenon, in its formative stage, and much in ferment. Given the uncertainty surrounding the nature of black theology, James Cone is perhaps its most exacting spokesman.

We shall single out Cone's Christology as central to his theological endeavor and at least illustrative of a trend in black theology. And we shall attempt to critique his effort within a historical perspective.

AUTHOR'S PURPOSE

Cone states his theological objective:

> The present work seeks to be revolutionary in the sense that it attempts to bring to theology a special attitude permeated with black consciousness. It asks the question, What does the Christian gospel have to say to powerless black men whose existence is threatened daily by the insidious tentacles of white power?[1]

---

*While this paper concerning Black theology happened to be the one available for publication from the annual meeting of ETS, a white person such as myself cannot speak for the Black evangelical. He can, at best, only hope to dialogue with him about their common faith and witness.

[1]J. Cone, *Black Theology and Black Power* (New York: Seabury, 1969) 32.

His statement of purpose reflects the historical setting of black theology in general and black Christology in particular.

Alistair Kee reminds us that "Black theology arises from the experience of black Christians in America, especially as they were caught up in the political sequence which began with the civil rights movement of the late 1950s and early 1960s."[2] There are, in fact, several stages in the development of "black consciousness." The earliest and most uncertain phase concerns the West African experience prior to settlement in the New World. For instance, some think that the African pervasive sense of the supernatural accounts at least in part for a more holistic attitude by the American black church. (By holistic we mean that which touches on life in all its religious, social, political, and economic facets.)

We are on less tenuous ground when we come to the black experience with slavery. Here we can proceed on the basis of known conditions and a later experience as it reflects an earlier disposition.

What were the peculiar conditions of black slavery in America? While slavery may never be a desirable lot, the American instance was especially disruptive to personal, societal, and cultural life. Oppression and paternalism combined to build a white economy on black shoulders.

We can also sense something of the impact of slavery through the extended experience of the black community. We can recognize a longing for freedom, often perpetuated by and through Christian symbols. And there was an accompanying feeling of despair that turned hope away from this life and to the next. There was also a degree of accommodation to the servile role that would compound the objective demand for it. Resentment was coupled with envy. All of these and other currents would merge in the future and provide greater visibility for the black response to slavery.

Black consciousness made its way from slavery through the reconstruction era to the civil rights movement at the middle of this century. Emancipation had become a critical political issue that justified other underlying concerns. The determination to protect the northern industrial complex was a major factor in the appeal to preserve the Union, and the emancipation of the slaves lifted the resulting conflict to the level of a crusade.

The reconstruction was a period of transition calculated more to restore the South than to preserve the Union. Black freedom was thus

---

[2]A. Kee (ed.), *A Reader in Political Theology* (Philadelphia: Westminster, 1975) 113.

something of a campaign promise of symbolic importance rather than personal or corporate conviction. In time the resolve of the national government and the public demand would weaken, allowing racial prejudice to take a new hold. The celebrated "black codes," while designed to meet the peculiar needs of the blacks in their adjustment as free men, really became persisting obstacles. As an example, the black could not testify in court except in cases involving his own race.

The plantation black became a lien tenant. One form of dependency replaced an earlier one. Freedom was postponed, and resentment was thereby nurtured.

Booker T. Washington is the key to understanding an earlier black response while W. E. B. DuBois suggests the persisting ambiguity and later expression of black consciousness. Washington emerged as the acknowledged black leader toward the close of the nineteenth century. He freely criticized the political solution imposed by the reconstruction and called upon the black community to exercise to the full the privileges now guaranteed by law. He urged blacks to improve their lot and whites "to lend a helping hand in the uplifting of the Negroes in order to further the prosperity and well-being of their region."[3]

Dubois reflects the black uncertainty as to their ability to compete with white advantage, and scepticism as to the whites' willingness to surrender that advantage. At one moment he would urge moderation, and the next retaliatory violence. He wrote of his own perception of black consciousness, "One ever feels this two-ness, an American, a Negro; two souls, two thoughts, two unreconciled strivings; two warring ideals in one dark body, whose dogged strength alone keeps it from being torn asunder."[4]

With DuBois the scene had been set for the civil rights movement which dates from 1954–1964. On May 18, 1954 the Supreme Court's *Brown vs. Board of Education* decision struck down the separate but equal concept. The desegregation of schools was ordered with all deliberate speed. In December of 1955 Rosa Parks's refusal to move to the back of her bus triggered a boycott led by Martin Luther King, Jr. Encouraged by the nonviolent tactic, the student movement began in 1958; by 1961 the first freedom rides challenged segregated facilities regulated by interstate commerce; in 1963 there was a major breakthrough in Birmingham regarding employment and public ac-

---

[3]M. Drimmer (ed.), *Black History* (Garden City: Doubleday, 1968) 338–9.
[4]Ibid., 355.

commodation. Finally, on June 2, 1964, a civil rights bill was enacted which anticipated the end of the civil rights movement as such and resulted in a call to political action.

The familiar lyrics of the time look back over the hard road the black had traveled in the civil rights movement and ahead to the demanding course of political action that still lay before him:

> We shall overcome
> We shall overcome
> We shall overcome, someday,
> Oh, deep in my heart,
> I do believe
> We shall overcome someday.

The road might be long, the way difficult, but black consciousness affirmed that "we shall overcome."

There is one more step in the development of black consciousness before the emergence of black theology. I refer to what has been termed *black power*. "What is black power? For some, it means anarchy in the streets. This is an unfortunate connotation. Black power means integrity and vitality for the race."[5] It suggests, in the litany coined by Jesse Jackson, "I am somebody."

Scripture enjoins us to love our neighbor as ourself (Matt 22:39), and the black power advocate reasoned that the appeal to love others could not be achieved until one had first come to love himself. One must come to accept and appreciate himself as a black. The conviction was born that "black is beautiful."

Black theology was the next logical step, given the precursors of black consciousness and power. While Kee is correct in the conclusion that "Black Theology comes from a situation created largely by factors outside the Christian Church and often hostile to Christianity as the religion of the white man and the Uncle Tom,"[6] it is no less the response of the black church to that situation imposed upon the black community.

Black theology, given the oppressive circumstances to which it addresses itself, takes on a predictably strident form. But it also offers hope, not only to the oppressed black, but to the white oppressor as well. Cone writes that "when blacks assert their freedom in self-determination, whites too are liberated."[7] Black theology works in the

---

[5]M. Inch, "Anatomy of a Symbol," *Christianity Today*, 13, no. 14 (April 11, 1969) 5.

[6]Kee, *Reader*, 116.

[7]Cone, *Black Theology*, 44.

presence of a threatening white power structure so as to fulfill a redemptive purpose in the lives of both blacks and whites. It is black faith assuming its peculiar redemptive calling.

Cone alerts us to the centrality of Christology to this theological endeavor: "Christianity begins and ends with the man Jesus—his life, death, and resurrection. He is the Revelation, the special disclosure of God to man, revealing who God is and what his purpose for man is. In short, Christ is the essence of Christianity."[8] No topic assumes a higher priority as black theology turns to its agenda.

THE QUESTION

To what question is "Jesus Christ" the answer? Cone responds: "What, then, is God's Word of righteousness to the poor and the helpless? 'I became poor in Christ in order that man may not be poor. I am in the ghetto where rats and disease threaten the very existence of my people, and they can be assured that I have not forgotten my promise to them. My righteousness shall vindicate your suffering!'"[9] *Jesus Christ* answers the question of why the black community suffers.

Cone acknowledges that the time of lynching blacks has passed, but views the repressive white culture as forcing the blacks into poor urban ghettos, there to suffer from deprivation and adversity. The "I Am" of the burning bush becomes the "I-am-in-the-ghetto" (as the Divine participant with the black people of God).

Jesus Christ is also the answer to how the black community is to respond to white oppression. Cone observes that "though the decisive battle against evil has been fought and won, the war, however, is not over."[10] There can be only one answer to white racism, and it is to fight back. Carry the triumph of the cross into the arena of contemporary American life; wage warfare, knowing that Christ has already struck the enemy a mortal blow.

One would be indeed insensitive if he were not to identify with those suffering or rejoice in the ability of their faith to cope with the problem of theodicy. However, the issue is more basic than this. We must ask whether Cone has framed the right question(s) for *Jesus Christ* to answer. What is the proper Christological question?

Dietrich Bonhoeffer comments: "Who are you? Are you God himself? This is the question with which Christology is concerned."[11]

---

[8] Ibid., 34
[9] Ibid., 46.
[10] Ibid., 40.
[11] D. Bonhoeffer, *Christology* (Cleveland: Collins, 1966) 30.

"Who" is the question of transcendence; "how" is the question of immanence. Bonhoeffer poses the question of transcendence, and Cone the question of immanence.

Bonhoeffer's approach is Christologically correct except that it presupposes the person of Jesus. Wolfhart Pannenberg explains: "As Christians, we know God only as He has been revealed in and through Jesus. All other talk about God can have, at most, provisional significance. In this sense it may be very meaningful and necessary, even a presupposition, for the message of Christ."[12] The Christian attests that *Jesus* is the Christ.

"Who are you?" was the question put to a Galilean rabbi of nearly two thousand years ago. The fact that we can still pose the question depends on the prior circumstance that gave rise to it. Had there been no Jesus, there could be no Christ and no question concerning His transcendence.

Once we have qualified Bonhoeffer's polemic, his conclusion appears in order. The proper Christological question is "who," and not "how." Its concern is with transcendence rather than immanence.

Bonhoeffer elaborates his thesis: "The question 'Who?' expresses the strangeness and otherness of the encounter, and at the same time reveals itself as the question of the very existence of the inquirer himself. He inquires about the being which is alien to his own being, about the boundaries of his own existence. Transcendence puts his own being in question."[13] Another, any other, expresses a strangeness and otherness from myself. The "I" and "not I" distinction leads to the questions, "If not I, then who are you?"

This discontinuity is radically asserted by the Divine otherness we experience with Jesus. "For as the heavens are higher than the earth, so are my ways higher than your ways, and my thoughts than your thoughts" (Isa 55:9). The varied ways of men resemble diverse paths crossing the earth's surface as compared with God's course through the heavens.

The proper response to Jesus' Christological otherness is silence. "Teaching about Christ begins in silence," Bonhoeffer reminds us. "This has nothing to do with mystical silence which, in its absence of words, is, nevertheless, the soul secretly chattering away to itself. The Church's silence is silence before the Word."[14] This is a silence that blocks out all voices in order to hear Jesus' reply. It is illustrated by

---

[12]W. Pannenberg, *Jesus, God and Man* (Philadelphia: Westminster, 1968) 19.
[13]Bonhoeffer, *Christology*, 31.
[14]Ibid., 27.

Paul's inquiry, "'Who are you, Lord?' And he said, 'I am Jesus whom you are persecuting'" (Acts 9:5, RSV).

The proper Christological question reminds us that Jesus is ultimately the Stranger. For all that he may volunteer to share with us along this pilgrim way, it is never exhaustive knowledge. We ought therefore never to presume upon Jesus as if we had him boxed into our own experience. He remains the Divine other who challenges our complacency.

Cone must take care not to uncritically baptize the black power struggle as a Christian crusade. The black power movement is not without its faults or need for repentance. We can best address the sins of others when sensitive to our own.

Cone may also be too categorical concerning the oppressive character of the white community. He sounds at times like the disciples who inquired, "Lord, do you want us to bid fire come down from heaven and consume them?" (Luke 9:54, RSV). Or if not at that moment, they must have felt the impending judgment could not be far removed. But Jesus cautioned a more temperate spirit for his disciples.

We have attempted to get the question put correctly before coming to the proper Christological reply. Cone seems to miss the question in his anxiety to wrestle with the experience of black suffering. This is the kind of well-meaning but shortsighted approach that has proved so ineffective in the past. The result has been that we not only failed to address the ultimate issues, but the pressing concerns were served poorly as well. Karl Barth reminds us of this classic error: "Theology . . . went overboard—and this was its weakness—insofar as confrontation with the contemporary age was its decisive and primary concern."[15]

We err by rushing into any of the modern dilemmas without respect for the distance of Christ from our most cherished assumptions. The prior question is not how Christian teaching relates to this or that concern, but "Who are you?"

THE ANSWER IN BRIEF

Cone means to stand in the Chalcedonian tradition. The creed (A.D. 451) affirmed, in answer to the question of Christ's person, that he was "perfect in Godhead and perfect in manhood, truly God and truly man." Cone gladly concurs with the observation that he "is God himself coming into the very depths of human existence for the sole

---

[15]K. Barth, *The Humanity of God* (Richmond: John Knox, 1972) 19.

purpose of striking off the chains of slavery, thereby freeing man from ungodly principalities and powers that hinder his relationship with God."[16] Thus he intends to identify with orthodox Christology and resist Ebionite and docetic heresies whether in classical or current form.

Cone's intent is not at issue: the question is whether he can properly reach such a conclusion through his theological method. Here we must remain sceptical. He may defer to an earlier theological opinion but undercut it as a result of an alien technique.

Cone seems somewhat aware of the problem when he admits that his approach "may appear to overlook Barth's earlier emphasis on 'the infinite qualitative distinction between God and man.'"[17] Nonetheless, he persists in the face of the risks and without what seems to me an adequate estimation of the Christological issue.

Wolfhart Pannenberg in the title of his work on Christology anticipates the direction in which one must develop an orthodox Christological confession: *Jesus, God and Man.* The figure of Jesus walking across the pages of history solicits the inquiry, "Who are you?" The orthodox reply is, "God and Man." We cannot change the setting and expect to get the same certain results.

AN ASSOCIATED CONCERN

I am also uneasy with what seems to be an effort to circumvent the church. Cone concedes that "contemporary theology from Karl Barth to Jürgen Moltmann conceives of the theological task as one which speaks from within the covenant community with the sole purpose of making the gospel meaningful to the times in which men live."[18] Cone continues, "There is ... a desperate need for a *black theology* (seeing the failure to address the issue), a theology whose sole purpose is to apply the freeing power of the gospel to black people under white oppression."[19] It does not follow that we ought to or can replace "the covenant community" as the locus of theology. Even when we stand outside the church hierarchy, it must be in the name of the church. "The nearer the church, the further from God" is one of those misleading cliches that needs careful qualification so that it does not undercut responsible theology.

---

[16]Cone, *Black Theology,* 35.
[17]Ibid., 38.
[18]Ibid., 31.
[19]Ibid.

It is within the church that Jesus is recognized as the Christ. It is there and there alone, not in alternative centers, even granting that they may have been endowed by the Christian "spirit."

The world's memory is short when it comes to recalling the gospel, if indeed it ever comprehends it. The church must provide the link between the past and present as it reaches back for renewal and the commission to evangelize. We shall not succeed by standing outside the church if we have failed standing devoutly within it.

But here Cone's reference to the church's failure has relevance: "unfortunately, Christianity came to the black man through white oppressors who demanded that he reject his concern for this world as well as his blackness and affirm the next world and whiteness."[20] Insofar as his analysis is correct, the church has failed to be the church. It has confused the idea of church unity with conformity to a particular cultural expression. It has allowed black Christians only as they have accepted a white way of thinking and the hope of heaven at the cost of relinquishing abundant life in the present.

Although Christianity came to the black man in an unfortunate setting, nevertheless it came. And Paul would seem to add "only that in every way, whether in pretense or in truth, Christ is proclaimed; and in this I rejoice, yes, and I will rejoice" (Phil 1:18). The alternative leads us to depreciate the church and our oneness in Christ. As a result we turn our backs on those brothers with whom we disagree and fail to experience the grace of Christ in healing our alienation from one another.

Black Christians would err if they categorically rejected those theological insights which have accompanied the bringing of the gospel. No people, black or white, need start from scratch; to do so is only to impoverish themselves. (Conversely, those who convey the gospel should be prepared to have their faith challenged, revised, and renewed by those who embrace its teaching. White Christians need to bear the hurt, protest, and challenge of their black brothers.)

There is one church, and that is Christ's church. Christ laid its foundation, and we build upon it, no matter how discouraging it may be at times or tempting to look elsewhere. Only within the church can we assert with confidence who Jesus really is.

FINISHING OFF

Bonhoeffer directs us to the concluding feature of our Christological study: Where is Christ? "If we look for the place of Christ, we are

---

[20] Ibid., 33.

looking for the structure of the 'Where?' within that of the 'Who?' We
are thus remaining within the structure of the person. Everything
depends on Christ's being present to His Church in space and time."[21]
We are still on a different course than when we press for the "How?"
We are dealing with the Divine transcendence by way of *uncovering*
immanence.

Where is Christ? Bonhoeffer succinctly replies that "he stands *pro
me*. He stands in my place, where I should stand and cannot."[22] Christ
pro me means that he intends to fulfill my life and extend my service to
others. Emil Brunner aptly states, "It is precisely the man whose first
concern is not culture but the kingdom of God that has the necessary
distance from cultural aims and the necessary perspective to serve
them in freedom, and to grasp that order which prevents the various
sections of civilization from monopolizing the totality of life."[23]

Christ does not stand where I stand in my self-centeredness. "The
fact that Christ is the centre of our existence does not mean that he is
the centre of our personality, our thought and our feeling. Christ is
our centre even when he stands on the periphery of our consciousness."[24] He is not *my* center but God's center; he does not stand where
I can, but where I cannot and should.

As such, Christ mediates between God and man. "For there is one
God, and one mediator also between God and men, the man Christ
Jesus" (1 Tim 2:15).

Christ also mediates between man and man. I am reminded of
Pastor Bodelschwingh's refusal to allow his patients to perish so as to
ease the drain on resources for the Nazi war efforts. "He had no other
weapon for that battle than the simple affirmation that these were
men and women made in the image of God, and to destroy them was
to commit a sin against God which would surely be punished."[25] The
pastor-director of the hospital had no defense on pragmatic grounds,
but appealed to Christ as the center between man and his fellow man.

Christ likewise mediates between man and his environment. This is
so whether we think in terms of the natural creation or our legacy
from past generations.

Christ finally mediates between man and himself. This seems the

---

[21]Bonhoeffer, *Christology*, 61.

[22]Ibid.

[23]E. Cell (ed.), *Religion and Contemporary Western Culture* (Nashville:
Abingdon, 1967) 74.

[24]Bonhoeffer, *Christology*, 62.

[25]L. Newbigin, *Honest Religion for Secular Man* (Philadelphia: Westminster,
1966) 62.

proper place to comment on the black arts. The black artist should represent reality as he understands it, out of integrity to himself and honesty with others. Christ calls him to be a man and a black man in particular.

There is a dimension of reality restricted to the black Christian. It differs from that of other blacks and other Christians. It nevertheless follows that what the black spokesman affirms by way of his Christian faith must bear the scrutiny of the larger black community and the larger Christian community as well. He cannot shift weight from one foot to the other in order to escape the discomfort of fully accepting his identity as a black and as a Christian. This may be viewed as a creative tension rather than unduly burdensome. As Jesus taught, "For My yoke is easy, and My load is light" (Matt 11:30).

Man is freed by Christ to a creative interplay with God, man, the creation, and self. And with this liberation theme we come to the cutting edge of Cone's approach. He assumes from Jesus' pronouncement "to set free those who are downtrodden" (Luke 4:18) that the oppressed peculiarly enjoy Divine favor and function in turn as a redemptive agent. But this unqualified perspective confuses social oppression with bondage of the spirit. Paul forged the necessary distinction when he testified, "I would to God, that . . . all who hear me this day, might become such as I am, except for these chains" (Acts 26:29, RSV). He was free in Christ although bound with Roman chains.

Part of the confusion at this point may arise from the popular impression that the church from early days was a movement of the oppressed. Kenneth Scott Latourette's speculation is likely more accurate when he says that "it may well have been that the proportion of the educated, the socially prominent, and the poor in the Christian communities was about that in the Empire as a whole. This would entail a predominance of the uneducated, but it would not necessarily mean that Christianity was associated with a movement to win more privileges for the proletarian elements in the great cities."[26] That is to say, Christianity is primarily a religious faith with implications for personal and social ethics. It ought never to be thought of as a social ethic qualified only with a religious sanction.

Indeed, Jesus ministered to the socially deprived but not to them alone or through them alone. Every person is in a manner of speaking the means of Christ's ministry to another, whether that individual actively cooperates or not.

---

[26]Kenneth Scott Latourette, *A History of Christianity* (New York: Harper & Row, 1975), 1.80-1.

The process of liberation implies a reciprocity, and Cone seems to grasp only a one-sided ministry. He observes that "Christ in liberating the wretched of the earth also liberates those responsible for the wretchedness."[27] That is, the oppressed become the channel for liberating the oppressors. But the grace of God flows both ways. It amounts to our being available to another, and allowing him to be available to us. The alternative is condescension rather than community.

Finally, Cone points out that "mature freedom is burdensome and risky, producing anxiety and conflict for free men and for the brittle structures they challenge. The call for Black Power is precisely the call to shoulder the burden of liberty in Christ, risking everything to live not as slaves but as free men."[28] Mature freedom certainly does imply such risk, but the risk involves the demand to be allowed to serve others and be available for the ministry of others. It risks by casting aside an uncritical dependence on any establishment or cause. It risks by calling a friend wrong and an enemy right. It risks by asserting the lordship of Christ. It risks by surrendering the one thing Cone grasps firmly to—the subjective certainty of his faith. He explains this as "an existential certainty which grips the whole of one's being in such a way that now all actions are done in the light of the Ultimate Reality."[29] But this subjective certainty can be the subjectification of our cultural ideal and may be in opposition to the liberating purpose of the Almighty. We still raise our cultural idols (some black, some white) in preference to serving the living God.

Cone has done us a significant service in probing the Christian faith from the perspective of black consciousness. My own remarks are offered in the spirit of theological dialogue. Through candid dialogue we may come to better understand and more faithfully apply the truth once revealed.

---

[27]Cone, *Black Theology*, 42.
[28]Ibid., 42–3.
[29]Ibid., 60.

13

The Current Status of Dispensationalism and Its Eschatology

Earl D. Radmacher

THE CONCEPT OF DISPENSATIONS

The growing rapprochement that has been taking place between covenant and dispensational theologians of orthodox persuasion over the last decade or so is demonstrated by a comparison of two articles done by Roy Aldrich, former president of Detroit Bible College, in *Bibliotheca Sacra*—one in 1955 entitled "An Apologetic for Dispensationalism" and the other in 1963 entitled "A New Look at Dispensationalism." In the earlier article Aldrich tends to fuel the fire of division when he states, "Those who object to seven dispensations usually also object to finding two dispensations in the Bible. They confuse law and grace."[1] In the later article, separated by almost a decade of interaction, Aldrich states, "All Bible students recognize at least two dispensations and most would acknowledge four or five."[2] He then goes on to demonstrate this by Charles Hodge, R. B. Kuiper, Floyd Hamilton, and others.

In the earlier article Aldrich quotes favorably the statement of Lewis Sperry Chafer: "Any person is a dispensationalist who trusts the blood of Christ rather than bringing an animal sacrifice."[3] This is

---

[1] R. L. Aldrich, "An Apologetic for Dispensationalism," *Bib Sac* 112 (January 1955) 52.
[2] R. L. Aldrich, "A New Look at Dispensationalism," *Bib Sac* 120 (January 1963) 44.
[3] Aldrich, "An Apologetic," 47.

often quoted to prove that everyone is a dispensationalist, whether he owns up to it or not, simply because he holds to a concept of dispensations. In his later article, however, Aldrich shows that this is not really the issue: " ... it is safe to say that ninety percent of the Bible deals with only two dispensations *which are not in dispute.* In other words, dispensationalists are usually in ninety percent agreement with non-dispensationalists who see only two dispensations in the Bible."[4]

It is not a matter of whether or not one holds to a concept of dispensations, or how many, that makes one a dispensationalist. It is inaccurate to simplistically state that one who holds to a concept of dispensations is a dispensationalist. Any biblicist recognizes dispensations, but being a dispensationalist is something distinct from that. It is a *system* of interpretation of the Scriptures.

In his evaluation of dispensationalism, Millard Erickson, a nondispensationalist, affirms:

> The first strength of a dispensational system is that it is indeed a system. The word *system* evokes a negative reaction in many circles today, largely because of the influence of existentialism which is hostile to structure and order in reality and to the intellectualizing or rationalizing of truth. From the time of Sören Kierkegaard's attack upon Georg Hegel's system, in which everything fit neatly in its place, existentialism has been suspicious of any treatment of reality that brings the various elements into a coherent whole. Consequently, Biblical studies in recent years have been rather fragmentary in nature, emphasizing Biblical Theology and minimizing systematic theology. The dispensationalist, however, has attempted to synthesize or integrate the entire Biblical witness into a unified whole.[5]

Charles Ryrie highlights this same point by referring to that which has been developed since J. N. Darby as "Systematized Dispensationalism."[6]

THE BASIC PRINCIPLE OF DISPENSATIONALISM

What is it, then, that makes a dispensationalist to be a dispensationalist? What are the principles out of which this system grows? At this point much confusion has been propagated by both dispensationalists and nondispensationalists. Theological *conclusions*

---

[4]Aldrich, "A New Look," 44.

[5]M. Erickson, *Contemporary Options in Eschatology* (Grand Rapids: Baker, 1977) 122.

[6]C. C. Ryrie, *Dispensationalism Today* (Chicago: Moody, 1965) 74.

have been substituted for premises or *principles*. In response to the question, "What, then, is the *sine qua non* of dispensationalism?" Ryrie gives a threefold answer beginning with "(1) a dispensationalist keeps Israel and the church distinct."[7] And he agrees with Daniel Fuller that "the basic premise of dispensationalism is two purposes of God expressed in the formation of two peoples who maintain their distinction throughout eternity."[8] At this point we should remind ourselves that a *sine qua non* is an indispensable thing or that which is absolutely prerequisite. Thus, we are told that the absolute prerequisite of dispensationalism is two peoples of God that maintain their distinctions throughout eternity. This is fallacious, but in fairness to Ryrie, it should be noted that he says, "This is probably the most basic *theological* (italics mine) test of whether or not a man is a dispensationalist. . . ."[9] The seriousness of this confusion of principle and theological deduction is seen, however, when George Ladd picks up on Ryrie's *sine qua non* and states, "This conclusion rests upon a second principle: that of a literal system of interpretation."[10] One must confess that it is difficult to understand how a conclusion can be the first principle which rests upon a second principle.

---

[7]Ibid., 44.

[8]For a dispensational view that does not see the distinctions "throughout eternity," see W. Robert Cook's *The Theology of John* (Moody): "Contrary to some dispensational teaching which makes a firm distinction between Israel as God's earthly people and the Church as God's heavenly people, which distinction is to be maintained throughout eternity, the Biblical evidence seems to show a progressive blurring of such distinctions as history moves toward its climax. Beginning with the time of the rapture and resurrection of the saints these groupings, which during the outworking of God's historical purposes are legitimate to a certain degree, become less and less important. It should be observed that most passages dealing with the rapture and resurrection of the saints in the New Testament relate to individuals rather than to entities such as Israel or the Church. Beginning with the Millennium and continuing on into the Eternal Kingdom of God there is an inter-penetration of time and eternity, heaven and earth. During the Millennium saints with glorified bodies will relate to the people of earth. In the final form of the Kingdom, as set forth in Revelation 21:1ff., such an inter-penetration is clearly set forth (see especially verses one to seven, nine and ten) as the heavenly city comes down out of heaven to, or at least proximate to, earth. Thus it would appear that sharp distinctions between groups of saints in eternity is not Biblically warranted and tends to lead to an unnecessary and potentially divisive elitism."

[9]Ryrie, *Dispensationalism*, 45.

[10]G. E. Ladd, "Historic Premillennialism," *The Meaning of the Millennium: Four Views,* edited by R. G. Clouse (Downers Grove: InterVarsity, 1977) 19.

Why should one make such a fuss over a proper statement of the basic principle? Because it is so utterly fundamental to understand that the foundational premise of dispensationalism is not theological but hermeneutical. Ryrie cogently argues with respect to hermeneutics: "These principles guide and govern anybody's system of theology. They ought to be determined *before* one's theology is systematized, but in practice the reverse is usually true. . . . Most people know something of the doctrines they believe, but little of the hermeneutics on which they have been built."[11]

What, then, is this *basic* hermeneutical tenet? Erickson rightly analyzes that "the first tenet of dispensationalism is that the Bible must be interpreted literally."[12] In the same vein, Clarence Bass declares, "The basic implications of dispensationalism arise, not out of its chronology of eschatological events, but out of its principle of literal interpretation."[13] Again he states, "One great impetus to its growth has been its invariable insistence that the Bible must be taken literally as the Word of God and its meaning must not be 'spiritualized.'"[14]

Dispensationalists accept this evaluation and commit themselves to a single, not a dual hermeneutic. They disallow spiritualizing or allegorizing and in so doing maintain the tradition of evangelical Protestantism. As Bernard Ramm has stated: "It is still distinctively Protestant hermeneutics to be especially pledged to the literal interpretation of Scriptures."[15] With the sound of antiquity, William Tyndale exhorts:

> Thou shalt understand, therefore, that the Scripture hath but one sense, which is the literal sense. And that literal sense is the root and ground of all, and the anchor that never faileth, whereunto if thou cleave thou canst never err nor go out of the way. And if thou leave the literal sense, thou canst not but go out of the way. Nevertheless, the Scripture uses proverbs, similitudes, riddles, or allegories, as all other speeches do; but that which the proverb, similitude, riddle, or allegory signifieth is ever the literal sense, which thou must seek out diligently.[16]

---

[11]Ryrie, *Dispensationalism*, 86.

[12]Erickson, *Contemporary Options*, 115.

[13]C. B. Bass, *Backgrounds to Dispensationalism* (Grand Rapids: Eerdmans, 1960) 149.

[14]Ibid., 21.

[15]B. Ramm, *Protestant Biblical Interpretation* (Boston: Wilde, 1956) 92–3.

[16]Quoted by J. I. Packer, *Fundamentalism and the Word of God* (Grand Rapids: Eerdmans, 1958) 103.

CLARIFICATION OF THE BASIC PRINCIPLE

The latter part of Tyndale's statement concerning figures of speech has been the area where confusion has abounded. Many statements have been made which give the impression that figures of speech are antithetical to literal interpretation. Bass evidences this when he says, "Dispensationalists will not interpret the obviously literal as literal, and the obviously symbolical as symbolical. Everything must be literal."[17] Nor have dispensational writers helped to alleviate the confusion when they say that "some Scriptures are contextually indicated as containing figures of speech and not intended for literal interpretation."[18] More accurate is the statement of Ryrie that "the use of figurative language does not compromise or nullify the literal sense of the thing to which it is applied. Figures of speech are a legitimate grammatical usage for conveying a literal meaning."[19] Behind every figure of speech is a literal meaning, and by means of the historical-grammatical exegesis of the text, these literal meanings are to be sought out. As Ramm states:

> The literal meaning of the figurative expression is the proper or natural meaning as understood by students of language. Whenever a figure is used its literal meaning is precisely that meaning determined by grammatical studies of figures. Hence, figurative interpretation does not pertain to the spiritual or mystical sense of Scripture, but to the literal sense.[20]

The Syrian school of interpretation in Antioch in the early centuries of the church asserted that literal interpretation is both plain-literal and figurative-literal. The plain-literal sentence being one of straightforward prose and a sentence such as "The eye of the Lord is upon thee" being a figurative-literal sentence.[21] In other words, literalism is not the same as letterism.

More recently Robert Mounce has suggested similarly that "A writer may convey his thought either by the use of words in their directly denotative sense or he may choose the more pleasing path of figurative expression. But one thing must be kept clear: In either case

---

[17]Bass, *Backgrounds*, 23–4.
[18]J. F. Walvoord, *The Millennial Kingdom* (Findlay, OH: Dunham) vi.
[19]C. Ryrie, *The Basis of the Premillennial Faith* (New York: Loizeaux, 1953) 42–3.
[20]Ramm, *Interpretation*, 141.
[21]Ibid., 49.

the literal meaning is the same."[22] Mounce goes on to say: "An interpretation is literal only when it corresponds to what the author intends to convey with his statement." When Jesus spoke of Herod as "That fox" (Luke 13:32) he was not trying to tell us that a carnivorous mammal of the family *Canidae* had entered the human race incognito. He was only saying that the Galilean ruler was cunning, although relatively insignificant.[23] In like manner we realize upon our reading the statement of Jesus, "I am the door," that he is not a 2' 8" × 6' 8" birch door, but he is that which the figure literally signifies, namely, a way of entrance and, more specifically in the context, the way of entrance into eternal life. The literal meaning is the intention of the metaphor.

Very often Isaiah 55:12 is set forth as sort of an "Achilles' heel" to those who hold the literal interpretation. Exultingly Isaiah speaks: "For ye shall go out with joy, and be led forth with peace: the mountains and the hills shall break forth before you into singing, and all the trees of the field shall clap their hands." Here the writer is not speaking of that which would be an inherent contradiction, but he is marvelously portraying in word pictures that even all of nature shall rejoice when the king shall come to reign in his kingdom. By such a graphic word picture he has said more than could be said in several paragraphs of straight prose.

CREDIBILITY OF THE BASIC PRINCIPLE

Inasmuch as this plenary session is meant to focus on eschatology, the question needs to be asked, "When one applies this principle of literal interpretation consistently to prophecy, what is the result?" Loraine Boettner, a postmillennialist responds, "It is generally agreed that if the prophecies are taken literally, they do foretell a restoration of the nation of Israel in the land of Palestine with the Jews having a prominent place in that kingdom and ruling over the other nations."[24] The late Floyd Hamilton, an amillennialist, concurred: "Now we must frankly admit that a literal interpretation of the Old Testament prophecies gives us just such a picture of an earthly reign of the Messiah as the premillennialist pictures."[25]

---

[22]R. Mounce, "How to Interpret the Bible,"*Eternity* (May 1963) 21.

[23]Ibid.

[24]L. Boettner, "A Postmillennial Response," *The Meaning of the Millennium*, 95.

[25]F. E. Hamilton, *The Basis of the Millennial Faith* (Grand Rapids: Eerdmans, 1952) 38.

But does such a consistently literal approach to prophecy have any strong support in Scripture? The late professor of OT at Calvin Theological Seminary, Martin J. Wyngaarden, in his book, *The Future of the Kingdom in Prophecy and Fulfillment: A Study of the Scope of 'Spiritualization' in Scripture,* asked in the first chapter on "Wonders of Jehovah's Prophecy," "Were any Old Testament prophecies fulfilled literally?" He then proceeds:

> Few things can so stimulate one's faith in the revelation of God as the fulfillments of prophecy. Here we have, first of all, those fulfilled in Christ's ministry, in his sacrifice and resurrection. But there are also many others fulfilled in the history of great cities and mighty nations, in a most remarkable manner. The fulfillments are so precise, unmistakable, important and far-reaching as to recall the words of Isaiah, addressed to those inclined to reject Jehovah's predictions (Isaiah 41:21, 22). . . . and then we find many literal fulfillments of prophecy, in connection with Israel as the theocratic nation, and in connection with the surrounding nations referred to by the prophets serving under the theocracy,—the Old Testament kingdom of Jehovah. *Now the very remarkable thing is that those fulfillments are so exceedingly literal.*[26]

After such a statement it is perplexing indeed to discover that Wyngaarden concluded that much of the prophecy which is yet to be fulfilled must be fulfilled in another way other than literally. As he looked to certain unfilled prophecies he was convinced that there are those that must be spiritualized. "Even if we should say that prophecies are fulfilled literally, as a rule," he stated, "we find a series of exceptions to this rule, in the future state of Israel, in the eschatology of the theocracy, in the spiritualization of the kingdom of priests—the holy nation."[27] For these reasons, he concluded, "The problem thus raised is one of great interest, with a view toward attempting to discover the sphere in which the spiritualization of prophecy takes place."[28]

It would seem that, without theological predispositions, one would conclude that the prophecies which have been fulfilled are to form the pattern in the interpretation of prophecy that has not yet been fulfilled. If we have seen that so long as we have the history of the Jews to compare with the prophecies concerning them—that is, up to this time—a certain mode of interpreting those prophecies is ren-

---

[26]Martin J. Wyngaarden, *The Future of the Kingdom in Prophecy and Fulfillment: A Study of the Scope of the "Spiritualization" in Scripture* (Grand Rapids: Eerdmans, 1955) 13–14.

[27]Ibid., 28.

[28]Ibid., 14.

dered indispensable, then why not simply continue that same mode of interpretation, when we have prophecy alone not yet illustrated by history? If prophecies concerning the Jews, delivered two or three thousand years ago, be proved, by the history of the interim up to our own days, to have been fulfilled in the literal sense, and, therefore, to demand a literal interpretation, upon what principle can it be alleged that other prophecies, delivered in similar language by the same prophets, are not to be similarly interpreted after our days?

The logic resulting from a study of the history of fulfillment is obvious. Why then would anyone depart from it? Albertus Pieters states:

> No one defends or employs the allegorizing method of exegesis. Calvin and the other great Bible students of the Reformation saw clearly that the method was wrong and taught a now generally accepted 'grammatical—historical' interpretation, so far as the Scriptures in general are concerned. That they retain the spiritualizing method in expounding many of the prophecies was because they found themselves forced to do so in order to be faithful to the New Testament.[29]

One might question here whether it is faithfulness to the NT which forces this deductive principle of spiritualization, or whether it might more correctly be stated that it is faithfulness to a particular theological interpretation of the NT. If the latter is the case, then one might certainly question the wisdom of overthrowing the literal interpretation which is a proven biblical principle, for the unproven deductive principle of spiritualization.

At any rate the use of a dual hermeneutic which applies the literal hermeneutic to the great majority of Scripture and the spiritualizing hermeneutic to a *portion* of prophecy, namely, that portion which is future only and not even all of that, has its dangers. It is easy to see how such a method of interpretation could easily get out of hand. For example, while the evangelical believes that the prophecy of the second coming of Christ will have a future literal fulfillment, the liberal theologian applying the spiritualizing principle erases any hope of a literal return of the Lord to the earth for his saints.

Because of this possibility, therefore, the evangelical has certain regulative principles in addition to his deductive principle. Hamilton states:

> But if we reject the literal method of interpretation as the universal rule for the interpretation of all prophecies, how are we to interpret them?

---

[29]Albertus Pieters, "Darbyism vs. The Historic Christian Faith," *Calvin Forum* 2 (May 1936) 225–8.

Well, of course, there are many passages in prophecy that were meant to be taken literally. In fact a good working rule to follow is that the literal interpretation of the prophecy is to be accepted unless (a) the passages contain obviously figurative language, or (b) unless the New Testament gives authority for interpreting them in other than the literal sense, or (c) unless a literal interpretation would produce a contradiction with truths, principles, or factual statements contained in the non-symbolic books of the New Testament....[30]

If one examines each of these suggested regulative principles carefully, he will discern that none of them is necessitated by a proper understanding of literal interpretation.

APPLICATION OF THE BASIC PRINCIPLE

Literal interpretation, then, is the "bottom-line" of dispensationalism. Although certainly one would not claim absolute consistency among dispensationalists in the application of the principle, there are areas of unanimity among them which have become theological tenets in their system. Undoubtedly, the most significant of these is the maintaining of a distinction between Israel and the church. The roots of this go in two directions, first, the OT covenant promises to Abraham stated in Genesis 12:2-3 and established unconditionally in Genesis 15:6-21, and second, the NT revelation of the mystery of the church as established in Acts 2:41-47 and explained in Ephesians 3:1-6. In the minds of dispensationalists it is the Abrahamic covenant promises—particularly the land and seed promises—that have suffered most from spiritualization in interpretation. Presenting the logic of this very simply, Ryrie asks two questions:

(1) Does the Abrahamic covenant promise Israel a permanent existence as a nation? If it does, then the Church is not fulfilling Israel's promises, but rather Israel as a nation has a future yet in prospect; and (2) Does the Abrahamic covenant promise Israel permanent possession of the promised land? If it does, then Israel must yet come into possession of that land, for she has never fully possessed it in her history.[31]

---

[30]Hamilton, *Basis*, 53-4.

[31]Ryrie, *The Basis of the Premillennial Faith*, 48-9. For further discussion of the distinction between Israel and the church, see Earl D. Radmacher, *What the Church Is All About* (Chicago: Moody, 1978) 281-7; C. C. Ryrie, *Dispensationalism Today* (Chicago: Moody, 1965) 132-44; R. L. Saucy, *The Church in God's Program* (Chicago: Moody, 1972) 69-97.

One of the most probing recent works on this subject was done by
one who would not likely be called a dispensationalist, namely, Arnold
A. Van Ruler, the late Professor of Dogmatic Theology at the University of Utrecht. In his work of 1955 translated in 1971 by Geoffrey
Bromiley, *The Christian Church and the Old Testament,* he states:

> To the very depths of Old Testament expectation, the people of Israel
> as a people, the land, posterity, and theocracy play a role that cannot
> possibly be eliminated. This role cannot be altered by regarding Christ
> and his church as the fulfilment, in other words, by spiritualizing.
> There is a surplus in the Old Testament, a remnant that cannot be
> fitted into the New Testament fulfilment.[32]

He continues:

> I believe that the NT never says that the people of Israel . . . is defi-
> nitively rejected. It simply says that the people of Israel is blind and
> hardened and indeed with a view to a new development. This develop-
> ment has an eschatological range: it contains the solution to the riddle
> of the world (Rom. 11:15).[33]

And then he raises the key question:

> How are we, as the Christian church standing in the New Testament in
> the light of God's act in Jesus Christ, to handle the Old Testa-
> ment? . . . A renewal of allegorizing may seem to offer a way of assign-
> ing an authentic function to the Old Testament in the Christian situa-
> tion. . . . I believe that we must resist to the last the temptation lurking in
> this idea. The idea is in fact a temptation, for it seems that allegorizing
> can solve all the problems of the Christian church in relation to the
> Old Testament. . . . (It) gives the appearance of making it perfectly
> plain that the Old Testament is wholly and exclusively the book of the
> Christian church, which can be exploited fully by it alone.[34]

It is difficult to resist continuing the quotation from Van Ruler
because his remarks are so cogent, but it is that key phrase of his—
"surplus in the Old Testament"—which catches one's attention. It is
that surplus which has so often been spiritualized to find its fulfillment in the church. But when interpreted literally it demands an
earthly reign of Christ such as this earth has never seen. Thus, it is the
nature of the earthly reign of Christ as predicted in the OT and not

---

[32]A. A. Van Ruler, *The Christian Church and the Old Testament* (Grand
Rapids: Eerdmans, 1971) 45.
[33]Ibid., 55.
[34]Ibid., 57.

simply the *length* of that reign in the millennial prophecy of Revelation 20 that provides the basis for dispensational premillennialism.

Continuing to apply this basic principle of literal interpretation, the dispensationalist not only finds significant eschatological distinctions within God's kingdom program, but he is confronted with a unifying philosophy of history which presents a majestic and climactic victory within history on this earth. In his system, history is not simply an endless series of cycles of testing, apostasy and judgment moving nowhere. Rather, history has meaning and purpose, and this is seen in its progressive movement toward its grandest demonstration of its doxological purpose. Thus, with intensity and expectation God's children pray the Disciples' Prayer, "Our Father in heaven, hallowed be your name, your kingdom come, your will be done on earth as it is in heaven" (Matt 6:9, 10, NIV). The King, the Second Adam, is coming and he is going to reign until he has reversed the curse on this earth and subjected every shred of rebellion precipitated by Satan and his opposing kingdom of darkness "so that God may be all in all" (1 Cor 15:28).[35]

Too often theological systems, or their applications, have narrowed God's kingdom purpose down to a redemptive purpose. They have become redemptocentric rather than theocentric; consequently, they have minimized or spiritualized activities in the Word that do not have

---

[35]W. Robert Cook observes in *The Theology of John,* p. 95: "Those dispensationalists who object to considering Jesus Christ as King today suffer from the same problem in reverse as do the anti-dispensationalists who refuse to recognize Israel and the Church as distinct entities. The dispensationalist tends to compartmentalize his theology to such a degree he does not admit any relationship of saints from one dispensation with those of another. Although he may affirm, and rightly so, that the cohesiveness of his theological system is a doxological theocentricity (rather than the redempto-centric theme of the Covenant theologian) this rarely is demonstrated in practice. He often fails to remember that this theocentricity must have as its vehicle of expression a form of theocracy. The glory of God must be the dominant note of all theology and practice but He is supremely glorified only when the sovereign King of the universe is allowed to extend His rule in every sphere of reality. This includes the Church, of which Christ is Head *and* King (Eph. 1:22–23; I Tim. 6:13–16). By the same token, only in the opposite direction, the anti-dispensationalist unnecessarily lumps all saints into one amorphous group failing to see that the one grand theme of the universe, the glory of God, may be served by several lesser purposes. When a historico-grammatical hermeneutic is consistently applied to Scripture the future of Israel as a separate entity from the Church is substantiated without sacrificing either the concept of covenant or kingdom."

immediate relation to the redemption of man. In this they fall short of an adequate philosophy of history for they fail to account for all of created reality.

On this subject one must listen to Van Ruler again in his chapter "The Necessity of the Old Testament for the Christian Church."[36]

> ... the Christian church really has to make something out of the Old Testament. It is unquestionably the book of the people of Israel. ... In the Old Testament this original and final element, this faithfulness to the earth and time, is more plainly visible. In my view this means that, in this respect, we have to speak most emphatically of the greater value of the Old Testament as compared with the New. The Old Testament has a more positive concern with creation and the kingdom, with the first things and the last, with the image and the law, with sanctification and humanity, with ethos and culture, with society and marriage, with history and the state. These are precisely the matters at issue in the Old Testament. For this reason the Old Testament neither can be nor should be expounded Christologically, but only eschatologically, in other words, *theocratically*. There is in it a profound confidence in the goodness of the world, the serviceability of man, and the possibility of *sanctifying the earth* [italics mine]. ... For the consciousness of the Christian church throughout the centuries there has always been a surplus in the Old Testament that it could not assimilate. This surplus is not just the cultus. The church has spiritualized this or brought it into its own liturgy or used it as a witness to the message of Golgotha or simply said that it has been superseded by Christ. ... In my view Martin Buber is completely correct to level against the Christian church throughout the centuries the accusation that it has never really been faithful to this Old Testament belief, this grand vision of the God of Israel, this visionary faith in the possibility of the sanctification of the earth. From the necessity of the cross of Christ, which the church has accepted on the basis of the New Testament, the false conclusion has been drawn that no more can be made of the earth. ... The Christian church has treated the Old Testament just as uncertainly and unsuitably as it has treated the Jews. ... Does everything end in the church? Does everything, not only Israel, but history and creation exist for the sake of the church? Or is the church only one among many forms of the kingdom of God, and does its catholicity consist precisely in the fact that it respects, acknowledges, and holds dear all forms of the kingdom, for example, even the people of Israel?

Just a few years after Van Ruler raised those questions, another Dutch theologian, Gerrit C. Berkower, observed a new openness among his colleagues to the Chiliast's philosophy of history:

> Time was when most theologians regarded Chiliasm as a fantastic, earth-bound eschatology. ... A remarkable change has taken place. ...

---

[36]Ibid., 75–98.

While the critics of Chiliasm find its description of the millennial times objectionable and unacceptable, the same critics praise the Chiliast's fidelity to God's purpose for the earth. It is this motif, they say, which has made Chiliasm a current that has never been wholly set aside in the Church. The Chiliast's hope for Christ's kingdom on earth is sometimes called the anti-spiritualistic motif in millennialism. It is the faith that God's salvation has meaning not only for heaven, but for earth as well. For *this* earth![37]

Yes, the dispensationalist is optimistic about what God is yet going to do with this earth. The greatest and grandest display of God's glory is yet to come when the multiformity of his kingdom program will consummate in a many splendored unity. The earliest prophecy of God's Word, Genesis 3:15, presents in microscopic fashion, God's twofold solution to a twofold problem occasioned by sin, "And I will put enmity between you and the woman and between your offspring and hers; he will crush your head, and you will strike his heel" (NIV). The problem was (1) how to reclaim his usurped kingdom, and (2) how to provide redemption for mankind. Two prophesied bruisings or crushings are the key. "He will crush your head" portrays the final destruction of Satan and his kingdom provided for in Christ's death on the cross. "You will strike his heel" pictures Christ's death as also the basis for God's redemptive program. In his work, *Biography of a Great Planet,* Stanley Ellisen shows the progressive unfolding of this twofold purpose in the rest of the Scripture.[38]

The Lord chose two men of faith through whom he inaugurated these programs.[39] With Abraham he made a covenant promising among other things a seed that would bless all nations. This seed Paul identified as Christ who would bring redemption to men, fulfilling the redemptive program (cf. Gal 3:6–16). To fulfill his kingdom purpose, God chose David out of the same line and made a covenant about a kingdom and a royal seed (2 Sam 7:12–16). This royal seed would rule, not only over Israel, but over the whole world. Through the seed of David, God would fulfill his kingdom program by destroying the rebels and ruling the world in righteousness. The victory will be won where the battle was started. Ellisen concludes: "Although these two functions of Christ are inextricably related throughout the Bible, they are distinct in their purposes. The kingdom purpose is primarily for God, having to do with his reclaiming what was lost from his kingdom.

---

[37]G. C. Berkower, "Review of Current Religious Thought," *Christianity Today,* 6 (October 27, 1961) 40.

[38]S. A. Ellisen, *Biography of a Great Planet* (Wheaton: Tyndale, 1975) 22–6.

[39]Note Matt 1:1, "The son of David, the son of Abraham."

The redemptive purpose relates primarily to man, providing the basis of his salvation."[40]

The apostle John relates these two functions in Revelation 5:12: "Worthy is the Lamb who was slain, to receive power and wealth and wisdom and strength and honor and glory and praise!"(NIV). He will have shown not only his right but his worthiness to rule as God's Lion, having been slain as God's Lamb. In grand consummation Christ will present the reclaimed kingdom to the Father "so that God may be all in all" (1 Cor 15:24, NIV).

---

[40]Ellisen, *Biography,* 25. For a presentation of the progress of this philosophy of history in earth's history, see R. E. Showers, *What on Earth Is God Doing?* (Neptune, New Jersey: Loizeaux, 1973).

PART
TWO

BIBLICAL THEOLOGY

14

The Future of Biblical Theology

Gerhard F. Hasel

Biblical theology is today in a state of disarray. The disturbing fact that "there is no one definition of this field on which biblical scholars can unanimously agree"[1] is highlighted by the diversity of approaches in the unprecedented volume of recent publications. No less than eleven different theologies of the NT appeared in the period from 1967 to 1977[2] and at least twelve different theologies of the OT were

---

[1]K. Stendahl, "Biblical Theology, Contemporary," *IDB* 1. 418.

[2]H. Conzelmann, *Grundriss der Theologie des Neuen Testaments* (Munich: Chr. Kaiser, 1967), Eng. trans. *An Outline of the Theology of the New Testament* (New York: Harper & Row, 1969); K. H. Schelkle, *Theologie des Neuen Testaments*, 4 vols. (Düsseldorf: Patmos, 1968–74), Eng. trans. *Theology of the New Testament*, 4 vols. (Collegeville, MN: Liturgical Press, 1971–77); W. G. Kümmel, *Die Theologie des Neuen Testaments nach seinen Hauptzeugen: Jesus-Paulus-Johannes* (Göttingen: Vandenhoeck & Ruprecht, 1969), Eng. trans. *The Theology of the New Testament According to Its Major Witnesses: Jesus-Paul-John* (Nashville: Abingdon, 1973); A. T. Nikolainen, *Uuden Testamentin Tulkintin ja tutkimus* (Porvo-Helsinki: Urvo, 1971); J. Jeremias, *Neutestamentliche Theologie. Erster Teil: Die Verkündigung Jesu* (Gütersloh: G. Bertelsmann, 1971), Eng. trans. *New Testament Theology: The Proclamation of Jesus* (New York: Harper & Row, 1971); M. G. Cordero, *Teología de la Biblia II et III: Nuevo Testamento*, 2 vols. (Madrid: Biblioteca de Autoies Cristianos, 1972); G. E. Ladd, *A Theology of the New Testament* (Grand Rapids: Eerdmans, 1974); C. K. Lehman, *Biblical Theology, 2: New Testament* (Scottdale, PA: Herald, 1974); E. Lohse, *Grundriss der neutestamentlichen Theologie* (Stuttgart: W. Kohlhammer, 1974); L. Goppelt, *Theologie des Neuen Testaments*, 2 vols. (Göttingen: Vandenhoeck & Ruprecht, 1975–76); S. Neill, *Jesus Through Many Eyes. Introduction to the Theology of the New Testament* (Nashville: Abingdon, 1976); R. Kieffer, *Nytestamentlig teologi* (Stockholm: VerBum, 1977).

published between 1970 and 1978.[3] An analysis of these theologies of
the OT and NT reveals basic disparities regarding the nature, function, method, and scope of biblical theology.[4] Deep historical, theological, philosophical, and methodological problems are underlying
these divergences and call for creative reflection.

In view of the complexity of this situation we deem it advisable to
discuss the subject of the future biblical theology by stating a number
of theses that deal respectively with the place, method, content, task,
structure, and challenge of biblical theology. In the course of the
discussion of each thesis we attempt to engage in dialogue with various opinions and to present some new directions for the future of
biblical theology.

I

*Biblical theology takes its place as the crown of biblical studies and is limited
by the boundaries of the OT and NT canons and the final form of their texts.*

This thesis reflects critically and hopefully creatively on some
trends in modern scholarship which interpret biblical theology in radically new ways. The English-speaking world of biblical scholarship
has witnessed the rise and decline of the so-called "Biblical Theology
movement" as part of the liberal scholarly tradition. Its peak period
existed between 1945 and 1960 and is ably described for the American scene by B. S. Childs[5] and beyond by J. Barr.[6] Although it "now

---

[3]G. E. Wright, *The Old Testament and Theology* (New York: Harper & Row,
1970); Th. C. Vriezen, *An Outline of Old Testament Theology* (2d ed.; Newton,
MA: Branford, 1970); C. K. Lehman, *Biblical Theology I: Old Testament*
(Scottdale, PA: Herald, 1971); A. Deissler, *Die Grundbotschaft des Alten Testa-
ments* (Freiburg i. Br.: Herder, 1972); G. Fohrer, *Theologische Grundstrukturen
des Alten Testaments* (Berlin/New York: W. de Gruyter, 1972); W. Zimmerli,
Grundriss der alttestamentlichen Theologie (Stuttgart: W. Kohlhammer, 1972),
Eng. trans. *Old Testament Theology in Outline* (Atlanta: J. Knox, 1978); J. L.
McKenzie, *A Theology of the Old Testament* (Garden City, NY: Doubleday,
1974); D. F. Hinson, *Theology of the Old Testament* (London: SPCK, 1976); S.
Terrien, *The Elusive Presence: Toward a New Biblical Theology* (San Francisco:
Harper & Row, 1978); W. C. Kaiser, *Toward an Old Testament Theology* (Grand
Rapids: Zondervan, 1978); C. Westermann, *Theologie des Alten Testaments in
Grundzügen* (Göttingen: Vandenhoeck & Ruprecht, 1978).

[4]See the studies by the present writer, *Old Testament Theology: Basic Issues in
the Current Debate,* 2nd ed. (Grand Rapids: Eerdmans, 1975); *New Testament
Theology: Basic Issues in the Current Debate* (Grand Rapids: Eerdmans, 1978).

[5]B. S. Childs, *Biblical Theology in Crisis* (Philadelphia: Westminster, 1970)
13–87.

[6]J. Barr, "Biblical Theology," *IDBSup,* 104–11.

belongs to the past history of [liberal] biblical studies,"[7] it has given stimulus to a "new Biblical Theology."[8]

Proposals for a "new Biblical Theology" come from B. S. Childs. He insists that "the canon of the Christian church is the most appropriate context from which to do Biblical theology."[9] For the enterprise of biblical theology the historical-critical method is outrightly rejected. The reason: because the historical-critical method "sets up an iron curtain between the past and the present, it is an inadequate method for studying the Bible as the church's Scripture."[10] Childs argues for a biblical theology that employs a canonical and theological method that seems to be confessional in nature. Biblical theology is conceived as a "distinctively Christian discipline, a part of Christian theology [dogmatics], because it uses the OT and NT as Scripture."[11]

Does this mean that Childs understands OT theology and NT theology as part of biblical theology? Not at all. Childs separates biblical theology which is part of dogmatic theology from OT and NT theology which follows the historical-critical method. He writes, "The enterprise of Biblical theology is a different discipline from either OT or NT theology. I try to maintain a sharp distinction in method."[12] The fact is that Childs's new biblical theology "is a distinctively Christian discipline, [and] a part of Christian theology"[13] which stands over against OT and NT theology as a separate but "legitimate field" while the latter is seen "chiefly as a descriptive enterprise."[14]

The methodology of Childs posits a dichotomy between the "normative"[15] canonical-theological enterprise of biblical theology as part of Christian theology or dogmatics[16] and OT and NT theology as a chiefly descriptive, nonnormative historical-critical enterprise. The assignment of biblical theology to dogmatics implies, of course, that it is no longer a part of biblical studies. In terms of the history and development of biblical theology this means that Childs links his ap-

---

[7]Barr, "Biblical Theology," 111.

[8]Hasel, *OT Theology*, 49–55.

[9]Childs, *Biblical Theology in Crisis*, 99.

[10]Ibid., 141–2.

[11]Private communication of Prof. Childs of Sept. 25, 1973.

[12]Ibid.

[13]Ibid.

[14]Ibid.

[15]Childs, *Biblical Theology In Crisis*, 100, "To do Biblical Theology within the context of the canon involves acknowledgment of the *normative* quality of the Biblical tradition" (italics his).

[16]Childs, private communication of Sept. 25, 1973, "I do not think that one can move directly from OT to constructive Christian theology (dogmatics)."

proach of a "new Biblical theology" to a pre-Gabler era when biblical theology was not separated from dogmatic theology.[17] Childs has not spelled out what role biblical theology has within dogmatics and what it means that it has normative status within the enterprise of dogmatics.

Another recent approach for biblical theology stands in sharp contrast to the one of Childs. It takes its starting-point from the traditio-historical method and remains firmly grounded in a diachronic historical criticism. The OT scholar Hartmut Gese has outlined its basic approach[18] which has found a recent supporter in the University of Tübingen NT scholar Peter Stuhlmacher.[19] This diachronic approach to biblical theology is indebted to Gerhard von Rad and seeks to overcome the hiatus between the Testaments with the 200-year separation of biblical theology into OT and NT theology[20] by means of the process of tradition which is said to establish continuity between the Testaments.[21] The basic thesis is that biblical theology is "theology as formation of tradition" in the sense that the unity of the Testaments "exists already because of tradition history."[22] The NT is but an extension of the process of tradition out of which the OT emerges, so that "the New Testament presents the goal and end, the *telos* of the path of Biblical tradition."[23] Continuity between the Testaments rests in the "one single tradition process at the end and goal of which the New Testament appears."[24] This model of biblical theology as forma-

---

[17]Hasel, *NT Theology*, 14-25.

[18]H. Gese, "Erwägungen zur Einheit der biblischen Theologie," *ZTK* 67 (1970) 417-36, reprinted in *Vom Sinai zum Zion. Alttestamentliche Beiträge zur biblischen Theologie* (München: Chr. Kaiser, 1974) 11-30; H. Gese, *Zur biblischen Theologie. Alttestamentliche Vorträge* (München: Chr. Kaiser, 1977); H. Gese, "Tradition and Biblical Theology," *Tradition and Theology in the Old Testament*, ed. D. A. Knight (Philadelphia: Fortress, 1977), 301-26.

[19]P. Stuhlmacher, *Schriftauslegung auf dem Wege zur biblischen Theologie* (Göttingen: Vandenhoeck & Ruprecht, 1975); P. Stuhlmacher, *Historical Criticism and Theological Interpretation of Scripture* (Philadelphia: Fortress, 1977); P. Stuhlmacher, "Zum Thema: Biblische Theologie des Neuen Testaments," *Biblische Theologie heute*, ed. K. Haacker (Neukirchen-Vluyn: Neukirchener Verlag, 1977), 25-60.

[20]Georg L. Bauer (1755-1806) separated OT theology from NT theology by publishing separate volumes on each in 1796 and 1800-02 respectively. See Hasel, *OT Theology*, 22-3.

[21]Gese, *Vom Sinai zum Zion*, 14; Stuhlmacher, "Zum Thema," 25-6.

[22]Gese, "Tradition and Biblical Theology," 322.

[23]Ibid.

[24]Ibid.

tion of tradition also maintains that the NT tradition process played a material part in the shaping of the OT. "The Old Testament was closed through a reform in the spirit of Pharisaism which rejected the Hellenistic Old Testament."[25] What this means is that the theory of the late closing of the canon at Jamnia, which is highly problematical in itself, manifested the spirit of Pharisaism which was anti-Hellenistic and produced a much reduced OT canon. These hypotheses concerning the influence of Pharisaism, the open Hellenistic canon, the late closing of the canon, and the influence of the NT in this process[26] are foundational for the approach to biblical theology as formation of tradition. It rejects the boundaries of the OT and NT canons for the enterprise of biblical theology. It is evident that if any of these hypotheses should turn out to be unsupportable, then this model of biblical theology cannot stand.

These two recent models of biblical theology are symptomatic of some major issues and the disarray of the discipline. Both of these models have hardly anything in common with each other except the use of the same name. The new biblical theology proposed by Childs shifts it into the seemingly safe haven of Christian dogmatics. The Gese-Stuhlmacher model maintains continuity with the historical-critical method but the metamorphosis of biblical theology into a "theology as formation of tradition" separates it from the final form of the biblical text.

Biblical theology should be conceived as a rather different enterprise. It must maintain its place as the crown of biblical studies. It must maintain its intimate connection with OT and NT theology. It should neither be reduced to a chapter in dogmatic theology nor should it be transformed into a diachronic and immanent "theology as formation of tradition."

Biblical theology must integrate OT and NT theology in a dynamic way that overcomes the present juxtaposition of OT and NT theology. This can be creatively accomplished once biblical theology recognizes as its boundaries the full biblical canon and deals with the biblical texts in the final form in which they meet the eye. Since the two Testaments produce *one* Bible, it is difficult to look at OT theology in a totally isolated way "as if the New Testament did not exist."[27] Likewise a NT theology can hardly be produced as if the OT did not exist. W. Eichrodt has observed correctly that there is a "historical movement from the Old Testament to the New [and] there is a cur-

---

[25]Ibid., 323.
[26]Gese, *Vom Sinai zum Zion*, 16–18; Stuhlmacher, "Zum Thema," 26.
[27]McKenzie, *A Theology of the Old Testament*, 319.

rent of life flowing in reverse direction from the New Testament to the Old. This reverse relationship also elucidates the full significance of the realm of OT thought."[28] Only where this reciprocal relationship between the Testaments is understood and reflected do we find the correct place and definition of biblical theology. Biblical theology must be open to the full biblical context and must not be allowed to be dominated by such limiting theological notions as an authoritative core, a depreciating use of progressive revelation,[29] or a canon within a canon.[30]

Evidently the future of biblical theology is not at all certain. We maintain, however, that biblical theology can and must have a future. But it appears that this future can only be guaranteed within sound biblical studies that recognize the validity of the canon of the OT and NT and that build on the final or canonical form of the texts as they meet the eye.

II

Biblical theology employs the theological-historical method which takes full account of God's self-revelation embodied in Scripture in all its dimensions of reality.

From the latter part of the eighteenth century when Johann P. Gabler defined biblical theology as having an "historical character, transmitting what the sacred writers thought about divine matters,"[31]

---

[28]W. Eichrodt, *Theology of the Old Testament* (Philadelphia: Westminster, 1961), 1. 26.

[29]G. Vos, *Biblical Theology: Old and New Testaments* (Grand Rapids: Eerdmans, 1948) 25, "The method of Biblical Theology is in the main determined by the principle of historic progression." Vos does not seem to depreciate the early periods of revelation as being inferior to later periods as seems to be the case by M. S. Augsburger who claims that "the New Testament is at a higher level than the Old Testament" (in Lehman, *Biblical Theology I: OT*, 12). On progressive revelation ideas in liberal theology, see D. L. Baker, *Two Testaments: One Bible* (Downers Grove: InterVarsity, 1977) 76–80.

[30]I. Lönning, *"Kanon im Kanon." Zum dogmatischen Grundproblem des neutestamentlichen Kanons* (München: Chr. Kaiser, 1972); E. Käsemann, ed., *Das Neue Testament als Kanon* (Göttingen: Vandenhoeck & Ruprecht, 1969); G. F. Hasel, "Whole Scripture or 'Canon Within the Canon,'" *The Channel* 2 (April 1978) 25–50.

[31]J. P. Gabler, "Oratio de iusto discrimine theologiae biblicae et dogmaticae regendisque recte utriusque finibus," *Kleine theologische Schriften,* eds. Th. A. Gabler and J. G. Gabler (Ulm: Pustet, 1831), 2. 183.

biblical theology followed by and large a historical method which in the course of time rendered it incapable of affirming the divine dimension to which the Bible testifies. It is within this context that H. J. Kraus points out that "one of the most difficult questions confronting Biblical theology today is that of the starting-point, the meaning and function of historical-critical research."[32] This is not the place to review the crisis in which the historical-critical method finds itself today,[33] whether it is bankrupt[34] or whether its end has actually come.[35] What matters is not even so much whether the method can be made to have "openness to transcendence."[36] The fact remains that "historical criticism brings a concept of truth to the Bible that is not able to give full access to reality in history."[37] None other than G. von Rad had come to recognize this. He notes perceptively that it is impossible for "a consistently applied historico-critical method . . . really to do justice to the Old Testament scripture's claim to truth."[38] We may add that this is true also for the NT Scripture's claim to truth. P. Stuhlmacher who likes to open the historical-critical method for transcendence still points to the dilemma. He points out that the historical-critical method leads to "a conflict between theological intention and the tendentiousness of the method or introduces historical criticism into theological thought as a disturbing or destructive element."[39] The dilemma can only be resolved with a method that does justice to all dimensions of reality to which the biblical texts testify.

The theological-historical method seeks to be faithful to all dimensions of reality. It does maintain the transcendent-supratemporal dimension of reality and shows sensitivity to the spatial-temporal di-

---

[32]H. J. Kraus, *Die Biblische Theologie* (Neukirchen-Vluyn: Neukirchener Verlag, 1970) 377.

[33]Hasel, *NT Theology,* 19 ns. 32–5, 207–11.

[34]W. Wink, *The Bible in Human Transformation: Toward a New Paradigm for Biblical Study* (Philadelphia: Fortress, 1973) 1–18.

[35]G. Maier, *The End of the Historical-Critical Method* (St. Louis: Concordia, 1977).

[36]Stuhlmacher, *Historical Criticism and Theological Interpretation of Scripture,* 84–5.

[37]E. Krentz, *The Historical-Critical Method* (Philadelphia: Fortress, 1975) 81.

[38]G. von Rad, *Old Testament Theology* (Edinburgh, Oliver and Boyd, 1965), 2. 417.

[39]P. Stuhlmacher, "Zur Methoden- und Sachproblematik einer interkonfessionellen Auslegung des Neuen Testaments," *Evangelisch-Katholischer Kommentar zum NT. Vorarbeiten* Heft 4 (Neukirchen-Vluyn. Neukirchener, 1973) 46.

mension of reality. It does not seek to skip one in favor of the other but seeks to be theological and historical from the beginning. It has been demonstrated that scholars have engaged in historical-critical research on the exegetical level in naturalistic explanations and then moved on to speak of the acts of God on the level of theology, biblical theology.[40] The central historical-critical and theological issues remain in this two-level dichotomy in a state of confusion. The result was a "theology of the historical and prophetic tradition"[41] and now it is a "theology as formation of tradition" or a return to the history-of-religions theology[42] where William Wrede is said to be right after all for calling for an "Early Christian History of Religion."[43]

A biblical theology conceived as theological-historical from its starting point puts exegesis also into a theological-historical frame of reference.[44] This means among other things procedures that are open to the full biblical context. In this connection the call for a reorientation of exegetical science within context-open research and theme-oriented perspectives has a place and fills an urgent need.[45]

III

Biblical theology is in content a theology of the Bible and not a theology that has its roots in the Bible or takes the Bible as its starting point.

---

[40]See P. Hanson, *Dynamic Transcendence* (Philadelphia: Fortress, 1978), 23–7. Hanson notes perceptively that well-known Biblical theologians "describe the *bruta facta* within a modern scientific understanding of reality, then switch to speak confessionally of acts of God perceived by the 'eyes of faith,' without giving a philosophical explanation of how the two realms relate" (25–6). He argues for a "hermeneutic of engagement" (76–94) which seems to have certain similarities to aspects of the model of Gese-Stuhlmacher.

[41]This is the epoch-making diachronic approach developed by von Rad, *OT Theology*, 2 vols., who designates his enterprise forthrightly as a theology of Israel's historical and prophetic traditions. See D. G. Spriggs, *Two Old Testament Theologies* (London: SCM, 1974) 39–60.

[42]So J. M. Robinson, "The Future of Biblical Theology," *Rel S Rev* 2 (1976) 20.

[43]W. Wrede, *Über Aufgabe und Methode der sogenannten Neutestamentlichen Theologie* (Göttingen: Vandenhoeck & Ruprecht, 1897), 80; cf. R. Morgan, *The Nature of New Testament Theology* (London: SCM, 1973) 116, who translates incorrectly "early Christian history of dogma" from "urchristliche Religionsgeschichte."

[44]Kraus, *Die Biblische Theologie*, 369.

[45]H. J. Kraus, "Probleme und Perspektiven Biblischer Theologie," *Biblische Theologie heute*, 112.

The name biblical theology is equivocal. It can refer to a theology that is biblical in the sense that it is rooted in the Bible, or is in harmony with the Bible, or is drawn from the Bible.[46] It can also refer to a theology that is biblical in the sense that it presents the theology which the Bible contains or simply a theology of the Bible.[47] The former conception takes biblical theology as part of the realm of theological studies whereas the latter conception conceives biblical theology as part of biblical studies. We have suggested that biblical theology is the theology of the Bible. Accordingly, the content of biblical theology is determined by the Bible and not by philosophical or theological models of Judeo-Christian thought.

In harmony with the perimeters of the Bible, the subject matter of biblical theology is provided in the sixty-six books that make up the Bible. There are other fields of study that draw upon material from the Bible such as the history of ancient Israel, the religion of Israel, or a history of early Christianity. Biblical theology is however not identical with them.[48] This is not the place to engage in an extended discussion of the differences between these endeavors, their materials and purposes.[49] May it suffice to say that the endeavors other than biblical theology proceed along the lines of historico-genetic relations with the surrounding realm of sociocultural settings. Biblical theology on the other hand focuses upon the biblical faith in all its variety and richness. It is certainly not oblivious to the data of other ancient Near Eastern religions, yet it is not a history of Israelite and/or early Christian religion.

IV

Biblical theology has the task of providing summary interpretations of the final form of the individual biblical documents or groups of writings and of

---

[46]So for example D. Schenkel, "Die Aufgabe der Biblischen Theologie in dem gegenwärtigen Entwicklungsstadium der theologischen Wissenschaft," *TSK* 25 (1852) 42–4.

[47]See O. Merk, *Biblische Theologie des Neuen Testaments in ihrer Anfangszeit* (Marburg: Ewert, 1972), 7–8; G. Ebeling, "The Meaning of Biblical Theology," *Word and Faith* (Philadelphia: Fortress, 1963) 79–81.

[48]Among the OT theologians who wrote separate volumes on the religion of ancient Israel are Th. C. Vriezen, *The Religion of Ancient Israel* (London: Lutterworth, 1967); W. Eichrodt, *Religionsgeschichte Israels* (Bern/München: Francke Verlag, 1969); G. Fohrer, *Geschichte der israelitischen Religion* (Berlin: W. de Gruyter, 1969).

[49]Wrede, *Über Aufgabe und Methode*, 15–79, argued at length that NT theology should be a purely historical discipline which should include all early Christian literature and should not be restricted to the NT canon.

presenting the longitudinal themes, motifs, and concepts that emerge from the biblical materials.

The conception of this two-pronged task for biblical theology tends toward an inclusion of the maximum of biblical revelation. It attempts to ward off a one-sided emphasis on an authoritative core within either the OT or NT or one that is common to both Testaments.[50] The basic openness toward the whole of the Bible is in harmony with the holistic idea with which the NT treats the OT. NT Christianity obviously did not see the Torah in the OT as the primary authoritative core, but conceives the whole of the OT as Scripture and prophetic in nature. Evidence of this is found in the NT affirmation of the tripartite OT canon (Luke 24:44)[51] and the undifferentiated citations of the OT from all its sections.[52] Several NT writers use the term γραφή for the whole OT with an emphasis on its unity and totality.[53]

As regards the NT the holistic concept of biblical theology is again guided by the same openness toward the entire NT. It has been evident time and again that in biblical theology greater attention is accorded to certain NT writings,[54] usually the Johannine and Pauline corpus or parts thereof,[55] at the expense of other parts of NT Scripture.[56] If the fullness of biblical revelation is to come to expression in biblical theology, then the theology of all biblical documents or blocks of writings must be presented in their full polychromatic richness and with all variety of thematic perspectives.

The emphasis on the final form of the biblical texts for biblical theology is of utmost importance. The conception of biblical theology

---

[50]The affirmation of such an "authoritative core" for OT theology has come forth from G. E. Wright, *The Old Testament and Theology* (New York: Harper & Row, 1969) 179–83.

[51]See also the reference to other parts of the Hebrew canon in Matt 5:17; 7:12; Luke 24:27. S. Z. Leiman, *The Canonization of Hebrew Scripture* (Hamden, CN: Shoestring Press, 1976).

[52]D. Guthrie, "Canon of the New Testament," *ZPEB* 1. 732–3.

[53]Cf. Matt 22:29; 26:54; John 7:38, 42; 13:18; 19:24, 28, 36; Rom 1:2; 7:12; 15:4; 16:26; Gal 3:8, 22; 1 Pet 2:6; 2 Pet 1:20. See G. Schrenck, "γραφή," *TDNT* 1. 751–5.

[54]For example, W. G. Kümmel, *The Theology of the New Testament According to its Major Witnesses: Jesus-Paul-John* (Nashville: Abingdon, 1973), stresses the theology of Jesus, Paul, and John and leaves out of consideration all the rest of the NT witnesses.

[55]For example, R. Bultmann, *Theology of the New Testament* (London: SCM, 1965), places the theology of Paul in the center of his discussion.

[56]The typical stepchildren of NT theology are the letters of Hebrews, James, Jude, 1–2 Peter, and Revelation.

here advanced conceives its task in totally different ways than the various conceptions proposed by diachronic approaches. We have emphasized this already in terms of its distinction from a "theology of historical and prophetic traditions,"[57] or a "theology as formation of tradition,"[58] or a "theology of the history of redaction."[59] These diachronic approaches that are part of historical criticism in our century seek to penetrate behind the text to its supposed stages until it was fixed in final form. They are largely if not totally uninterested in the totality of the final form of the biblical text as it meets the eye and the dynamics of its canonical context. We envision an approach for biblical studies of which biblical theology is the crown that conceives the respective texts as coherent with its own inner dynamics, that shows deep concern for each document as a totality[60] within the larger totality of the entire Bible. This holistic task ultimately yields summary interpretations of the biblical documents and causes the longitudinal themes, motifs, and concepts to emerge in the fullness of the totality of biblical revelation.

V

Biblical theology's structure must be capable of encompassing the multiform materials of the Bible without forcing upon them molds extraneous to the respective biblical materials and its contents.

The appropriate structure for a biblical theology is not easy to come

---

[57]So for the OT G. von Rad, *Old Testament Theology:* vol. 1, *The Theology of Israel's Historical Traditions;* vol. 2, *The Theology of Israel's Prophetic Traditions.*

[58]Proposed by H. Gese, see n. 18 above.

[59]Here we think of the usage of redaction criticism on the Gospels of Matthew, Mark, and Luke in particular. Cf. N. Perrin, *What is Redaction Criticism?* (Philadelphia: Fortress, 1970); N. Perrin, "The Interpretation of the Gospel of Mark," *Int* 30 (1976) 115-24; H. C. Kee, "Mark's Gospel in Recent Research," *Int* 32 (1978) 353-68; C. H. Talbert, "Shifting Sands: The Recent Study of the Gospel of Luke," *Int* 30 (1976) 381-95; E. Rasco, *La teología de Lucas: Origen, desarrollo, orientaciones* (Rome: Pontifical Biblical Institute Press, 1976).

[60]There are two directions from which this emphasis is heard in current study. One comes from the so-called "new criticism" which conceives the text as a work of art to be appreciated in its totality (see Hasel, *NT Theology,* 214-15 n. 41). The other is structuralism (see J. D. Crossan, "Perspectives and Methods in Contemporary Biblical Criticism," *BR* 22 [1977] 39-49), although it is interested primarily in the para-history of the text in order to penetrate from the surface structures to the deep structures.

by. Despite such highly revered procedures of systematizing the theological thoughts of Scripture along the lines of "concepts-of-doctrine" (*Lehrbegriffe*)[61] or the closely related dogmatic structure of Theology-Anthropology-Soteriology,[62] we will have to admit that they can succeed only by a *tour de force* if they seek to encompass the whole of biblical truth. The Bible does not order its material and its theology in such a way. Likewise the cross-section structures,[63] the genetic structures,[64] and the topical structures[65] reveal the problems of bringing together the fullness of the biblical realm of revelation.

A favorite approach of uniting the rich variety of OT and NT revelation is by means of a center, theme, key concept, or focal point.[66] It is not necessary to deal *in extenso* with the problem of the center of the OT[67] or the NT[68] as it relates to the structuring or

---

[61]It was used still by B. Weiss, *Lehrbuch der Biblischen Theologie des Neuen Testaments* (Berlin: W. de Gruyter, 1868), Eng. trans. from 3rd ed. *The Theology of the New Testament* (London: Cambridge Univ., 1892). See Hasel, *NT Theology*, 35-6.

[62]For R. Bultmann, *Theology of the NT*, the heart of NT theology is Pauline anthropology. On the whole issue, see W. Harrington, *The Path of Biblical Theology* (Dublin: Gill and Macmillan, 1973) 244-59.

[63]Typical examples are by W. Eichrodt, *Theology of the Old Testament*, 2 vols.; Th. C. Vriezen, *An Outline of Old Testament Theology;* W. C. Kaiser, *Toward an Old Testament Theology*.

[64]Recently used by C. K. Lehman, *Biblical Theology I: Old Testament* (Scottdale, PA: Herald, 1971); C. K. Lehman, *Biblical Theology II: New Testament* (Scottdale, PA: Herald, 1974).

[65]Typical are J. L. McKenzie, *A Theology of the Old Testament*; A. Richardson, *An Introduction to the Theology of the New Testament* (London: SCM, 1958); K. H. Schelkle, *Theology of the New Testament*, 4 vols. (Collegeville, MN: Liturgical Press, 1971-78).

[66]In NT theology a prominent trend is the concept of salvation history (Heilsgeschichte) which has rather diversified emphases by O. Cullmann, *Christ and Time* (2d ed.; London: SCM, 1962); O. Cullmann, *Salvation in History* (New York: Harper & Row, 1967); G. E. Ladd, *A Theology of the New Testament* (Grand Rapids: Eerdmans, 1974); L. Goppelt, *Theologie des Neuen Testaments*, 2 vols. (Göttingen: Vandenhoeck & Ruprecht, 1975-76). See Hasel, *NT Theology*, 111-32.

[67]See G. F. Hasel, "The Problem of the Center in the Old Testament Theology Debate," *ZAW* 86 (1974) 65-82; W. C. Kaiser, Jr., "The Centre of Old Testament Theology: The Promise," *Themelios* 10 (1974) 1-10; W. C. Kaiser, "Wisdom Theology and the Centre of Old Testament Theology," *EvQ* 50 (1978) 132-46; W. Zimmerli, "Zum Problem der 'Mitte des Alten Testamentes'," *EvT* 35 (1975) 97-118.

[68]K. Haacker, "Einheit und Vielfalt in der Theologie des Neuen Testaments," *Themelios* 4 (1968) 27-44; A. Stock, *Einheit des Neuen Testaments*

systematizing of the respective theologies. Some scholars propose a center, theme, or key concept that unites OT and NT theology. For example, G. Klein suggests the "'kingdom of God' as the central concept"[69] for both Testaments by means of which a biblical theology should be structured. H. Seebass suggests for the same purpose the concept of the "rulership of God"[70] whereas H. Wildberger believes the "election" theme[71] will do it. F. C. Fensham argues for the "covenant"[72] and G. Fohrer for "the *rule* of God and the *communion* between God and man."[73] Other attempts could be added.

This sampling of suggestions indicates that there is no consensus. The reason rests in the variety of biblical revelation.[74] Therefore J. Barr has ventured to speak of a "plurality of 'centres' "[75] which make many different organizations possible. In this instance the choice of the center and the structure of a biblical theology is again moved into the subjective realm. Those who would structure or systematize on the basis of a center or centers ultimately have to superimpose it or them upon the rich and manifold encounters between God and man over a long period of time or they are able to deal adequately only with those parts of total biblical revelation that fit into the framework and perimeters of the chosen center(s). We have not been persuaded that a "centered" approach to biblical theology will be adequate when it comes to its structure and its content.

On the positive side, the OT indeed betrays an all-pervading center.

(Zurich: Benziger, 1969); H. Riesenfeld, "Reflections on the Unity of the New Testament," *Rel* 3 (1973) 35-51; E. Lohse, "Die Einheit des Neuen Testaments als theologisches Problem. Überlegungen zur Aufgabe einer Theologie des Neuen Testaments," *EvT* 35 (1975) 139-54. For additional literature and discussion, see Hasel, *NT Theology,* 140-70; B. L. Martin, "Some Reflections on the Unity of the New Testament," *SR* 8/2 (1979) 143-52.

[69]G. Klein, "'Reich Gottes' als biblischer Zentralbegriff," *EvT* 30 (1970) 642-70.

[70]H. Seebass, "Der Beitrag des Alten Testaments zum Entwurf einer biblischen Theologie," *Wort und Dienst* 8 (1965) 20-49.

[71]H. Wildberger, "Auf dem Wege zu einer biblischen Theologie," *EvT* 19 (1959) 70-90.

[72]F. C. Fensham, "Covenant, Promise and Expectation in the Bible," *TZ* 23 (1967) 305-22; F. C. Fensham, "The Covenant as Giving Expression to the Relationship between Old and New Testament," *TB* 22 (1971) 82-94.

[73]G. Fohrer, "Der Mittelpunkt einer Theologie des Alten Testaments," *TZ* 24 (1968) 161-72 (italics his).

[74]H. Clavier, *Les variétés de la pensée Biblique et le problème de son unité. Esquisse d'une Théologie de la Bible sur les textes originaux et dans leur contexte historique* (Oxford: Oxford Univ., 1976).

[75]J. Barr, "Trends and Prospects in Biblical Theology," *JTS* 25 (1974) 272.

God is the beginning, center, and future of the OT.[76] The NT
likewise betrays an all-pervading center in Jesus Christ in whom God
has revealed himself. But we must make a significant distinction with
regard to the matter of the center. The fact of the center and unity of
biblical thought, i.e., the issue as to whether there is something that
appears as undergirding unity in spite of all diversity, must be clearly
separated from the question of a center, theme, concept, or the like
on the basis of which a biblical theology is structured or on the basis of
which one engages in "content criticism," distills an authoritative core,
or finds a "canon within the canon."[77]

Where does that leave us when it comes to the structure of a biblical
theology? We have argued elsewhere for a multiplex approach[78]
which translates itself among other things in avoiding a juxtaposition
of OT theology and NT theology. The multiplex approach consists
basically of two major steps as regards the structure of biblical theology: (1) The first step consists of a presentation of the theologies of
the various OT and NT books or groups of writings so that *each*
biblical witness stands next to the others in all its richness, variety, and
diversity. This procedure allows ample opportunity for every biblical
thought to emerge and be heard. On principle these book-by-book
and group-by-group theologies provide opportunity of recognizing
both differences *and* similarities between them and of revealing the
growth of the divine self-disclosure. (2) The second step is equally
crucial. It consists of a presentation in the form of a multitrack treatment of the longitudinal themes, motifs, and concepts that have
emerged from the book-by-book and group-by-group presentations.
On the basis of the longitudinal thematic perspectives the totality of
the unity of the Bible can be perceived without forcing a single uni-
linear approach upon the Bible itself. The unity that emerges through
the appearance of the multiple interrelationships between the Testaments and within each Testament will certainly not mean uniformity
nor will it destroy diversity, but it will demonstrate the fullness of the
unity within diversity. Neither Testament is in itself monochromatic,
but the full spectrum of colors within each Testament and between

---

[76]Hasel, "The Problem of the Center in the OT Theology Debate," 80-2.

[77]Note F. Mildenberger, "Die Gegenläufigkeit von historischer Methode
und kirchliche Anwendung als Problem der Bibelauslegung," *Theologische
Beiträge* 3 (1972) 57-64; G. Maier, "Einer biblischen Hermeneutik entgegen?
Zum Gespräch mit P. Stuhlmacher und H. Lindner," *Theologische Beiträge* 8
(1977) 148-60; P. Stuhlmacher, "Biblische Theologie und kritische Exegese,"
Theologische Beiträge 8 (1977) 88-90.

[78]Hasel, *OT Theology*, 129-43; Hasel, *NT Theology*, 204-20.

the Testaments can be expected to reveal a compatible, rich, and dynamic blend.

VI

Biblical theology presents probably the most profound challenge for the biblical scholar in the latter part of the twentieth century.
This thesis is highlighted by the fact that modern biblical scholarship has found it most difficult, if not nearly impossible, to speak of and to present a way of engaging in biblical theology. The fact that B. S. Childs as we have observed moves the discipline into the field of dogmatics is symptomatic of the problem. James M. Robinson's negative reaction to "The Future of New Testament Theology"[79] with his attempt at redirecting this discipline into a "History of Primitive Christian Religion"[80] gives further support to the problem. J. Barr would like to "amalgamate both these interests,"[81] namely that of the history-of-religions and that of biblical theology. The definition of biblical theology as a "theology as formation of tradition"[82] along a diachronic tradition history[83] implies a radical transformation of biblical theology into a theology of a tradition process.[84] The latter transformation reflects also the assessment of E. Käsemann who has stated that "the *one* Biblical theology which grows from a single root and maintains an unbroken continuity is a wishful dream and a phantom."[85] In short, the future of biblical theology along these and similar paths is dim indeed.

There is, however, a future of biblical theology that is bright, promising, and challenging. It cannot be restricted to a methodology for biblical studies that does not account for the total reality expressed in Scripture. Thus a truly biblical theology cannot be oriented merely on a "purely historical" approach of an immanent understanding of

---

[79]J. M. Robinson, "The Future of New Testament Theology," 17-23.

[80]Ibid., 20. He follows consistently the program of W. Wrede proposed in 1897. See n. 43 above.

[81]Barr, "Biblical Theology," 110.

[82]Gese, *Vom Sinai zum Zion*, 18-30.

[83]Seconded by P. Stuhlmacher. See n. 19 above.

[84]Incisive reactions against this approach have come from H. J. Kraus, "Theologie als Traditionsbildung?" *Biblische Theologie heute*, 61-73; reprinted from *EvT* 37 (1976) 498-507; H. H. Schmid, "Unterwegs zu einer neuen Biblischen Theologie?" *Biblische Theologie heute*, 75-95.

[85]E. Käsemann, *Exegetische Versuche und Besinnungen* (Göttingen: Vandenhoeck & Ruprecht, 1964), 2. 27.

world and history, because in the biblical view "history is a display (*Veranstaltung*) of God."[86] The theological-historical approach to biblical studies in general and biblical theology in particular seeks to be open to the fullest claims of biblical revelation within the context of Scripture.

A biblical theology along these lines will have a future. It will force the challenge of the old and the new, the letter and the spirit, the law and the gospel, the old covenant and the new one, ethnic Israel and the believing community, particularity and universality, etc., from the perspectives derived from the context of Scripture in its final form and with a methodology built upon and in harmony with the claims of the Bible and its reality. Promise and fulfillment are evident in both Testaments. Salvation history is part of both Testaments. God's plan for redemption, life, and creation is present in both Testaments. Typology functions within both Testaments. Both Testaments share a unity of perspective on many levels not the least of which is the eschatological orientation of the future of man and world.[87] The NT completes the incompleteness of the OT, and both Testaments together make the one Bible which is the source of biblical theology and which contains the great prediction of the One who is guiding all history to its goal in the great and final *eschaton* that is yet to be realized. The future of that *eschaton* is the ultimate goal of biblical theology.

---

[86]L. Koehler, *Theologie des Alten Testaments* (3rd ed.; Tübingen: F. C. B. Mohr, 1953), 78.
[87]Vriezen, *Outline of OT Theology*, 123.

15

On the Concept of Development in Pauline Thought

Richard N. Longenecker

Since Auguste Sabatier's attempt in 1870 to trace out what he called the "progressive character of Paulinism,"[1] the question of development in Paul has been very much to the fore in NT scholarly circles.[2] In opposition to both "the orthodoxy of the past" and "the rationalistic criticism of the Tübingen School"—both of whom in their own ways and for their own purposes, as he saw it, denied "the existence of progress and development in Paul's doctrine" and thereby turned the figure of the apostle into something resembling the frigid, stone statuary of Europe's cathedrals—Sabatier took as his purpose "to write not a general biography of Paul, but a biography of his mind, and the history of his thought."[3]

Sabatier's thesis of development in Pauline thought was viewed with a rather jaundiced eye by more orthodox scholars for a number of reasons. In the first place, he was obviously affected by the ideas of development and genealogical relationships that were so much in the air as a result of Darwin's publication in 1859—which dependence he readily and almost unconsciously acknowledged in the opening

---

[1] A. Sabatier, *The Apostle Paul: A Sketch of the Development of His Doctrine*, trans. A. M. Hellier (London: Hodder & Stoughton, 1896, from 1870 French original).

[2] For an annotated bibliography of scholars advocating a theological development in Paul's thought, see J. C. Hurd, Jr., *The Origin of I Corinthians* (London: SPCK, 1965), 8–9, ns. 2 and 3; 11, n. 1.

[3] Sabatier, *Apostle Paul*, v–xiv, 1–2.

statement in explication of his thesis: "The law of development is so inseparable from the idea of life that we always assume its action, even when we cannot trace it."[4] Secondly, he could be faulted at many points in his handling of the data in the Pauline letters in support of his thesis, which did not serve to endear his proposal to those who numbered themselves among the unconverted in this matter. And thirdly, his developmental thesis, while meant for entirely other purposes by Sabatier himself, was taken by many of more conservative persuasion to only add fuel to the fire in the claimed dichotomy between Paul and Jesus that was asserted by the Tübingen School in the nineteenth century and was argued on a religionsgeschichtliche basis by such radical critics as William Wrede and Wilhelm Heitmüller at the beginning of the twentieth century.[5]

Now it is not our purpose here, space and time being at a premium, to enter into the specific details of Sabatier's thesis or to interact with the various favorable or unfavorable responses that have been made to it. Much of what is in Sabatier's own exposition and of how it was received was rooted in the situation of that day and reflects on all sides some degree of "hidden agenda." What I would like to do in this presentation, if possible, is to start afresh on the question of development in Pauline thought and to ask in an initial fashion, with an eye upon the data in the apostle's letters themselves, three elementary (though, admittedly, rather explosive) questions: (1) Is there evidence for development in Paul's thought? (2) Can such development be traced out? and (3) Of what nature is that development? In addition, I would like to conclude by suggesting some initial implications for our study of Paul in particular and for our reading of the NT and our writing of Christian theology in general.

I. IS THERE EVIDENCE FOR DEVELOPMENT IN PAUL'S THOUGHT?

To the first question regarding what evidence there might be in Paul's letters for development in the apostle's thought, two types of data immediately come to mind. In the first place, there are those Pauline statements that reflect a consciousness of life before God as being a process of growth into the full attainment of God's purposes. In Galatians 4:1-7, for example, he employs such language in his

---

[4]Ibid., 2.

[5]Cf. W. Wrede, *Paul*, trans. E. Lummis (London: Green, 1907, from 1905 German original); W. Heitmüller, "Zum Problem Paulus und Jesus," *ZNW*, 13 (1912) 320-37.

illustration of Israel under the law as being like that of "a child (νήπιος)... under guardians and trustees (ὑπὸ ἐπιτρόπους καὶ οἰκονόμους; cf. ὁ παιδαγωγός of 3:24-25) until the time set by his father," and in going on to speak of "the full rights of sonship" (ἡ υἱοθεσία) now given to God's people through Christ Jesus the Son. Likewise in 1 Corinthians 3 he employs in a variety of ways the language of growth and development in rebuke of the party spirit that had broken out within the Corinthian church: first by describing his quarrelsome converts as "mere infants (νήπιοι)in Christ" for whom he desires full maturity (vv. 1-4); then, changing the metaphor, by depicting the church as a field in which he "planted the seed, Apollos watered it, but God made it grow" (vv. 5-9); and finally, changing the metaphor again, by speaking of the church as a building for which he laid the foundation and "others are building on it" (vv. 10-15).[6] And in the prayers that head up each of his so-called Prison Epistles (i.e., Col 1:9-14; Philem 6; Eph 1:15-23; Phil 1:9-11), there are repeated emphases upon his desire for growth in his converts' lives—perhaps most obviously indicated in such expressions as "growing in the knowledge of God" of Col 1:10, "that you may know him better" of Eph 1:17, and "that your love may abound more and more in knowledge and depth of insight" of Phil 1:9.

More particularly, however, and of greater significance among the apostle's statements reflecting a consciousness of life before God as being a process of growth, are those where Paul speaks of his own spiritual and mental development. In 1 Cor 13:8-12 he laments his incapacity to grasp all the riches of the gospel, contrasting his present knowledge with that which shall be revealed:

> Where there is knowledge, it will pass away. For we know in part and we prophesy in part, but when perfection comes, the imperfect disappears. When I was a child, I talked like a child, I thought like a child, I reasoned like a child. When I became a man, I put childish ways behind me. Now we see but a poor reflection; then we shall see face to face. Now I know in part; then I shall know fully, even as I am fully known.

And in Phil 3:12-16, which was probably written just a few years before his death, Paul speaks most revealingly of his attitude toward the concept of development. In the course of expressing his desire "to attain to the resurrection from the dead," he says:

> Not that I have already obtained all this, or have already been made perfect, but I press on to take hold of that for which Christ Jesus took

---

[6]See also Col 2:7, where these metaphors allusively come to expression again in describing Christian growth.

hold of me. Brothers, I do not consider myself yet to have taken hold of
it. But one thing I do: Forgetting what is behind and straining toward
what is ahead, I press on toward the goal to win the prize for which God
has called me heavenward in Christ Jesus.

And in the last two verses of that passage he indicates that the progress in question has as much to do with his mental development as
with his moral perfection: "All of us who are mature should take such
a view of things. And if on some point you think differently, that too
God will make clear to you. Only let us live up to what we have already
attained."

The second type of data that presents itself to us when we consider
the possibility of development in Pauline thought consists of those
conceptual and expressional evidences of growth in Paul's doctrinal
affirmations and ethical statements that appear repeatedly throughout his writings. For example, almost everyone would acknowledge
that his "in Christ" (ἐν Χριστῷ) formula, which shares equal billing
with his "of Christ" (τοῦ Χριστοῦ) phraseology in the earlier letters,
comes to dominant expression in Colossians and Ephesians and serves
to encapsulate the essence of the apostle's understanding of what it
means to be a Christian. Likewise, his "body of Christ" (τὸ σῶμα τοῦ
Χριστοῦ) imagery, which was employed more illustratively in 1 Corinthians and Romans, becomes the controlling figure by way of defining the nature of the church universal in Colossians and Ephesians. But these represent only the tip of the iceberg, for implicit in all
of Paul's doctrinal and ethical pronouncements is the idea of development, which surfaces continually as the apostle speaks his message at various times and under various circumstances. As William
Ramsay in 1907 aptly said:

> Paul is penetrated from first to last with this idea. He looks at every-
> thing as a process of growth, not as a hard stationary given fact. The
> true life is a making towards perfection through growth, culminating in
> fruit. How frequently there appears in his letters this thought of pro-
> ducing fruit, a development leading towards an issue in riches and
> usefulness. The good seems never to occur to his mind as a mere qual-
> ity, but as a law of progress. . . . His whole philosophy rests on this idea
> of growth and development. The world is always to him fluid and
> changing, never stationary. But the change is towards an end, not mere
> flux without law: it is either degeneration towards death or increase
> towards perfection and true life.[7]

---

[7] W. M. Ramsay, *The Cities of St. Paul: Their Influence on His Life and Thought*
(Grand Rapids: Baker, 1960 reprint of 1907 original) 33.

To demonstrate the truth of Ramsay's assertion would require a full-scale exposition of the teachings of Paul, which, obviously, we are unable to enter into now. Suffice it here to say that as for the question "Is there any evidence for development in Paul's thought?" we feel ourselves compelled to answer in the affirmative, both because of the apostle's direct statements on moral and mental perfection as being something of a process and because of the many indications in his letters of conceptual and expressional developments in his thought.

II. CAN DEVELOPMENTS IN PAUL'S THOUGHT BE TRACED OUT?

But if it be accepted that there is development in Paul's thought, the question arises: "Can such development be traced out?" Numerous *a priori* objections against such an enterprise have been raised that, as Murray Harris aptly phrases it, "form easily discernible signposts which remind travellers of the hazards of the way."[8] And it is well that we be forewarned of such matters at the start of our inquiry and keep them constantly in mind as we proceed.

First of all, there is the question of the extent of the Pauline corpus itself, which in our day is not a mitigating factor for nine of the letters but does pose real problems with regard to Ephesians and the so-called Pastoral Epistles. Then there are problems having to do with the chronological sequence of and historical relations between not only the letters themselves but also, in some cases (e.g., the Corinthian correspondence), material within our present form of the letters. In addition, all of the extant letters fall within a relatively brief period of the apostle's life—roughly speaking, a fifteen-year period corresponding to the second half of his life as a Christian—when he might reasonably be supposed to have reached a certain level of maturity in his thought. Further, the pastoral and polemic nature of much that Paul says in his letters requires that we treat them more circumstantially than systematically, both as regards their inclusion of subject material and their manner of argumentation in response to various problems within the churches. A fifth objection often voiced, and one that legitimately arises when the pastoral and polemic nature of the correspondence is appreciated, is that the argument from silence, which has frequently been employed in support of various develop-

---

[8] M. J. Harris, "2 Corinthians 5:1–10: Watershed in Paul's Eschatology?," *Tyndale Bulletin*, 22 (1971) 33.

mental theories, is notoriously insecure. In conjunction with this, a sixth objection has relevancy as well: that the paradoxical nature of Christian truth makes it exceedingly difficult to classify Paul's theology, either in its parts or in whole, according to any schema of successive stages of development. And, finally, what exactly constitutes growth of understanding and development of thought remains an open question with many, which serves to heighten the difficulty of talking about a concept of development and explicating its features without an agreed upon definition or model.[9]

Now it cannot be said that Paul himself, though he spoke of moral and mental maturity in terms of a process and though his letters give evidence of conceptual and expressional growth during his ministry, had any interest in tracing out the stages of his own personal development. Jewish teachers of the first century thought more in terms of ultimates than of mediate causation or stages of development, and in this regard Paul was a man of his people and of his day. His own rationale for his Gentile ministry, for example, is usually expressed in terms of the revelation he received on the journey to Damascus (cf. Gal 1:12; Rom 16:25–26; Eph 3:2–9; as also in Acts 26:16–18), even though at various places in his letters and the portrayals of Acts there are indications that a full appreciation of what was involved in that original revelation was only attained by means of a process involving various levels of understanding at various times in his ministry.

Nevertheless, Luke, being a Greek, seems to have been interested in growth, advances, and developments. In his Gospel, for example, alone of the evangelists, he tells us that the boy Jesus "grew in wisdom and stature, and in favor with God and men" (Luke 2:52), and in his Acts he relates that the new convert Saul "grew more and more powerful" in speaking about the messiahship of Jesus among Damascene Jews (Acts 9:22). Furthermore, as is commonly recognized, throughout Luke's two-volume work there is the explication of the themes of growth, advance, and development, not only with regard to geography, as in the movement of the gospel from Galilee to Jerusalem in the third Gospel and from Jerusalem to Rome in the Acts, but also ideologically, as the seed planted by Jesus in his life, death, and resurrection comes to flower through the ministries of the apostles and the church. And it is the Lukan perspective on redemptive history that furnishes the initial impulse to treat Pauline thought along the lines of a developmental hypothesis—though, it must be insisted, the data

---

[9]Cf. Harris, ibid., 32–3, for an abbreviated form of this listing; and Hurd, *Origin of I Corinthians,* 9–12, for an elaboration of issues two and three.

able to be drawn from the apostle's own letters is not adverse to such an understanding and endeavor, despite the fact that he might not have been interested in pursuing such a line of inquiry himself.

III. WHAT IS THE NATURE OF THE DEVELOPMENT IN PAUL'S THOUGHT?

Probably the most difficult and vexing issue in any discussion of the concept of development has to do with the meaning of the term itself. And this is true with regard to our discussion of development in Paul as well. If we allow (if only for the sake of argument) that there is a measure of development in Pauline thought and that it can to some extent be traced out, we must then ask the basic question: What do we mean by development generally and by development in Paul's thought specifically? Two matters in particular call for definition: (1) the course of the development envisaged, and (2) the continuity inherent within that development. The first has to do with the forms or shapes taken by the phenomena in the process of development. In an earlier day, based on a biological model, this was usually assumed to be from the simple to the more complex, though in the history of thought such a model has been often found wanting and at times directly opposed by the evidence. The second matter regarding continuity is in our day of even greater concern, and therefore requires further comment here before testing out those various hypotheses that have been proposed against the data from the Pauline letters.

While almost everyone today is prepared to speak of the development of Christian doctrine over the past two millennia, and while many would also speak of development within the canonical Scriptures (whether under the rubric of "progressive revelation" or the more mundane "evolution of religion"), three quite different models have been proposed to describe the relationship of latter formulations to earlier foundations.[10] In the first place, there are those who take that relationship to be essentially one of identity or sameness, with what appear to be innovations in later formulations but actually are only more precise explications and applications of what was already implicit in the earliest statements. The analogy to be drawn is that of a syllogism, wherein what appears to be an innovation in the conclusion is really only the logical deduction already contained in the major and

---

[10]On these three models, see M. F. Wiles, *The Remaking of Christian Doctrine* (London: SCM, 1974) 4–9.

minor premises and new only in the sense that it has not been explicitly seen to be the case before. This was the attitude of the Alexandrian fathers (e.g., Clement of Alexandria, Origen),[11] and continues to be the understanding of development in many Catholic, Reformed, and Puritan circles more traditionally oriented.

A second model proposed for understanding the concept of development is one that stresses both continuity with an unchanging foundational core and genuine growth of conceptualization and expression. It is a model that appeals by way of illustration to the relationship of a growing plant to its original seed, and which argues that real growth always involves genuine innovations of structure and expression (e.g., the stalk, leaves, and flower of a plant are not just reproductions of the original seed), yet with that growth being always controlled and judged by what is inherent in the seed itself. It is a model that encourages us to look for germinal expressions of doctrine in the life of the early church, with such germinal expressions incorporating within themselves some indications of a proper line of development by which to test all succeeding developments, and that calls upon us to trace out the various and oft-times varying stages of growth as they appear at various times and under various circumstances thereafter. This was the approach of the Antiochean fathers (e.g., Chrysostom, Theodore),[12] and it has come to characterize the methodology of the more constructive and moderate biblical theologians of our day, whatever their particular confessional stance.

A third understanding of development is that which emphasizes innovations in the growth of doctrine and minimizes any necessary propositional connection with the foundational core. Its stress is on environmental and ideological changes in the course of history that have caused innovative, even contradictory, reformulations of Christian doctrine. And it justifies its use of the adjective *Christian* in these reformulations not on any propositional correspondence to earlier formulations, but on the similarity of religious aim and faith. This is the model of an existentialist writing of theology with its insistence on the historically unconnected and momentary nature of God's encounter with men, and it has come to most vocal expression in NT circles through the writings of Rudolf Bultmann and his many disciples.

---

[11]On a static "Alexandrian" approach to Pauline thought among the Ante-Nicene fathers, see M. F. Wiles, *The Divine Apostle: The Interpretation of St. Paul's Epistles in the Early Church* (Cambridge: University Press, 1967) *passim.*

[12]On a developmental "Antiochean" approach to Pauline thought among the Ante-Nicene Fathers, see ibid., *passim.*

The question that confronts us here, of course, is, "Which of these three models of understanding, if any, most closely approximates what is true of Paul as judged by the data of his letters, even though he might not have formally espoused such a construct himself?" Sadly, neither space nor time allows opportunity here to deal with the evidence itself (which it is my hope to spell out shortly in a monograph on "Continuity and Development in Pauline Thought"). Suffice it only to say that I believe it is the second, and would suggest that it is possible to understand the multifaceted flow of thought and the variety of presentations in the letters of Paul along the lines of the following four captions: (1) revelational immediacy; (2) historical continuity; (3) conceptual growth; and (4) circumstantial expression.

Basic to all of Paul's thought as a Christian was the experience of having been confronted by the risen Christ on the road to Damascus.[13] It was the great turning point of his life which gave him not only a new perspective on all he knew as a Pharisee about Jesus of Nazareth and acceptance before God, but also started him on a quest that was to engage his heart and mind for the rest of his life: an experiential understanding of what Christ has done, of who Christ really is, and of what is God's will in light of what God accomplished in Christ. Revelational immediacy undergirds all of Paul's thinking. Yet it is a revelational immediacy not in a Gnostic sense of a full-blown content deposited, but in the biblical sense of a relationship established from which understanding grows. Indeed, as an immediate consequence of having been confronted by Christ as he was (cf. Acts 9:1–19), Paul undoubtedly had impressed upon his consciousness certain foundational truths about himself (e.g., that his life under the law lay under the judgment of God), about Jesus of Nazareth (e.g., that he is alive, exalted, and in some manner to be identified with God the Father, whom Israel worships), about eschatology (e.g., that the hope of Israel must be restructured to highlight the realized and inaugurated features associated with Jesus), about the nature of Christ's church (e.g., its organic and indissoluble unity with Christ himself), and about his mission in life as a result of having been confronted by the exalted Christ (e.g., to bear Christ's name before Gentiles as well as Jews). But such immediate perceptions, while fundamental to all he would later do and think, were his at first only in embryonic form. Each was to receive further development of both form and content as time went on.

If, therefore, we are to understand Pauline thought in its fulness, it

---

[13]Cf. J. Jeremias, "The Key to Pauline Theology," *ExpTim*, 76 (1964–65) 27–30.

is necessary to couple to the theme of *revelational immediacy* the further factors of *historical continuity,* of *conceptual development,* and of *circumstantial expression.* On the one hand, Paul's frequent employment of early Christian catechetical and hymnodic confessional material and his many kerygmatic allusions to Jesus' earthly life indicate that he sought constantly to validate his message by reference to what God had done redemptively in Christ Jesus, as that information was mediated to him through the traditions of the church.[14] And his ample use of Scripture in the so-called *Hauptbriefe* (Romans, 1 and 2 Corinthians, Galatians) illustrates that he also sought for continuity with God's redemptive activity within the nation Israel by means of a Christocentric re-evaluation of Holy Writ.[15] On the other hand, his letters clearly reveal (in a manner that I must beg my readers' indulgence to spell out more fully at another time) that his thought was in a process of continual development, both as to its form and as to its content, as a result of the Spirit's working both internally and externally to sharpen his perceptions and extend his understanding— often, it appears, using difficulties and opposing positions as catalysts in his thought. Likewise, his letters indicate that often he expressed his message in terms suited to the interests, appreciation, and apprehension of his readers, with even at times the various cultural situations and ideological environments supplying him with certain vehicles of expression that could appropriately be employed to proclaim the gospel more effectively.

In sum if we are to understand Pauline thought, I suggest that we must seek to understand it along the lines of the second model above: in terms of both continuity with an unchanging foundational core (i.e., items one and two of our proposed grid) and genuine growth of conceptualization and expression that came about through the Spirit's

---

[14]D. M. Stanley rightly says: "What is crucial for a correct understanding of Paul . . . is to see clearly that he never depreciated in any way the value of the traditions regarding Jesus' earthly life, transmitted by the primitive community in Jerusalem to himself and others. To imagine that Paul's gospel diverged from that created by the Twelve, because Paul restricted himself to what he had learned of Christ at his conversion or through other visions, is to make Paul a crank and an 'enthusiast.' What is worse, it is to contradict his own most emphatic asseveration that 'there is no other gospel' (Gal 1:6-9)" (*Boasting in the Lord: The Phenomenon of Prayer in Saint Paul* [New York: Paulist, 1973] 34). Cf. G. N. Stanton, "Jesus in Paul's Preaching," *Jesus of Nazareth in New Testament Preaching* (Cambridge: University Press, 1974) 86–116.

[15]Cf. my *Biblical Exegesis in the Apostolic Period* (Grand Rapids: Eerdmans, 1975), 104–32.

inward guidance coupled with the external catalyst of circumstances (i.e., items three and four of that same grid).

IV. SOME IMPLICATIONS FOR THE STUDY OF PAUL, THE NT, AND CHRISTIAN THEOLOGY.

NT scholars have become masters in the art of dissection, but are still bunglers when it comes to understanding continuities between and developments within various theological expressions of the first-century Christian church. Bultmann's program of dichotomizing the various strata of NT material, form criticism's tendency to atomize every biblical discussion, and the fear of so-called "Early Catholicism" on the part of many Protestants (interestingly, on the part of both those most radical and those most conservative theologically) have resulted in a rising disinterest in matters having to do with continuity and development in the NT. Certainly, as Ernst Käsemann pertinently though somewhat over-piously warns, we must resist every effort to so organize the biblical materials as to encourage any attempt to control and calculate their message instead of reverently listening and obeying.[16] Nevertheless, if we really believe that God has acted historically and progressively in redemption, we are called upon in our scholarly studies to give attention to features of that redemption having to do with continuity and development—both as that redemption has been progressively unfolded by God and as it has been progressively understood by man.

The NT comes to us not as a treatise on theology or as a compendium of ethics. It presents itself as the record of God's self-manifestation and redemptive activity in first-century Palestine through the ministry, death, and resurrection of Jesus of Nazareth, and as the apostolic interpretation of that revelation and redemption to various people in their diverse cultural situations and varying ideological environments. As such it speaks in the language of the day to the issues and interests of the day, employing such approaches, methods, and arguments in support as were then current, in order to

---

[16]E. Käsemann, "Justification and Salvation History in the Epistle to the Romans," *Perspectives on Paul,* trans. M. Kohl (London: SCM, 1971) 63: "In no case should what we call the divine plan of salvation be absorbed by an immanent evolutionary process whose meaning can be grasped on earth, or which we can control and calculate. This would make the divine and the human interchangeable and would allow the church ultimately to triumph over its Lord, by organizing him instead of listening and obeying."

win the allegiance of all it addresses to Jesus, Israel's Messiah and mankind's Lord.

Furthermore, the message it proclaims appears in the record not only in diverse cultural forms but also in various stages of development, which reflect not only the capabilities of the particular audiences addressed but also the growing comprehension of the respective writers themselves. It is necessary, therefore, in our understanding of that message not only to focus attention upon the situation of the addressees in question but also upon the state of the writers' mind when writing. And this is especially important in our understanding of the Pauline message, which, in the form we have it, was delivered over the space of approximately fifteen years in a variety of circumstances and situations.

Conservative interpreters of Paul, in their desire to emphasize unity and continuity within the early church, have tended to overlook differences and developments. Radical interpreters, on the other hand, in their highlighting of diversity, have failed to come to grips with the common core of conviction that underlies the various NT presentations and the continuity of thought that exists amidst the diversity. Both groups, however, in their own ways, have been unbalanced in their treatments of the evidence, for factors of both continuity and development (or, as more commonly expressed of late, of unity and diversity) must be taken into consideration if we are to understand the NT generally and Paul in particular aright.

What is needed in our scholarly study of Paul, our interpretation of the NT, and our writing of Christian theology today is a methodological approach that stresses both (1) continuity with an unchanging foundational core of revelation and conviction, and (2) development of conceptualization and expression as brought about by God's Spirit, often employing circumstances and alien ideologies as a catalyst. To divorce the developments from their foundational core is to devalue the adjective *Christian* in the expression *Christian Theology,* turning it into a description more of the kind of person who happens to be writing theology than anything denoting content.[17] On the other hand, to deny developments in Paul, the NT, and/or Christian theology is to devalue the noun of that same expression, turning it into a symbol for the mere repetition of past formulations rather than a discipline that is both constructive and properly creative.

Our brief review of the concept of development in Pauline thought

---

[17]Which is, sadly, what M. F. Wiles has done by his "non-incarnational" approach in *The Remaking of Christian Doctrine* (1974).

suggests that the apostle must be understood in terms of both continuity and development, with circumstances and alien ideologies often being employed by God's Spirit to stimulate thought. And what has been suggested as being true for Paul encourages us to think along similar lines in our understanding of the rest of the NT materials and in our writing of Christian theology generally.

16

Is There a Distinctive Future for Ethnic Israel in Romans 11?

O. Palmer Robertson

The renewal of a national identity for ethnic Israel in the Promised Land in the twentieth century has brought a new high in speculation concerning God's ultimate intention for the seed of Abraham. Always some have declared boldly their expectations concerning a distinctive future for Israel at the end of the church age. But now this expectation has reached new intensity. In these circumstances, few dare to deny the likelihood of a special providence toward ethnic Israel in the days of the end time.

Romans 11 generally is marked off as that distinctive chapter of Scripture which presents the unique future for Israel in the plan of God. More than any other passage in the Bible, this chapter is cited to support the proposition that God still has special plans for ethnic Israel yet to be realized.

The present study intends to evaluate exegetically the evidence in this chapter which might be interpreted as supporting the view that God intends in the future to deal with the Jews in a way which is distinctively different from the way in which he deals with them currently. Repeatedly in the history of the church, this material has been subjected to careful exegetical scrutiny. But the current circumstances merit a renewal of this kind of investigation.

Two matters will be examined in pursuing this theme as it appears in Romans 11: I. evidence that Romans 11 deals with God's present intention for ethnic Israel, and II. possible references in Romans 11 to God's intention to deal distinctively with ethnic Israel in the future.

I. EVIDENCE THAT ROMANS 11 DEALS WITH GOD'S PRESENT INTENTION FOR ETHNIC ISRAEL

It would be difficult to read Romans 11 without noting that in many places Paul presents God's purpose for the Jew in the present age. This theme of the significance of the Jew in the gospel age plays a vital role throughout Romans. When Paul first sets the stage for this great epistle, he underscores the present significance of the Jew. The gospel of Christ currently is the power of God unto salvation "to the Jew first, and also to the Greek" (Rom 1:17). Following this initial emphasis, the place of Israel in God's present execution of his plan for salvation finds an extremely prominent role throughout Romans. Chapters 9 and 10 continue this emphasis on the present significance of Israel (*cf.* Rom 9:1-5, 24; 10:1, 11-13). It would be surprising indeed if Romans 11, fitted so integrally into the unit of Romans 9-11, would omit entirely any reference to Israel's present significance.

Most commentators are aware of the references in Romans 11 to God's current saving activity among the Jews. However, the pervasiveness of these references, as well as their significance for the total thrust of the chapter, generally is overlooked. Several key verses may be noted particularly for their emphasis on the present significance of Israel in the plan of God:

> I say then, God has not rejected His people, has He? May it never be! For I too am an Israelite, a descendant of Abraham, of the tribe of Benjamin (Rom 11:1, NASB).

In answer to the question, "Has God cast off his people?" Paul identifies himself as current living proof that God's purposes for Israel are being realized in the present era. He himself is a present trophy of the grace of God.

It is worth noting that the apostle does not respond to his own question by asserting specifically that God has not cast off his people Israel with respect to some distinctive future reserved for them. This conclusion might be reached by inference; but the apostle specifically points instead to the concrete realities of God's activity among the Jews in the present. He himself is an Israelite, thus indicating that the grace of God is working currently among Judaism.

> In the same way then, there has also come to be at the present time a remnant according to God's gracious choice (Rom 11:5, NASB).

Paul emphasizes specifically the present position of Israel by the phrase "in the present time" (ἐν τῷ νῦν καιρῷ). Dramatically in the current situation a remnant of Israel remains.

These two references orient this first paragraph of Romans 11 (vv 1–10) to the question of God's dealing with Israel in the present hour. Paul's discussion of the OT remnant-concept in these verses as it has been manifested throughout redemptive history intends to alleviate his readers' concern over the present condition of Israel. Not all Jews currently are believing the gospel, to be sure. But never has the salvation of the totality of ethnic Israel been God's determination.

> But I am speaking to you who are Gentiles. Inasmuch then as I am an apostle of Gentiles, I magnify my ministry, if somehow I might move to jealousy my fellow countrymen and save some of them (Rom 11:13, 14, NASB).

The "provoking to jealousy" and the "saving" of some in Israel must be taken in the context of God's present dealing with the nation. Paul describes the hoped-for consequences of his own current ministry as an apostle to the Gentiles. By this current ministry he expects to see Jews moved to jealousy when they see Gentile believers sharing in the blessings of the messianic kingdom.

This reference to the present saving of some in Israel by the provoking of them to jealousy (vv 13, 14) connects immediately with the "receiving" of the Jews in the following verses (vv 15, 16). The "for if"(ϵi $\gamma \acute{\alpha} \rho$) of verse fifteen connects the "receiving" of the Jews with the present ministry of the apostle Paul in the gospel era. By his present ministry among the Gentiles, the apostle hopes to move the Jews to jealousy, and thereby to save some from among Israel. Their "saving" as described in v 14 corresponds to their "reception" in v 15. In each case Paul describes the hoped-for consequence of his current ministry.

Thus the middle section of this chapter has as a major concern the current consequences of Paul's apostolic ministry. The possibility of discovering a reference to a distinctive role for Israel in the future will be considered in the second portion of this paper. But let it be noted at this point that current saving activity among the Jews certainly is a central feature throughout this section.

The third major paragraph of the chapter (vv 17–24) also concerns itself with the expectation of a positive response of Israel to the present preaching of the gospel. Paul's kinsmen will be "grafted in" even as the Gentiles. "If they do not continue in unbelief," they shall participate in the promises. This participation by being "grafted in" cannot be postponed to some future date, while each and every Gentile believer immediately experiences the blessings of the covenant. Equally with every (current) Gentile believer, so every (current) Jewish believer shall be grafted in. Just as in the case of previous sections in Romans 11, this paragraph also underscores the significance of the Jew in the present time as it relates to God's purposes of salvation.

> For just as you once were disobedient to God but now have been shown mercy because of their disobedience, so these also now have been disobedient, in order that because of the mercy shown to you they also may now be shown mercy (Rom 11:30, 31, NASB).

The threefold "now" (νῦν) of these concluding verses indicates that Paul's emphasis on the present responsiveness of Israel continues to be his central concern. Gentiles *now* have obtained mercy; Jews *now* have been disobedient, that they also *now* may obtain mercy.[1] The summary statement of verse 32 strengthens this emphasis on the current significance of the Christian gospel for Jew as well as for Gentile. God "has shut up all in disobedience that he might show mercy to all" (Rom 11:32). The argument of Romans 9–11 essentially is no different from the argument of Romans 1–3. The gospel is the power of God unto salvation for the Jew first, and also for the Gentile.

The point originally indicated may be reiterated. Neither the pervasiveness in Romans 11 of references to God's present intention for Israel nor the significance of these references for the total thrust of the chapter has been noted adequately. These references do not exclude by necessity parallel references to some future purpose of God with Israel. They do, however, warn the exegete against assuming too hastily that the entirety of Romans 11 deals with Israel's distinctive future. Even further, the presence of references to the present role of Israel in every major section of the chapter indicates that the exegete must take into account the significance in Paul's thinking on this present role of Israel, regardless of the particular section of the chapter under consideration.

II. POSSIBLE REFERENCES IN ROMANS 11 TO GOD'S INTENTION TO DEAL DISTINCTIVELY WITH ETHNIC ISRAEL IN THE FUTURE

References to God's present dealings with Israel in Romans 11 have been ignored by and large. At the same time, portions of the chapter

---

[1] The textual problem of the third νῦν is rather difficult. However, the combination of ℵ and β and the uncertain state of the reading in p46 support the inclusion of the third "now."

which could be understood as referring to a special intention on God's part for Israel in the future have been assumed to be focal to the chapter.

However, a more careful examination of these portions may lead to a different perspective on the major outlook of the chapter. Several sections in particular deserve special consideration:

1. Romans 11:1, 2a (NASB)

> I say then, God has not rejected His people, has He? May it never be! For I too am an Israelite, a descendant of Abraham, of the tribe of Benjamin. God has not rejected His people whom He foreknew.

The denial on Paul's part that God has cast off his people generally is understood as indicating that God still must intend to deal distinctively with Israel in the future. This interpretation relies heavily on a very particular reading of the apostle's question. Paul's proposed query, "Has God cast off his people?" is read subconsciously to mean "Has God cast off ethnic Israel with respect to his special plan for their future?"

Obviously placing such a construction on Paul's question immediately prejudices the case in favor of those advocating a distinctive future for ethnic Israel. Once the question has been assumed to have this thrust, the "God forbid" of the apostle simply verifies that which is inherent in the assumed form of the question.

But the context of the apostle's question suggests an entirely different understanding of its thrust. The question is not "Has God cast off ethnic Israel with respect to his special plan for their future?" The inquiry of this apostle to the Gentiles implies something even more radical. He asks, "Has God cast off ethnic Israel *altogether* as they might relate to his purposes of redemption?" Is there any hope for the continuation of a saving activity of God among Israelites? Have they stumbled that they might fall (altogether)? (v 11).

Ethnic Israel had rejected their Messiah. They had crucified the Christ. Would it not therefore be quite logical to conclude that God would reject ethnic Israel? If a Gentile rejects Christ, he is lost. Israel rejected the Christ nationally. Should they not be lost nationally? Why should God continue to act savingly within Israel? They received all the special favors of the Lord (Rom 9:4, 5), and yet rejected the Lord's Christ. Why should they not be cast off completely?

The evidence cited by Paul in Romans 11:1b to support a negative answer to his question indicates the actual thrust of his thought. Has God cast off his people? No, for the apostle himself is an Israelite!

Paul does not marshal evidence relative to some hypothetical future for the Jews in order to answer his question. He points instead to the realities of God's working in the present. He himself is an Israelite, thereby establishing once and for all that God continues to include Jews in his purposes of redemption. The apostle's answer deals not with the state of Israel in the distant future, but with the condition of Israel in the present age. The apostle himself is an Israelite, and yet shares in the salvation brought by Messiah.

Romans 11:5 further summarizes Paul's answer to the question posed in verse 1. "Has God justly cast off ethnic Israel so that no hope of redemption within the nation remains?" No, for "at this present time also," in conformity with God's dealings with Israel in the past, "there is a remnant according to the election of grace."

Paul's answer to his own question in no way spells out the details of a massive turning of the Jews to Christ at some distant date in the future. His answer deals with the present state of Israel in the gospel era. Indeed, the apostle's answer does indicate that ethnic Israel has a "future." But this "future" is integrated explicitly with the current era of gospel-proclamation.

2. Romans 11:12, 15 (NASB)

> Now if their transgression be riches for the world and their failure be riches for the Gentiles, how much more will their fulness be! ... For if their rejection be the reconciliation of the world, what will their receiving be but life from the dead?

From any interpretive perspective, it should be recognized that the apostle is describing a temporally sequential situation in these verses. The Jews reject their Messiah; the Gentiles believe; the Jews are provoked by jealousy and return in faith; the world receives even richer blessing as a consequence of this return of the Jews.

One interpretation of these contrasting experiences of Israel assumes that the experience of "falling" and "casting away" coincides with the present gospel age, while the experience of "fulness" and "receiving" will occur subsequently, either at the very end of the present era, or after the present age of gospel proclamation has ended.

However, this temporal sequence may be viewed from another perspective. The whole cycle could be considered as having fulfillment in the present era of gospel proclamation. In context, Paul compares the experience of Israel to the experience of the Gentiles. According to v 30, Gentiles once were disobedient, but now have received mercy. In the same manner, Israel now is found disobedient, that they also now may receive mercy. Both in the case of Gentiles and of Jews, the full cycle of movement from a state of disobedience to a state of mercy occurs in the present age.

From this perspective, the "receiving" of Israel would refer to the ingrafting of believing Jews throughout the present era, which would reach its consummation at the point in time at which their "fulness" would be realized. The parallel experience of the Gentile world offers no support to the idea that Israel's period of "falling" and "casting away" coincides with the present gospel age, while their "receiving" and "fulness" is reserved for a subsequent era.

Most crucial to the understanding of these particular verses is Paul's statement that by his current apostolic ministry to the Gentiles he hopes to "save some" of the Jews (v 14). This saving of "some" ought not to be regarded as the deliverance of some pitiful minutia of Judaism hardly worthy to be compared with the "fulness" to be effected at the end of time.

Much to the contrary, this saving of "some" should be viewed as conjoining integrally with one of the major themes of Romans 11. As Paul says, there remains at the present time a "remnant" according to the election of grace (v 5). It is not that "some" which the apostle hopes to save is equivalent in number to the "remnant" which he discusses throughout the passage. But the saving of "some" and the maintaining of a "remnant" are interrelated ideas. Paul's hope that "some" would be saved through his current ministry is based on the principle that a "remnant" would remain throughout the ages.

The concept of the "remnant" too easily is prejudged as containing the idea of smallness and insignificance. But the "remnant according to the election of grace" encompasses exactly the same individuals included in the "fulness" of Israel. The remnant concept in and of itself does not determine the proportion of the whole to be saved. It speaks instead of the sovereign intervention of God in the salvation of men despite the expectation humanly speaking that all might perish.[2]

---

[2]*Cf.* The remark of V. Herntrich in "λεῖμμα, etc." in *TDNT* 4 (1967) 204, "If the remnant is preserved only by God's action, the concept cannot be a quantitative one in the sense that the remnant has to be small. The concept certainly contains a reference to the greatness of the judgment, but not to the small number of those who are delivered (though *cf.* Deut 4:27; 28:62; Isa 10:22)." Herntrich points to Mic 4:7, in which the remnant is paralleled to a "strong people" and Mic 5:6, 7, in which the remnant is compared to the dew. In other passages not specifically describing a people-remnant, the concept is applied to the "very much" land "left" to be taken after Joshua's conquest (Josh 13:1) and to the wood "left over" in the making of an idol (Isa 44:17, 19). While the concept of a remnant admittedly may refer to a small number, most basically it refers simply to that which is "left," whether small or great.

It is therefore quite appropriate to interpret the "fulness" and the "receiving" of Israel from the perspective of God's current activity of salvation among Jews. The apostle's argument builds on the consistency of a principle that has worked throughout redemptive history. Although outwardly it may appear as though God has cast off the Jews, he nonetheless is working sovereignly to save. The "receiving" of the "full number" in Israel will be realized in no way other than the way in which Israelites currently are being "received" and added to the number. The eye of man cannot tell whether this number is few or many. But the eye of faith is confident that the "full number" is being realized. For this reason, it is neither necessary nor appropriate to posit some future date in which the "remnant" principle will be superseded by a newly-introduced "fulness" principle. The completed number of the "remnant" of Israel is identical precisely with the "fulness" of Israel.

3. Romans 11:17-24

This entire passage, with its reference to the regrafting of Israel, frequently is considered in terms of a distinctive future for ethnic Israel. It is assumed that the figure of regrafting necessarily implies corporate inclusion at a future date when God will deal distinctively with Israel.

However, the argumentation of Paul specifically includes a paralleling of the experience of Israelite believers with that of contemporary Gentile believers. Gentiles currently are being "grafted in" among the people of God to receive the blessings of redemption *as they believe* (v 20). Ingrafting occurs at the point of their exercising faith.

What happens to Jews who believe? As they are provoked to jealousy through the apostle's current ministry, what relationship do they have to the true stock of God?

Nothing in the imagery of regrafting suggests a delay in the incorporation of the believing Israelite. As each Jew believes, he becomes a partaker of the blessings of the olive tree. The current ministry of the gospel provides the catalyst for the salvation of the Jews precisely in the same manner as it does for the Gentiles. The major thrust of the apostle's argument about the grafting process is that Israelites experience salvation and incorporation among God's people precisely in the same manner as the Gentiles. Nothing in the figure of ingrafting necessarily communicates the idea of a distinctive and corporate inclusion of the Jews at some future date.

4. Romans 11:25–26a (NASB)

> For I do not want you, brethren, to be uninformed of this mystery, lest you be wise in your own estimation, that a partial hardening has happened to Israel until the fulness of the Gentiles has come in; and thus all Israel will be saved.

These verses pinpoint the crux of the controversy. They continue to anchor the argument favoring a distinctive future for ethnic Israel. Three phases in particular should be noted:

a. "Hardening in part has happened to Israel" (v 25)

ἀπὸ μέρους often is interpreted as having a temporal reference. The passage is thus read: "for a while hardening has happened to Israel."

This understanding of ἀπὸ μέρους has little to support it. It is very doubtful that a single instance may be found in the NT in which the phrase has temporal significance.[3] The phrase declares either that "partial hardening" has happened to Israel, or that "part of Israel" has been hardened. Either of these understandings would relate meaningfully to the earlier discussion of Paul concerning a remnant from Israel that shall be saved. Probably the apostle is saying that a part of Israel has been hardened. But in either construction, "in part" has no temporal significance. This phrase does not provide an exegetical basis for the suggestion that God intends to initiate special saving activity among Israel some time in the future.

b. "Hardening . . . until the fulness of the Gentiles has come in" (v 25)

The critical point in this phrase centers on the weight to be given to the "until" (ἄχρις οὗ). Initially it would appear that the concept of "hardening until" inevitably implies that a time will come after which the hardening of Israel no longer shall continue. After the fulness of the Gentile has been realized, then the hardening which has affected part of Israel will be lifted.

However, further consideration of this key phrase indicates that the weight most frequently given to "until" in Romans 11:25 has been estimated wrongly. As a matter of fact, the term in itself cannot settle the question of a distinctive future for ethnic Israel. Several factors require this reappraisal:

(1) The nature of the "hardening" involved.

---

[3] BAG, 507, cites only Rom 15:24 as a case in which the phrase has temporal significance. But even this case is highly uncertain.

Failure to consider the precise nature of the "hardening" to which Paul refers may encourage too facile a treatment of precisely what the apostle is asserting in this context. Paul uses the terminology of "hardening" earlier in the chapter. He asserts that the elect in Israel obtained salvation, but the rest "were hardened" (Rom 11:7). By modifying the phraseology of his supporting quotation from the OT, the apostle underscores divine sovereignty in this "hardening." Instead of maintaining the negative form of the assertion in Deuteronomy to the effect that God had not given Israel a heart to know, eyes to see, or ears to hear (Deut 29:4), Paul turns the phrase into a positive affirmation: "God *gave* them a spirit of stupor, eyes to see not, and ears to hear not" (Rom 11:8).

"Hardening" in this earlier verse of Romans 11 clearly is bound up with God's sovereignty in electing some in Israel. Those who are not chosen are "hardened" by God.

The same usage of the terminology of "hardening" is found in John 12:40, which explains why the Jews did not believe Jesus' message:

> For this cause they could not believe, for Isaiah said again, "He has blinded their eyes, and he hardened their heart..." (John 12:39, 40, NASB).

Other New Testament passages using the terminology of hardening may refer either to men's hardening their own hearts in sin, or to God's hardening of their hearts (cf. 2 Cor 3:14; Mark 3:5; 6:52; 8:17; Eph 4:18). The situation is similar to the "hardening" of Pharaoh's heart as presented in the Exodus narrative, which attributes the hardening sometimes to God and sometimes to Pharaoh himself.

In any case, the "hardening" that has happened to part of Israel according to Romans 11 fits integrally into the historical outworking of the principle of election and reprobation. The reference to "hardening" does not concern itself merely with hard-heartedness on the part of some Israelites. It relates instead to the very mystery of the origins of God's grace in salvation. From among the numbers of humanity considered as dead in their sin, God in the sovereignty of his grace has elected some to everlasting life, while the rest were hardened.

The integral role of "hardening" in the processes of salvation through all the ages should make one pause before asserting too quickly that this "hardening" shall cease. It ought to be noted that Romans 11:25 does not make this assertion. The text does not say "hardening shall cease among Israel." Certainly it is not declared that the overarching principle of God's electing some and hardening of others someday will have no application in Israel.

Instead the text affirms a continuation of hardening within Israel throughout the present age. God's decrees of election and reprobation continue to work themselves out in history. As a sovereign distinction was made between the twins Jacob and Esau, so throughout the present age, hardening shall continue.

But what about the future? Does not the apostle say explicitly that hardening shall continue "until" a certain point in time? Would not this assertion imply an end to the hardening? The answer to this crucial question hinges on the precise force of the phrase which is rendered "until" (ἄχρις οὗ) in Romans 11:25.

(2) The precise force of the phrase which is rendered "until" (ἄχρις οὗ) in Romans 11:25.

It should be noted at the outset that the phrase essentially is terminative in its significance. More particularly, it has a *terminus ad quem* rather than a *terminus a quo* significance. The phrase brings matters "up to" a certain point, or "until" a certain goal is reached. The phrase does not determine in itself the precise state of affairs after the termination. This circumstance can be learned only by the context in which the phrase is used. The significance of this point becomes apparent when the nature of the termination envisioned is analyzed more carefully.

In many cases, the termination envisioned in ἄχρις οὗ has a finalizing aspect which makes irrelevant questions concerning the reversal of circumstances which had prevailed prior to reaching this termination point. This consideration is made obvious particularly in cases in which physical or figurative termination points are involved. Several examples from Scripture make the point plain:

Acts 22:4 states that Paul persecuted Christians "up to" or "until" death. The point of the "until" is not that Paul's activity of persecution ceased after the Christians died. Instead, the point is that he persecuted Christians "up to" the ultimate point, the point of finalization.

Hebrews 4:12 declares that the sword of the Spirit pierces "until" or "up to" the dividing of soul and spirit. Once more, the significance of the "until" is not that the piercing ceases and another condition prevails from that point on. Instead, the "until" has a finalizing significance. The piercing continues as far as is possible. If there were any possibility of a deeper piercing, the process would continue.

The use of ἄχρις οὗ in the NT in eschatological contexts also may serve to illustrate the essentially terminative character of the phrase. The phrase carries actions or conditions to the ultimate point in time, without intending to stress the reversal of prevailing circumstances afterwards.

According to 1 Corinthians 11:26, the Christian community is directed to show forth the Lord's death "until" he come. The point respecting termination in this context is not that the apostle wishes to stress that a day is coming in which the Lord's Supper no longer will be celebrated. Instead, he intends to emphasize that this celebration shall continue "until" the end of time.

In Matthew 24:38, the people of Noah's day ate and drank "until" Noah entered the ark. The point of this assertion is not that a day came in which the people no longer ate and drank. Instead, the point is that they continued with their eating and drinking until their "eschaton" arrived.

1 Corinthians 15:25 declares that Christ must reign "until" he has put all his enemies under his feet. The intended stress is not that a day will come in which Christ no longer will reign. Instead, the point is that he must continue in reigning until the last enemy is subdued at the resurrection.[4]

In the same manner, the "hardening... until" of Romans 11:25 speaks of eschatological termination. Throughout the whole of the present age, until the final return of Christ, hardening will continue among part of Israel. "Hardening... until" too frequently has been understood as marking the beginning of a new state of things with regard to Israel. It hardly has been considered that "hardening... until" more naturally should be interpreted as eschatologically terminating in its significance. The phrase implies not a new beginning after a termination point in time, but instead the continuation of a prevailing circumstance for Israel until the end of time.

In any case, the ἄχρις οὗ phrase does not in itself confirm the concept that a period of time will exist after the fulness of the Gentiles has been realized in which the partial hardening of ethnic Israel will be lifted. The phrase "hardening... until" more naturally is interpreted as possessing a *terminus ad quem* significance. The least that can be said is that this phrase "hardening... until" cannot in itself bear the weight of determining the question as to whether or not Romans 11 positively proposes that God shall deal distinctively with ethnic Israel in the future in a manner in which he is not dealing with the Jews today.

With this background in mind, attention now focuses dramatically on the crucial wording of Romans 11:26. If clear reference to a dis-

---

[4]J. Jeremias in *The Eucharistic Words of Jesus* (New York: Charles Scribner's Sons, 1966) 253, makes the following evaluation: "Actually, in the New Testament ἄχρι οὗ with the aorist subjunctive without ἄν regularly introduces a reference to reaching the eschatological goal, Rom. 11:25; I Cor. 15:25; Lk. 21:24."

tinctive future for ethnic Israel does not occur either in the phrase "in part" or in "hardening... until" of Romans 11:25, such reference must depend on the much-disputed statement of Romans 11:26.

c. *"And so all Israel shall be saved" (v 26a)*

At this point it should be remembered that the question under consideration concerns a distinctive future for ethnic Israel different from that which Israel continues to experience throughout the gospel era. It cannot be disputed that Jews have been saved and will continue to be saved throughout the present dispensation. This kind of "future" for the descendants of Abraham is granted on all sides. The question instead is whether or not the phrase under consideration speaks of some distinctive conversion-activity of God among ethnic Israel immediately prior to or in conjunction with the return of Christ.

Immediately prevalent false impressions concerning the weight of this phrase must be removed. Generally the passage is read as though it were saying: "And *then* all Israel shall be saved." The phrase καὶ οὕτως is interpreted as though it possessed primarily a temporal significance. "Hardening" has happened to part of Israel "until" the fulness of the Gentiles has come in; but *then, after that,* all Israel shall be saved.

Such a rendering of the phrase καὶ οὕτως obviously resolves the question at hand in favor of a distinctive future for ethnic Israel. The present "hardening" is set in radical contrast with a yet-future salvation.

However, it is rather difficult to support this rendering of the phrase καὶ οὕτως simply because the phrase does not mean "and then." Instead, it means "and in this manner" or "and in this way." Of the approximately 205 times in which the term occurs in the NT, the lexicon of Arndt and Gingrich does not cite a single instance to support the concept of a temporal significance.[5] Paul does not say καὶ τότε, "and then," but καὶ οὕτως, "and in this manner."

A dramatic recoloring of Romans 11:26 emerges as a result of this

---

[5]Outside the verse under consideration, Paul himself uses the term approximately 70 times. All of these uses are nontemporal, and include four cases in Rom 9–11.

Several passages may be cited in an effort to establish temporal significance for οὕτως. The leading instances include John 4:6; Acts 17:33; 20:11; 28:14. But in each of these cases, a nontemporal significance provides a better rendering. F. F. Bruce, *The Epistle of Paul to the Romans. An Introduction and Commentary* (Grand Rapids: Eerdmans, 1963) 222, affirms the temporal significance of the phrase, but offers no supporting evidence.

more precise rendering of Paul's actual words. "And in this manner all Israel shall be saved." In such a manner, by such a process, thus, by this means, in the way described, Israel shall be saved. The rendering of the *New English Bible,* "when that has happened," appears to support the popular idea of the significance of καὶ οὕτως. But this understanding of the phrase is difficult to support as properly representing the actual wording of Paul.

The interpretation which understands Paul as referring to a temporal sequence by the phrase καὶ οὕτως in Romans 11:26 has penetrated the popular mind to the level of subconscious assumption. As a result, it is extremely difficult to give proper weight to the true significance of Paul's words. Yet it is essential that the resulting picture be appreciated.

By the phrase καὶ οὕτως as it introduces Romans 11:26, Paul does not look prospectively into the future beyond the "fulness of the Gentiles." Instead, he looks retrospectively into the past. He recalls to the mind of his readers the fantastic processes of God's salvation among the Jews as he just had described them. In accordance with the pattern outlined in the previous verses of Romans 11, "all Israel shall be saved." First the promises as well as the Messiah were given to Israel. Then, somehow in God's mysterious plan, Israel rejected its Messiah and was cut off from its position of distinctive privilege. As a result, the coming of Israel's Messiah was announced to the Gentiles. The nations then obtained by faith what Israel could not find by seeking in the strength of their own flesh. Frustrated over seeing the blessings of their messianic kingdom heaped on the Gentiles, Israel is moved to jealousy. Consequently they too repent, believe, and share in the promises originally made to them. "And in this manner" (καὶ οὕτως), by such a fantastic process which shall continue throughout the entire present age "up to" (ἄχρις οὗ) the point that the full number of the Gentiles is brought in, all Israel shall be saved.[6]

The final question to consider relates to the identification of the "all Israel" which is to be saved. Essentially five possibilities may be suggested: (1) "all Israel" refers to all ethnic descendants of Abraham; (2) "all Israel" refers to all ethnic descendants of Abraham living at a

---

[6]J. Murray, *The Epistle to the Romans. The New International Commentary on the New Testament* (Grand Rapids: Eerdmans, 1965), 2. 97f., suggests this interpretation of "and so" in Rom 11:26 leads to the relatively prosaic assertion that elect Israel will be saved. However, Paul is not simply asserting *that* all elect Israel will be saved. He is speaking instead of the fantastic manner ("and in this manner") in which this salvation will be accomplished. Paul's explanation of this manner of salvation for Israel hardly could be called prosaic.

future time at which God shall initiate a special working among the Jews; (3) "all Israel" refers to the "mass" or "majority" of Jews living at the time of a special saving activity of God in the future; (4) "all Israel" refers to all elect Israelites within the community of Israel; (5) "all Israel" refers both to Jews and Gentiles which together constitute the church of Christ, the Israel of God.

Since Scripture gives no hint of a "second chance" after death, the idea that all ethnic descendants of Abraham will be saved must be rejected. This conclusion finds explicit biblical re-enforcement in this context by Paul's assertion that "they are not all Israel that are of Israel" (Rom 9:6).

Perhaps the most popular view today is that "all Israel" refers to the "mass" or "majority" of Jews living at the time in which the "hardening" of part of Israel is lifted. However, this viewpoint contains a problem which cannot be dismissed very easily.

The problem in this viewpoint arises from the contradiction created by the proposal that a mass or majority, *though not all,* of Israel shall be saved when the "hardening" is lifted. For the "hardening" in this context refers to the historical outworking of the principle of reprobation, as indicated earlier. As Paul says so explicitly, the principle of hardening means that "God *gave* them a spirit of stupor, eyes to see not, and ears to hear not" (Rom 11:7, 8). If a day is coming in which the principle of reprobation is to be inactive among Israel, then it must be assumed that every single Israelite living at that time will be saved. If even one Israelite of that period is to be lost, then the principle of "hardening" or "reprobation" still would be active.

If a time is coming in which the principle of "hardening" no longer will be operative in Israel, the result will not be merely the salvation of the "mass." The cessation of this principle would have to mean the salvation of "all" in a completely inclusive sense.

Should it then be asserted that Paul's declaration that "all Israel shall be saved" means that some day in the near future every single living Israelite shall come to salvation? Is this the significance of the salvation of "all Israel"?

The person that chooses this interpretation of "all Israel" in Romans 11:26 ought to be fully aware of the peculiar position in which this view places him. First of all, this position proposes a set of circumstances wholly foreign and actually contradictory to the manner in which God has worked throughout all the ages. God never has obligated himself to save every single individual of a particular group of people. Always previously the principle of saving activity in and among those externally organized into a covenant community has prevailed. This principle has been in effect throughout the entire history of redemption, providing explanation for the distinction between Isaac and Ishmael (Rom 9:6–9), Jacob and Esau (Rom 9:10–13), those spared and those destroyed about the golden calf in Moses' day (Rom 9:14–16, citing Exod 33:19), faithful remnant and unbelievers in Elijah's day (Rom 11:2–4), enemies and companions in David's day (Rom 11:9–10), believers and disobedient in Isaiah's day (Rom 9:29; 11:8), and the saved and the lost of Israel in the present day (Rom 11:5, 7). Indeed, it may be asserted that in the future this principle of God's never guaranteeing the salvation of every individual in a certain externally-related group might be contradicted. But it should be recognized that such a contradiction would introduce a principle foreign to all God's previous redemptive activity, including activity under the gracious provisions of the new covenant.

A further complication arises from viewing the salvation of "all Israel" as referring to the salvation of every single Israelite living at some future date. This complication relates to the question of the identification of an "Israelite." More precisely, who is to be included in the "all Israel" that is to be saved?

Throughout the present paper it has been assumed, for the "sake of the argument," that a "Jew" was to be defined simply on the basis of ethnic considerations. But this assumption now must undergo serious question.

Benno Jacob, the notable Jewish commentator on Genesis, insists that ethnic descent was not the ultimate basis for determining participation in the old covenant. He says:

> Indeed, differences of race have never been an obstacle to joining Israel which did not know the concept of purity of blood. . . . Circumcision turned a man of foreign origin into an Israelite (Exod 12:48).[7]

At the time of the setting aside of Abraham, it was made plain that any Gentile could become a full-fledged Jew through the process of proselytism (Gen 17:12, 13). No legislation in Israel would forbid the marriage of an Egyptian proselyte to an Assyrian proselyte. The possibility of such a union, with its totally "non-Abrahamic" ethnic orientation, dramatizes the problem involved in supposing that "Israel" might be defined simply along ethnic lines.

From still another perspective, it also must be recognized that any ethnic descendant of Abraham might be declared a non-Israelite as a result of violation of the covenant (Gen 17:14). This real option underscores the fact that it is difficult to define "Israel" purely along ethnic lines.

---

[7]B. Jacob, *The First Book of the Bible, Genesis* (New York: KTAV 1974) 233.

But if it nonetheless is a certain fact that all those associated with Judaism one day soon shall be saved, should this fact affect the Christian's perspective on evangelism today? If a person rejects the Christian gospel, should he then be encouraged to consider Judaism as another alternative? If a person could be persuaded to become a Jew through following the route of the proselyte, would he not be fully assured of eternal salvation if he should be alive at the time that the proposed mighty working of salvation among "all Israel" begins? Since that beginning appears in the minds of some to be very close, should not Christians be active in encouraging as many Gentiles as possible to become Jews if they are not willing to become Christians?

Hopefully the absurdity of such a suggestion is obvious. Not by the wildest stretch of the imagination may it be supposed that the apostle Paul would countenance for an instant such a concept.

Yet if all who are Jews one day will be saved, and if it is possible to become a Jew by the process of proselytism, then how could this procedure be excluded as a possible way of salvation? At the very minimum, the Christian today would have to rejoice at every new proselyte added to the nation of Israel because of the prospect of future salvation which this "conversion" would hold.

The idea that the "all Israel" which is to be saved in Romans 11:26 refers specifically to ethnic Judaism is fraught with problems. This concept overlooks many aspects of a biblical definition of "Israel," and contradicts the concept that God does not guarantee that a person will be saved if he possesses certain external qualifications. These considerations argue against identifying the "all Israel" of Romans 11:26 with all ethnic descendants of Abraham living at some future date when God shall inaugurate a supposed special saving activity.

Who then is the "all Israel" that shall be saved? Does the phrase embrace the whole of the church of Christ, including all Jewish and Gentile believers?[8]

Contextual considerations point in another direction. Paul has referred too consistently in Romans 9–11 to a continuation of the community of the old covenant as "Israel." The principle of the preservation of a select number from within this community pervades this section of the apostle's argumentation, and includes the reference to "Israel" in the last phrase of Romans 11:25.

"All Israel" describes all elect people within the community of Israel. By the process described in the earlier verses of Romans 11, all of this "Israel" shall be saved. As particular members of the Jewish

---

[8] *Cf.* J. Calvin, *The Epistles of Paul the Apostle to the Romans and to the Thessalonians* (Grand Rapids: Eerdmans, 1961) 255.

community are "moved to jealousy" when they observe Gentiles relishing in the promises of the old covenant, they shall be grafted into the true community of God. And "in this manner," all Israel, all of the elect within the community of Israel, shall be saved.[9]

This conclusion finds confirmation by Paul's final citation as explained by his own interpretative comments. "All Israel" shall be saved *because* "it is written" (Rom 11:26b).

The apostle's ensuing quotation conflates passages from Isaiah and Jeremiah (Isa 59:20, 21; Jer 31:33f.). A comparison of the MT, LXX, and the NT texts uncovers an interesting emphasis in Paul's analysis of the significance of Isaiah's words as they relate to his current situation. The prophet had declared that a redeemer (גֹּאֵל) would come to (or for) Zion. More specifically, this redeemer would come to those turning from iniquity in Jacob. In the context of Isaiah, salvation would come in a situation in which many among Israel had been rebelling against the Lord (Isa 59:1–18). But in justice the Lord would send the redeemer.

The LXX chooses to emphasize that the redeemer would come "for the sake of" Zion (ἕνεκεν Σιών), which is an acceptable rendering of the Hebrew of Isaiah (לְצִיּוֹן). But Paul modifies this perspective by stating that the redeemer would come "out of" Zion (ἐκ Σιών).

It may be that Paul's slight change of perspective intends to place one final underscoring for emphasis on the remnant-concept that has played such a prominent role throughout the whole of the chapter. Out from among Israel shall come a single person, representing the ultimate point of reduction in remnant-theology. He shall redeem in himself all those who are of the true Israel.

Both Scriptures cited by Paul in Romans 11:26, 27 emphasize God's merciful act of forgiving sins as the basis for restoration. Throughout Paul's argumentation, this merciful action occurs because of God's sovereign and particular choice (Rom 11:28). It stands over against God's action of "hardening" in sin, in accordance with the counsels of his own will (*cf.* Rom 11:7).

The positive response of Israel to the gospel should be viewed from the perspective of the irrevocable "calling of God," even as Paul explicitly declares (Rom 11:29). This "calling" activity must be understood in terms of the Lord's sovereignty in salvation. According to his earlier discussion, Isaac (within "Israel") was chosen over his older

---

[9]The fact that the term *Israel* is used in two different ways in two consecutive verses (Rom 11:25, 26) should not be disturbing. When Paul says in Rom 9:6 that "they are not all Israel that are of Israel," he undoubtedly is using the term *Israel* in two different ways within the scope of a single phrase.

twin brother Esau (equally within "Israel") "in order that the pre-ordaining purpose of God might stand, not of works but of him who *calls*" (Rom 9:11, 12).

In the end, God's gracious activity of calling the elect within Israel to salvation is related solidly to the present hour by Paul's three-fold usage of an emphatic "now." Gentiles *now* have been shown mercy; Jews *now* have been disobedient, that they also *now* may be shown mercy (Rom 11:30, 31).

Give all glory to God! (Rom 11:33–35). Salvation is wholly of the Lord! Grace prevails! Never shall human merit-of-birth exercise a controlling effect on the free and unmerited working of God's grace. If ever a people could claim special consideration some day in the future on the basis of ethnic considerations, a coordinate cancelling of the sovereignty and freedom of grace would be effected. Yes, God shall see to the preservation of a number from Israel throughout every generation. But no individual may presume to claim race as somehow assuring his own election.

For of him and through him, and unto him, are all things. To him be the glory forever. Amen (Rom 11:36).

PART THREE

PHILOSOPHICAL THEOLOGY

17

Kant and the Problem of Religious Knowledge

John Jefferson Davis

The contemporary situation in both philosophy and theology is characterized by sharp dichotomies between the realms of fact and value. Positivistic philosophies operating with epistemological models based on the natural sciences concentrate on the "factual" dimensions of experience, bypassing the realms of value, interiority, and metaphysics. Existentialist philosophies concentrate on the realms of value and human subjectivity, bypassing the "objectifying" world of the natural sciences. The proponent of one option in contemporary philosophy is scarcely able to recognize an adherent of the opposing school as one who is engaged in a legitimate form of the philosophical enterprise. Positivistic philosophies in this century have been characterized by powerful refinements in techniques of logical and linguistic analysis, but at the same time they have tended to avoid grappling with the first order metaphysical questions that have traditionally comprised the chief concerns of classical philosophy and theology. Such metaphysical questions have, in the positivistic tradition, been understood to be either meaningless or entirely beyond the reach of philosophical reason. The existentialist tradition, on the other hand, has not avoided the questions of metaphysics and ultimate values. Its results, however, have generally lacked logical rigor and analytical clarity, and as a result have not been altogether satisfactory. In its concentration on human interiority, the existentialist tradition has also failed to integrate into its own outlook the objective world of the natural sciences.

Protestant theology since Kant has tended to operate within the "value" dimension of a fact-value dichotomy. Modern theology has attempted to minimize if not eliminate all possibility of conflict with the natural sciences by sharply distinguishing the types of knowledge claims that are proper to the respective disciplines. This attempt to delimit the respective spheres of theology and the natural sciences led to revised understandings of the nature of revelation and the nature of the relationship of faith and history. Revelation, it is said, does not communicate factual information about the spatio-temporal world, but is rather the medium through which God communicates *himself*.[1] Neither is God to be understood as a direct causal agent in the spatio-temporal nexus; biblical "miracles" are to be interpreted as the vehicles through which the biblical authors communicated the religious and existential import of saving events in the life of the covenant community—events that nevertheless can be understood within a naturalistic framework. This understanding of the nature of revelation and of God's relation to the natural order had the advantage of eliminating the conflicts with natural science that had proved to be so embarrassing for Christian theology in the past. In terms of the new understanding, conflict was simply not possible, since theology and the natural sciences dealt with two incommensurable dimensions of human experience.

In recent years, however, the problematic nature of this attempt to adjudicate between the disciplines has become more and more apparent. Both analytic philosophers and Protestant theologians have been raising fundamental questions about the adequacy of this way of understanding the problem. Langdon Gilkey has pointed out, for example, that phrases such as the "mighty acts of God" which are characteristic of the "biblical theology" school of G. E. Wright and Bernard Anderson do not have any empirically verifiable content. According to Gilkey, in this outlook " . . . the Bible is a book of the acts Hebrews believed God might have done and the words he might have said had he done and said them—but of course we recognize he did not."[2] Analytic philosophers such as Anthony Flew were quick to point out that this way of speaking of the "mighty acts of God" was not empirically falsifiable and hence bordered on the meaningless.[3] If, in

---

[1]The development of this concept of revelation is detailed in J. Baillie, *The Idea of Revelation in Recent Thought* (New York: Columbia University, 1955).

[2]L. Gilkey, "Cosmology, Ontology, and the Travail of Biblical Language," *JR* 41 (1961) 197. See also Gilkey's analysis in *Naming the Whirlwind: the Renewal of God-Language* (Indianapolis: Bobbs-Merrill, 1969).

[3]Cf. A. Flew, "Theology and Falsification," in Flew and MacIntyre, eds., *New Essays in Philosophical Theology* (London: SCM, 1955).

this neo-orthodox approach, God was not really considered to be a causal agent in the spatio-temporal world, what did it mean to say that God "acts" in such a world? What difference could such "action" possibly make in the real world? What objective basis, if any, does such a use of language have? Answers to these and similar questions were not readily forthcoming on the premises of neo-orthodox theology.

Similar questions arose in relation to the neo-orthodox concept of revelation. If "personal" and "propositional" revelation are to be distinguished so sharply, how are we to escape the conclusion that the *meaning* of the revelatory event is a purely subjective one, being attributed to the event from the side of the human subject rather than the divine Subject? If there is no normative interpretation of the revelatory event from the side of the divine Subject, it is difficult to see how theological statements can have any genuinely objective basis. On such predicates theology is vulnerable to the criticism of Feuerbach that all theological statements are reducible to anthropological ones. Such conclusions were being drawn in the "Death of God" theologies of the 1960's and led to the widespread discussion of the crisis in "God-talk." These developments have led to renewed efforts in Protestant theology to find more adequate ways of understanding both the nature of revelation and the nature of God's relation to the spatio-temporal world. Before exploring some of these efforts, however, it will be necessary to review one of the main contributing factors to the contemporary impasse in Protestant theology: the basic dualism between nature and freedom in the critical philosophy of Immanuel Kant. While almost all modern Protestant theology has been influenced in one way or another by the Kantian epistemological paradigm, few evangelical theologians have personally attempted a fundamental criticism of the Kantian premises. The Kantian strictures on metaphysical knowledge in the traditional sense have been in the liberal tradition, widely accepted as unquestionably valid. Given the magnitude of the contemporary impasse in theology relative to revelation, the knowledge of God, God-language, and God's relation to the world, such a basic re-examination seems to be very much in order.

Before examining some of the crucial features of Kant's epistemology in relation to the task of contemporary theology, it will be helpful to recall the Kantian problematic in terms of its own context and aims. Kant's critical philosophy was a comprehensive attempt to understand the fundamental coherence of human experience in its scientific, moral, and aesthetic dimensions. Kant's pervasive influence in modern theology and philosophy has in no little part been due to the architectonic nature of his vision. Kant attempted to comprehend in a single philosophical vision the standpoint of Newtonian physics, the reality of moral experience, and the valid insights of the idealistic and empirical traditions in philosophy. Kant believed that his critical philosophy had achieved three results of first order significance: the justification of the universality and necessity of scientific knowledge in the face of Hume's skepticism; the vindication of human freedom and the autonomy of moral experience in the face of the challenge posed by the mechanistic world of Newtonian science; and a decisive adjudication between the claims of conflicting metaphysical systems through the limitation of the use of theoretical reason to the sphere of spatio-temporal experience alone. Whether or not one agrees with the methods and results of Kant's philosophy, it is undeniable that the issues which he addressed are of fundamental importance for any modern philosophy. In the very comprehensiveness of the Kantian program is found much of the truth of the oft-cited thesis that one can philosophize with Kant or against him, but not without him.

KEY THEMES IN THE "CRITIQUE OF PURE REASON"

In terms of our particular concern for the problem of religious knowledge in modern theology, it will be helpful to focus on three key features of the Kantian paradigm: the constructive nature of the knowing process; the limitation of the categories to the sphere of possible experience; and the sharp distinction between the noumenal and phenomenal realms, with the attendant unknowability of the *Ding-an-sich.* Each of these doctrines was posited as part of the solution of the problematic that Kant had set for himself. In order to be in a position to assess the adequacy of Kant's solution, it will be helpful to first attempt a brief exposition of these three doctrines in the light of our own question of the problem of religious knowledge.

For Kant, knowledge is the result of an active construction of the human mind. Traditional epistemologies had assumed that knowledge is the result of the mind's conformity to external objects; in Kant's "Copernican revolution," knowledge is understood to be the result of the conformity of external objects to the *a priori* categories of the human mind. Kant's hypothesis arises from his belief that knowledge, in the proper sense of the term, must have an *a priori* character, exhibiting universality and necessity. His paradigms for such an understanding of knowledge are, of course, mathematics and the natural sciences. Kant presents his hypothesis in the preface to the second edition in the following manner:

Hitherto it has been assumed that all our knowledge must conform to objects. But all attempts to extend our knowledge of objects by establishing something in regard to them *a priori*, by means of concepts, have, on this assumption, ended in failure. We must therefore make trial whether we may not have more success in the tasks of metaphysics, if we suppose that objects must conform to our knowledge. This would agree better with what is desired, namely, that it should be possible to have knowledge of objects *a priori*, determining something in regard to them prior to their being given.[4]

In the past theologians have tended to forget the hypothetical nature of Kant's program, and have often treated Kant's doctrines as though they were irreducible facts. It is clear from Kant's own presentation, however, that his program presupposes a particular doctrine of the nature of knowledge which takes mathematics and the natural sciences as the paradigms for knowledge generally. If it should be the case that there were good grounds for questioning Kant's understanding the nature of science itself, or questioning his rather restrictive view of the nature of knowledge, then it would be clear that there would be no necessity in assuming that Kant's hypothesis is either the normative or most adequate one for the purposes of theology.

A second crucial feature of the Kantian program is the limitation of the speculative or theoretical use of the categories to the sphere of possible experience:

> *Knowledge,* which as such is speculative, can have no other object than that supplied by experience; if we transcend the limits thus imposed, the synthesis which seeks, independently of experience, new species of knowledge, lacks that substratum of intuition upon which alone it can be exercised.[5]

For Kant, possible experience is limited to sensory experience, since he believes that human nature has no capacity for intuiting a supersensible object. "Our nature is so constituted," he believes, "that our *intuition* can never be other than sensible; that is, it contains only the mode in which we are affected by objects."[6] In Kant's view there can be no direct religious or mystical experience of God to which the categories of the understanding might be applied. Kant believes that

---

[4]I. Kant, *Critique of Pure Reason* (New York: St. Martin's Press, 1929, 1965), B. xvi. All references to the *Critique* are to the text of the first (A) or second (B) edition given in this translation.
[5]A,471 = B,499.
[6]A,52 = B,76.

by limiting the categories in their constructive use to the realm of sensible experience, he can put an end to the constant strife and contradictions of competing systems that have characterized the history of metaphysics.

On the Kantian hypothesis, the conflicting claims of the various metaphysical systems arise from the mistaken attempt to extend the categories of the understanding beyond the sphere of their legitimate employment. Thus, while metaphysics is a "natural disposition" of the human mind, and the human mind is inevitably driven to consider the questions of the reality of God, freedom, and immortality, these questions admit of no speculative resolution. In the words of the preface to the first edition, the human mind has the peculiar fate of being burdened " . . . by questions which, as prescribed by the very nature of reason itself, it is not able to ignore, but which, as transcending all its powers, it is also not able to answer."[7]

For Kant, while "God" can be *thought,* i.e., the mind can form without contradiction a concept of a Supreme Good, a Supreme Reason, an *ens realissimum,* and so forth, God cannot be *known,* since no intuition of God is given in the spatio-temporal manifold. Modern theologians who have accepted the Kantian hypothesis have accordingly attempted to reconstruct theology on the basis of a noncognitive model of revelation and a noncognitive awareness of God. The results of this attempt, as we have seen, have not been altogether satisfactory.

A third important feature of the Kantian epistemology is the sharp distinction between noumenal and phenomenal realities, with the attendant doctrine of the unknowability of the *Ding an sich:*

> That space and time are only forms of sensible intuition, and so only conditions of the existence of things as appearances; that, moreover, we have no concepts of understanding, and consequently no elements for the knowledge of things, save in so far as intuition can be given corresponding to these concepts; and that we can therefore have no knowledge of any object as thing in itself, but only in so far as it is an object of sensible intuition, that is, an appearance—all this is proved in the analytical part of the Critique.[8]

This doctrine of the unknowability of the *Ding an sich,* which Kant believes that he is able to establish through transcendental argumentation, is essential to the structure of the entire critical philosophy. Without it, the Kantian analysis cannot be sustained. Kant believed that such a doctrine was essential for the achievement of two of the

---

[7]A, vii.
[8]B, xxvi.

major goals of his enterprise: ending the conflict of metaphysical systems through the limitation of the categories of the understanding to an empirical use, and preserving the autonomy of human moral experience and the possibility of freedom in the face of the necessity prevailing in the realm of phenomena. If the *Ding an sich* is held to be unknowable, then metaphysical conflicts are, of course, no longer a problem, since metaphysics in the classical sense of the term is deemed to be impossible. The possibility of human freedom is insured by limiting the applicability of the category of necessity to the phenomena which are the objects of knowledge in the natural sciences. Since human freedom is a noumenal reality, it escapes the necessary determinations of the phenomenal sphere. Since reason in its theoretical use is limited to the phenomenal realm, it is evident that human freedom, while not provable by theoretical reason, at the same time cannot be disproved by it. The way is accordingly left open to argue for the reality of freedom as a necessary postulate of reason in its practical use. Here again it is the case that one should not assume that agreement with Kant's goals (i.e., adjudicating metaphysical disagreements and making a place for human freedom) necessarily entails agreement with the solution offered by Kant. Protestant theology since Kant has tended to make such an assumption rather uncritically.

AN EVALUATION OF THE ADEQUACY OF THE KANTIAN PARADIGM

Having reviewed briefly some of the features of Kant's epistemology which are most pertinent to our concern about the nature of religious knowledge, we are now in a better position to attempt some preliminary evaluation of the adequacy of the Kantian paradigm.[9] It should be acknowledged at the outset that even one who is finally led to reject basic premises of Kant's position can nevertheless learn a great deal about epistemology from it. In particular, it seems undeniable that Kant brought to a sharp focus certain questions in the area of epistemology in a more profound manner than any thinker who preceded him. Kant called to our attention in a striking way the active nature of the mind in the knowing process. Modern studies in experimental psychology have demonstrated that visual perception is heavily influenced by the categories that are acquired through social

---

[9]It is beyond the purpose of this article to consider Kant's detailed analysis of the theistic proofs. The concern here is rather to question some of the assumptions which are presupposed by Kant in his treatment of the proofs.

238 Philosophical Theology

interaction.[10] While Kant was concerned with an *a priori* rather than merely empirical priority of the categories to experience, these modern studies nonetheless are in agreement with Kant insofar as they show that the mind is hardly a passive receiver of external stimuli.

Kant has also done philosophy an enduring service by pointing to the transcendental preconditions of experience and knowledge. The categories through which we experience the world are not simply abstracted from experience, but in some sense are necessary to have any experience of the world whatsoever. Kant rightly pointed out that a purely empirical understanding of the genesis of the categories could hardly account for the measure of unity, necessity, and generality which we actually encounter in our experience of the world. At the same time, the Kantian paradigm has the merit of not making transcendental preconditions the sole explanation of knowledge; knowledge, in Kant's view, consists in a synthesis of empirical and rational elements. In Kant's own words, "Thoughts without content are empty, intuitions without concepts are blind."[11]

We can also find ourselves in fundamental agreement with Kant's concern to limit the constitutive employment of the categories to the sphere of possible experience. This would seem to be in fundamental harmony with the biblical understanding of the finitude of human thought. The human mind is not an autonomous and originative source of knowledge, but is fundamentally dependent on that which comes to it from beyond itself. Kant, in arguing for the necessary empirical component in all knowledge, was making this point in his own way. While we might disagree with Kant in his estimation of the *range* of human experience, we can yet agree with his insight that many problems in philosophy arise from a misplaced use of the categories.

In spite of the many enduring insights provided by the critical philosophy, the impasse in modern philosophy and theology points to the need for a careful re-examination of Kant's basic premises. As we have seen, the rather uncritical appropriations of the Kantian paradigm in modern theology have led to apparently unresolvable dualisms between God and nature, the knowledge of God and knowledge of the world, and the realm of fact and the realm of value. In

---

[10]R. E. Ornstein in *The Psychology of Consciousness* (New York: Harcourt Brace Jovanovich, 1977) 4 cites the work of Jerome Bruner. Bruner's subjects did not "see" a *red* ace of spades flashed before them because it did not conform to their usual categories of perception.

[11]A,52 = B,76.

particular, questions need to be raised with respect to Kant's understanding of the nature of reason and experience, his concept of
knowledge, his model of the natural sciences, and his doctrine of God.
What follows here is in the form of exploratory questions and comments. This list of items itself suggests that the questioning should
take the form not merely of questions addressed to details of the
Kantian system from a standpoint within the system, but rather from
a standpoint without it, where the basic adequacy of the Kantian
paradigm is not assumed.

The Nature of Reason

Kant's "transcendental" critique of the powers and scope of human
reason has the rather paradoxical character of claiming to exercise
successfully during the course of the *Critique* by means of those powers of reason which are ruled out by its conclusions. As John E. Smith
has observed, "A peculiar fact about Kant's entire first *Critique* is that
nowhere does it have any place within itself for the type of knowledge
it purports to be."[12] That is, while Kant apparently believes that the
results of the first *Critique* constituted *knowledge* in some sense, the
critical analysis itself limited valid knowledge claims and the valid
application of the categories to the spatio-temporal manifold. Since
human consciousness for Kant is clearly not reducible to sensory
phenomena, but rather transcends the sensible world, how is it that
Kant can claim to have established knowledge claims about the supersensible range of reason? The Kantian premise which limits reason in
its constitutive use to the sensible sphere should be recognized for
what it is: a *hypothetical* premise postulated in order to achieve a particular philosophical aim (the elimination of conflicting metaphysical
claims). This philosophical goal itself is not self-evidently valid, but
needs to be examined in terms of its own presuppositions. The result
of this line of questioning is the recognition of the following state of
affairs: if the Kantian premise is accepted, then on Kant's own terms,
the conclusions of the *Critique* cannot be considered to be "knowledge" in the same sense in which it is understood in relation to mathematics and the natural sciences, which are paradigmatic for Kant. On
the other hand, if the *results* of the *Critique* are accepted as
"knowledge"—and it seems clear that this was Kant's own understanding of his analysis—then reason in its theoretical or constitutive use
cannot be limited to the sensible sphere alone. In either case, whether

---

[12] John E. Smith, "The Religious Implications of Kant's Philosophy," in *Reason
and God* (New Haven: Yale, 1961) 19.

the results are considered to be hypothetical or demonstrative in nature, there are sufficient grounds for calling into question the adequacy of the Kantian premise itself.

A further difficulty arises in connection with Kant's belief that reason in its critical use is completely "objective" and exempt from the dogmatic assumptions of traditional metaphysical systems. "The critique of pure reason," Kant claims, "can be regarded as the true tribunal for all disputes of pure reason; for it is not involved in these disputes . . . but is directed to the determining and estimating of the rights of reason in general."[13] Developments in philosophy since Kant have called into question Kant's belief in the objectivity and neutrality of critical reason. The internal developments in the tradition of linguistic analysis have gradually led to the recognition of the fact that disagreements are not only possible but virtually inescapable on the critical or metaphilosophical level itself.[14] It became evident, for example, that the criterion of meaning in terms of empirical verification postulated by the early proponents of logical positivism was not itself capable of empirical verification. In terms of Kant's own recognition of metaphysics as a "natural disposition" which inescapably leads to the consideration of the questions of God, freedom, and immortality, it is difficult to believe that Kant has sustained his claim

---

[13]A,751 = B,779. John E. Smith makes the following comment in regard to Kant's claims for the objectivity of critical reason: ". . . while Kant was viewing dogmatic philosophical standpoints as hopelessly involved in making transcendent claims about the nature of things, he was also regarding his critical standpoint as immune from criticism . . . From different standpoints . . . the Enlightenment philosophers set forth the limits of reason as coinciding with the bounds of sense. . . . But somehow the form of thought operative in these critical enterprises themselves managed to escape judgment and remain unaffected by the sceptical conclusions thus attained." "Hegel's Critique of Kant," *Review of Metaphysics* 26 (1973) 458, 459.

[14]J. E. Smith, "The Reflexive Turn, the Linguistic Turn, and the Pragmatic Outcome," *Monist* 53 (1969) 588–605. The thesis of Smith's article (603) is that ". . . belief in a secure, critical level of thinking, whether represented by the idea of a transcendental critique, a neutral form of analysis, or an absolute criterion of significance, is a mistake. There is no such level of thought which is incorrigible in itself and superior to some lower level which forms its object."

An extensive criticism of the claims for "neutral" standpoints in philosophy has been attempted by the Calvinistic philosopher Herman Dooyeweerd in *A New Critique of Theoretical Thought* (Philadelphia: Presbyterian and Reformed, 1969).

that reason in its critical use can establish in a completely disinterested and neutral manner reason's relationship to such matters of the highest existential import. While it is true that Kant recognizes the "existential" concern of reason in its practical use for the reality of God, freedom, and immortality, he nonetheless claims to be able to draw the boundaries between the two uses of reason in a completely neutral and objective manner, and it is precisely this assumption which must be called into question. In the understanding of the biblical writers, there is no neutral or value-free standpoint from which the actually existing individual can autonomously establish *a priori* reason's relationship to the transcendent Creator and Lord of reason. Such an *a priori* determination would be understood as symptomatic of man's alienation from and rebellion against God. Human reason in its existential actuality is characterized not by neutrality and autonomy with respect to divine realities, but by fallenness and alienation from its proper use.[15] This biblical concept of human reason as an integral function of the total selfhood in its actual alienation needs to be taken with renewed seriousness in Protestant theology today.

It can also be observed that Kant's model of reason is inherently *privatistic* in nature. John Macmurray has argued that the critical philosophy " . . . fails to do justice to, and even to allow for the possibility of our knowledge of one another; and this failure arises because its formal conception of knowledge excludes this possibility by postulating the 'I think' as the primary presupposition of all experience."[16] If the Cartesian "I think" is considered to be constitutive for the self and its knowledge, then, given the inherently privatistic nature of the *cogito,* it becomes difficult to give an adequate account of the reality of other selves. Since, on Kantian premises, the existence of other selves (including God) is virtually irrelevant to the thinker's program of establishing a self-grounded epistemological certainty, it then becomes very difficult if not impossible to incorporate the actions and words of other selves into the critical standpoint in an integral way. The possibility that the thinker's epistemological certainty is not self-grounded, but rather grounded at least in part in a *community* of selves whose deeds and words impinge upon the thinker from without, is virtually excluded from the outset by the privatistic model of reason in the critical philosophy. The scientific enterprise itself, which influenced Kant so strongly as an epistemological paradigm, points to the

---

[15]Cf. Jer 17:9; Rom 1:21; Eph 4:18.
[16]J. Macmurray, *The Self as Agent* (London: Faber and Faber, 1957, 1969) 73.

centrality of the living community of scientists as the actual and indispensable foundation for the certainty of scientific affirmations.[17] Given the fact that religious knowledge by its very nature involves the self being addressed from without by the divine "Thou" which is ontologically and epistemologically prior to it, it is quite evident that any standpoint which is inherently privatistic will have great difficulty in giving an adequate account of the cognitive awareness arising from the experience of such an encounter. The irreducible "givenness" and ontic reality of such an encounter simply cannot find an integral place in such a scheme. If the existential reality of such an encounter is an irreducible "given" of actual religious faith, then any *a priori* preclusion of the validity of such a given must be deemed illegitimate. *A priori* limitations of the possibility of religious knowledge must give way to the actuality of religious knowledge. If the self's encounter with the divine Thou is indeed an existential actuality, and is in fact constitutive not merely for human knowledge but for human selfhood itself, then the privatistic nature of the Kantian model of reason disqualifies it as an adequate one for the purposes of theology.

Experience

Kant's limitation of the theoretical employment of the categories to the sphere of possible experience presupposes a belief that "possible experience" cannot extend beyond the spatio-temporal manifold. The noumenon, while it can be thought without contradiction, cannot, in Kant's view, be known, since no intuition of it is given in sensible experience. Human nature, according to Kant, possesses no faculty for intuiting a supersensible reality: "Since ... such a type of intuition, intellectual intuition, forms no part whatsoever of our faculty of knowledge, it follows that the employment of the categories can never extend further than to the objects of experience."[18]

Two somewhat obvious comments are in order here. First, Kant's belief that "experience" is limited to sensory experience needs to be recognized for what it is: a doctrine, and not an undebatable fact. While one might share Kant's desire to find a way of adjudicating conflicting metaphysical claims, it should be recognized that there may be other ways of doing this besides limiting human intuition to the "bounds of sense." Second, Kant's doctrine simply denies the

---

[17]Michael Polanyi has made a persuasive case for such an understanding of the nature of the scientific enterprise in *Personal Knowledge: Towards a Post-Critical Philosophy* (Chicago: University of Chicago, 1958).

[18]B,309.

force of the testimony of countless individuals throughout human history to the reality of an intuition of divine things in various types of mystical and revelatory experiences. Kant's schematization of human experience leaves no room for religious and mystical awareness of its own terms. Today, when there is less willingness to limit the boundaries of valid human experience on the basis of a paradigm drawn from the physical sciences, Kant's rationalistic assumptions seem less persuasive than they might have seemed during much of the nineteenth century. Kant's doctrine has the further disadvantage of being something of a self-fulfilling prophecy, i.e., a definition of experience which excludes a direct awareness of the transcendent tends to reduce awareness of realities which do not conform to the definition. The power of an interpretative framework to bias one's awareness of the world has been attested by two modern writers, Arthur Koestler and Karen Horney:

> My party education had equipped my mind with such elaborate shock-absorbing buffers and elastic defences that everything seen and heard became automatically transformed to fit a preconceived pattern (Koestler, *The God that Failed,* London, 1950, 68).

> The system of theories which Freud has gradually developed is so consistent that when one is once entrenched in them it is difficult to make observations unbiased by this way of thinking (Horney, *New Ways of Psychoanalysis,* London, 1939, 7).[19]

These statements, the first by a former Marxist, and the second by a former Freudian, testify to the power of a system of categories to screen out certain aspects of one's experience of the world. The same would be true for Kant's philosophical assumptions about the nature of possible experience. If this is kept clearly in view, we may be less prone to find ourselves bewitched and mystified by "doctrine felt as fact."

Knowledge

For Kant, knowledge in the proper sense of the term is characterized by universality and necessity. Kant believed that such universality and necessity were found in Newtonian physics, and took the new scientific enterprise as an epistemological paradigm. The insistence on *necessity* as an essential element of valid knowledge appears to grow out of the search for epistemological *certainty* that has preoc-

---

[19]Cited by Polanyi, *Personal Knowledge,* 288.

cupied philosophy since Descartes. The development of philosophy since Descartes has tended to give increasing credibility to the view that such a necessitarian view of the nature of knowledge is overly restrictive.

An alternative understanding of knowledge as "justified true belief" rather than "universal and necessary truth" seems closer to the way in which the concept of knowledge actually functions in ordinary experience. As John Macmurray has pointed out, the Cartesian attempt to reach an indubitable "knowledge" through a process of suspending (or pretending to suspend) belief in propositions which I really do believe—*and have no good reason to doubt*—is in itself a highly artificial and quite dubious enterprise. Are firm epistemological foundations to be laid through an artificial exercise in which I pretend to disbelieve certain propositions, e.g., the reality of my physical body, which I have no good grounds for disbelieving? The fact that it may be *possible* to doubt a given proposition is not in itself an adequate ground for *actually* doubting that proposition. The act of doubting itself cannot be exempt from the normal requirement of having some ground for taking the positions (negative and affirmative) that we actually take. The Cartesian program, however, is based on a mistaken assumption of the legitimacy of positing doubt without the need for giving sufficient grounds for that doubt. The Cartesian program "canonizes" doubt and accords it a privileged epistemological position which itself has not been adequately justified.[20] Kant, insofar as he shares with Descartes a conception of knowledge involving self-grounded certainty, is open to the same line of criticism. If one holds that there are adequate grounds for rejecting a view of knowledge based on a self-grounded certainty as artificial and unduly restrictive, then it follows, of course, that one is hardly required to accept the Kantian hypotheses which were posited with such an understanding of knowledge in view.

A further difficulty with Kant's conception of knowledge, carried over from the rationalistic tradition, is his assumption that there must be a complete congruence or perfect "fit" between the categories of the understanding and the objects of knowledge. For Kant, this meant a complete "covering" or subsumption of the phenomena by the categories. Where, on Kant's assumptions, no such subsumption was possible, i.e., with respect to noumena, no knowledge at all was possible. On the basis of Kant's schematization, there is either a complete subsumption, or no subsumption at all, with no intermediate pos-

---

[20]These comments are indebted to the insights of Macmurray, *Self as Agent*, 75–78, and Polanyi, 269–98.

sibilities. On the basis of Kant's assumption of the need for a complete congruence between the category and its object, there is really no adequate place for a concept of an *analogical* knowledge.[21]

An analogical understanding of knowledge is based on the premise that a substantial, though not exhaustive, degree of congruence or isomorphism is required between the concept and its object in order for a knowledge claim to be affirmed. The need for such an analogical understanding of the relationship of our categories to reality has become evident through developments in modern quantum physics. It is now evident that events in the subatomic realm can only be related to our normal experience in an analogical fashion, rather than by way of a direct or exhaustive correspondence. The planetary model of the hydrogen atom proposed by Niels Bohr, for example, is not to be understood as a literal, miniature model of the atom. There are certain structural correspondences between the Bohr model and the actual hydrogen atom, but the model is not to be understood as a literal "picture" of the atom itself. Behavior in the subatomic world can be adequately described only in the abstract language of the differential equations of quantum mechanics. Nevertheless, working atomic scientists have no doubt about the reality of their actual knowledge of events in the subatomic world.

While the relationship between the experimental reality and the concepts of our common-sense world is in this case analogical rather than exhaustively congruent, it is nonetheless quite real. The state of affairs in modern physics demonstrates the need to adjust any preconceived notions concerning the relationship of categories to objects in a way that is appropriate to the subject matter at hand. It goes without saying that such a concept of analogical knowing is essential for the unique subject matter of theology. Once it is recognized that Kant's alternatives of either a complete congruence or complete lack of congruence between category and object are not the only possible ones, then the way is left open for a proper analogical understanding of the knowledge of God.

Natural Science

It is well known that one of Kant's central concerns in the first *Critique* was to show, in the face of Hume's skepticism, how the laws of natural science, considered by Kant to be grounded in *a priori* synthetic propositions, could be justified. Kant believed that scientific

---

[21]This point is made by Winfried Weir, "A Metacritique of Kant's Critique of Reason," *International Philosophical Quarterly* 8 (1968) 318–19.

laws, in order to be truly scientific, had to be characterized by a certain type of rational necessity. Hume, it will be recalled, had argued that experience yields only certain patterns of constant conjunction or regularity, but no causal relationships that could be characterized by an *a priori* necessity. Kant, on the other hand, while he did not believe that particular scientific laws could be deduced in their empirical particulars apart from actual experimentation, nevertheless believed that the generality of scientific statements were grounded in a real measure of rational necessity, and were to that extent *a priori.* The simple statement "Every effect has a cause" would, for Kant, be an example of an *a priori* synthetic proposition.

Now the tendency in twentieth-century philosophy, which has been predominantly of an empiricist character, has been to question or deny Kant's belief that scientific laws are *a priori* synthetic propositions. If we are to use Kant's terminology, the predominant view has tended to be that such laws are *a posteriori* synthetic propositions. Strict necessity of an *a priori* type, in this view, is simply not a feature of the lawlike statements of the natural sciences.

While philosophers standing within the idealist tradition such as F. H. Bradley, B. Blanshard, and A. C. Ewing have held a so-called "necessity" view with respect to natural laws, the most predominant view, represented by Karl Popper, Richard Braithwaite, A. J. Ayer, Rudolf Carnap, Carl Hempel, Ernest Nagel, and others, is the so-called "regularity" view. Here scientific laws are understood to be universal generalizations of observed patterns of regularity which are subject to experimental confirmation or disproval.

Whatever one might conclude with respect to this intramural debate within the philosophy of science, from the theological perspective another question is in order: Might it not be the case that Kant is fundamentally mistaken in seeking for *created* realities a type of necessity proper to the Creator alone? Moreover, the type of necessity which Kant seeks for natural laws is a *self-grounded* necessity, where the necessary character of physical law is not grounded in the Creator or even in the creation as such, but in the allegedly *a priori* and autonomous mental structures of the thinking subject.

In the perspective of biblical theology this might be seen as a denial of creaturely finitude and an expression of *hubris,* arrogating unto the creature the sovereign powers of legislating in the natural order that are proper to God alone. "Where were you when I laid the foundation of the earth?"[22] God's question to Job is intended to shatter his self-

---

[22]Job 38:4.

grounded confidence. In the light of the general tenor of biblical theology, which repeatedly affirms the complete ontological and epistemological priority of God over all forms of human self-certainty, Kant's search for a self-grounded certainty in the natural sciences appears suspect from the outset.

Yet another significant difficulty arises in connection with Kant's understanding of the nature of scientific laws. In the very sharp distinction which he makes between the phenomenal world of necessity and the noumenal world of freedom, Kant apparently fails to adequately appreciate the essentially *abstractive* nature of scientific statements. That is, scientific statements are abstractive in the sense that in making statements concerning, say, the motion of a physical object through space, the presence of personal agents who might influence the motion of the object are deliberately excluded or suppressed. For example, the equation $s = 1/2\ gt^2$, which describes the distance s through which an object will fall in a vacuum in time t, with g as the gravitational constant, prescribes the "necessary" behavior of a physical object only in a special context abstracted from the world of ordinary experience, i.e., the carefully constructed world of the experimental laboratory where the actions of personal agents upon the object are carefully excluded. It makes no sense at all to say that I am "breaking" a "necessary" law of physics when I suspend a weight in my hand over the floor and by an act of my will prevent it from falling freely; the equation for freely falling objects cited above presupposes the very special context abstracted from the world of our direct experience, where personal agents are continually acting to influence the behavior of physical objects and of other personal agents.[23]

Kant was attempting to salvage an area for the exercise of human freedom by sharply distinguishing the phenomenal and the noumenal worlds. Kant's hypothesis, has, however, the very serious defect of positing the complete unknowability of God and the human self, together with an irreconcilable dualism between the phenomenal and noumenal worlds. Once the *abstractive* nature of scientific statements is recognized, however, it is no longer necessary to posit with Kant a complete disjunction between the two areas of human experience in order to insure a place for the exercise of freedom. Scientific statements do not describe an ironclad "necessity" for the world of phenomena, but rather the behavior of such objects insofar as the actions of personal agents are directly excluded. The direct causal action of God in the world is not a "violation" of "necessary" laws,

---

[23]This analysis is indebted to Macmurray, *Self as Agent,* 218-20.

insomuch as physical laws describe the motion of bodies only under the special circumstances where, by hypothesis, the actions of personal agents have been suppressed.

The relationship between the world of physics and the everyday world of personal action is neither one of complete disjunction, or one of the subsumption of personal action under the categories of physics. The world of physics is actually a reduction of the everyday reality of personal action and is subsumable under it, rather than vice versa. The laws of physics prescribe the observable characteristics of our experienced world in a relative and contextual, rather than absolutely necessary sense. Such an understanding of the nature of natural law opens an avenue for thinking together the relative necessity of physical events, the reality of human freedom, and the action of God in the world, with his consequent knowability on the basis of that action. The barrier between a completely determined (and completely knowable) phenomenal realm and a completely undetermined (and completely unknowable) noumenal realm can be removed once it is recognized that the barrier was erected on the basis of mistaken assumptions about the nature of scientific law.

God

It is quite evident that the God of the rarefied world of the *Critique of Pure Reason* bears a closer resemblance to the God of Enlightenment deism than to the biblical God of "Abraham, Isaac, and Jacob." There is simply no room within the conceptual world of the *Critique* for the sovereign, almighty Creator of heaven and earth who acts in real space-time history to redeem his people from sin and bondage.

A properly trinitarian understanding of the God of the Scriptures is missing in the Kantian conceptuality. The biblical witness to the sovereign freedom of God to reveal himself through the creaturely realities of space, time, and human flesh in a real incarnation is ruled out beforehand by the Kantian presuppositions about the nature of knowledge and of God. Just as there is no real possibility on Kantian terms of appropriating the epistemological significance of the objective basis of revelation in the incarnation of God the Son, there is likewise no real possibility for comprehending the subjective reality of revelation in the outpouring of God the Holy Spirit.[24] God in his own sovereign act of self-revelation makes himself a genuine possibility for man's knowledge—a knowledge otherwise inaccessible to man—by

---

[24]Cf. T. Torrance, "The Epistemological Relevance of the Spirit," in *God and Rationality* (London: Oxford, 1971) 165–94.

taking man up into the divine self-knowledge of God as Father, Son, and Holy Spirit. Since the Kantian concept of God is not informed by the dynamics of the trinitarian life, there is no real possibility of appropriating the genuine reality of the knowledge of God on the basis of God's self-revelation as it is attested in Scripture.

At the root of the Kantian doctrine of the unknowability of God are some unbiblical assumptions concerning God's relationship to space. According to Kant, the concept of a supreme being is characterized by such attributes as "necessity, infinity, unity, *existence outside the world* . . . omnipresence as free from conditions of space . . . ."[25] These attributes of "existence outside the world" and "omnipresence as free (dom) from conditions of space" are, from the perspective of the biblical writers, only partial truths. The God who utterly transcends the bounds of space and time is also free to reveal himself in and through space and time. The Kantian conception of God, in common with the deistic one, gives no real place to the equally real immanence of God in the created order that is attested in Scripture. If for Kant God is completely "outside" the world of space and time, then it follows that no *cognitive* awareness of God is possible, since such awareness can only arise as the categories are applied to the intuitions given in the spatio-temporal manifold.[26]

Rather than understanding God's relationship to space deistically as Kant has done, it is necessary to understand the relationship more biblically in an *incarnational* or *sacramental* sense, where God, in the action of the Son and the Spirit, is really and spiritually present to his people through the medium of created forms, while at the same time transcending them. On the basis of such an incarnational and sacramental model of the divine presence, God on his own initiative gives himself to his people as the subject of possible experience, thus creating, through his real presence in space and time, the grounds of his own knowability.

This broad overview of selected features of the Kantian paradigm which are most pertinent to the constructive task of theology must now be brought to a conclusion. We have seen that while the basic Kantian concern to comprehend in a unified vision the basic unity of human experience can be affirmed, some of the basic premises of his thought concerning the nature of reason, experience, the natural

---

[25] A,642 = B,670.

[26] Thomas Torrance has pointed out how Kant seems to have taken over from Newton a faulty "receptacle" view of space which made it impossible to conceptualize God's real presence in space (*Space, Time and Incarnation* [London: Oxford, 1969] 39, 63).

sciences, and God's relation to the world are less than adequate for the contemporary theological task. It is my conviction that resources for an alternative, yet equally comprehensive paradigm are to be found in the writings of John Macmurray, Michael Polanyi, and Thomas Torrance. Such a paradigm would address the foundational questions of the basis for knowledge in the natural sciences, the reality of human freedom in a scientific milieu, and the actuality of the knowledge of God in human experience. While the outlines of such an alternative vision are already discernible, the full articulation of such a vision must wait for a later day.

18

Categories in Collision?

Gordon R. Lewis

Modern thought in the West has moved away from contemplation of changeless being to preoccupation with the kaleidoscope of change in space and time. The move from knowledge of absolutes has led to relativism and despair.

In *Modern European Thought* Yale University's Franklin Baumer traces the development of ideas away from continuity to change from 1600–1950. In contrast to earlier language about a world of static entities, modern man sees himself, society, history, and God as temporal and changing.[1] Under the impact of Darwinianism fixed and final conceptions that reigned for two thousand years in philosophy and theology passed away. The movement of interest away from the permanent to the changing transformed ways of knowing, morals, politics, and religion. By the time of Renan ultimate goals and eternal frames of reference looked endlessly dynamic. The historicist-evolutionary point of view impregnated nearly every department of thought. For Henri Bergson even the citadel of the self yielded to a succession of passing states, themselves ceaselessly changing.

It is not surprising that theologians respond differently to this trend away from talk about ontological being to the world of changing experience. Many evangelicals now seek to do theology without reference to the categories of changeless being, attributes, soul, spirit, body, or ontological entity.

---

[1] F. L. Baumer, *Modern European Thought: Continuity and Change in Ideas 1600–1950* (New York: Macmillan, 1977) 20–23.

The stance one takes regarding basic ways of thinking determines his formulations throughout the scope of biblical and theological studies. The issue is far from merely introductory. It has momentous consequences throughout theology as it has in thought at large.

We shall attempt a brief survey and evaluation of several influential evangelical writers who think that traditional metaphysical ways of thinking are in conflict with central categories of the Christian message so desperately needed in the world today. These writers and subjects include:

    I. Bruce Larson's Relational Categories
    II. G. C. Berkouwer's Functional Categories
    III. Helmut Thielicke's Existential Categories
    IV. John Bright's "Biblical" Categories
    V. Conclusion

I. BRUCE LARSON'S RELATIONAL CATEGORIES

Turning the spotlight away from changeless being to dynamic relationships has led to such colorful book titles as: Keith Miller's *Taste of New Wine, Please Love Me,* and *The Becomers;* Karl Olsson's *Come to the Party;* and Bruce Larson's *Ask Me To Dance* and *The Relational Revolution.*

Relational writers tend to displace the ontological and logical categories with the functional values of the biblical witness. In place of more traditional research are case-study, story, and repeated witness to personal experiences in relation to others and God. Larson expresses "a growing feeling that much of the 'orthodox theology' we have inherited from the past decades is not really biblical."[2]

Ignoring the universal knowledge of God's eternal *being* from creation (Rom 1:20) (the basis on which failure to lovingly worship God is inexcusable) Larson explains, "Relational theology simply emphasizes the central fact of all the Bible: man's relationship to God on his terms, a relationship between Forgiver and forgiven, between Lover and loved."[3] Larson adds, "In relational theology we say emphatically that the quality and scope of relationships and the ability and willingness to relate are marks of orthodoxy rather than doctrine, ethical performance or spiritual heroism."[4] "The primary biblical injunction

---

[2]B. Larson, *The Relational Revolution* (Waco, Texas: Word, 1976) 85.
[3]Ibid., 87.
[4]Ibid., 91.

is to relate in love to God, to self, and to others as the ultimate and authenticating mark of life in Christ."[5]

The Bible deals primarily with relationships, Larson says, and only indirectly with doctrine. "Despite that fact, throughout the history of the church and up to the present day a great deal more time has been spent on digging into the doctrinal aspects of theology than on exploring its relational aspects."[6] For example, the incarnation "has to do with the fact that people are people, and not disembodied concepts, and the greatest good news of all time is that God became one of those people in Jesus Christ."[7]

No follower of Christ can fail to appreciate an emphasis upon the supreme value of loving God with one's whole being and his neighbor as himself. Love, as Paul pointed out so eloquently (1 Cor 13), must be the supreme motivation of all that Christians do. But love is a fruit of the Holy Spirit developed in a person's character. Only a good tree can bring forth this good fruit. The heart and character is radically transformed by divine regeneration through repentance and faith. Relationships display the new nature in the believer's heart.

Larson has well said that the mere teaching of sound doctrine does not provide power to become what we ought to become. If theologians have given the impression that doctrine is a sufficient condition for living the Christian life, they have failed. Although gospel truths are a necessary condition the Spirit uses to bring people to life, they are not a sufficient condition. Apart from the Spirit's witness in the heart, systems of philosophy and theology are indeed lacking in power—including a relational theology!

Relational theologians wield a two-edged sword when they add, "The minute you theologize you are wandering one step away from life." But Walden Howard need not think he sidesteps this problem by preferring to speak about a "relational lifestyle."[8] If the theologian takes one step away from life while teaching a coherent view of redemption, is not a relational thinker one step away from relating in love to his neighbor while writing about it? Or is writing truth in love a way of relating lovingly to one's neighbor?

From another perspective, while orthodox theology has not paid sufficient attention to dynamic personal relationships, relational theology risks the danger of failing to do justice to the terms (entities,

---

[5] Ibid.

[6] B. Larson, *No Longer Strangers* (Waco, Texas: Word, 1971) 17.

[7] Ibid.

[8] "Unmasking: An Interview with Walden Howard" *Eternity* (August 1977) 11.

persons' characters) in relationship. Knowledge of terms need not exclude knowledge of relationships and vice versa. We need not decide against truths about God's being to present truths about his loving relationship to sinners. Rather, the significance of *his* love for the sinful can only be appreciated as we become aware not only of what he *did,* but of who he *is.*

II. G. C. BERKOUWER'S FUNCTIONAL CATEGORIES

The noted Reformed writer of an extensive series of volumes called *Studies in Dogmatics* summons evangelicals to reconsider their categories, reformulate their task, and revise their methodology.

The dogmatician's task, Berkouwer says, is not systematizing the Bible's teaching on a given subject as the teaching of God on that subject. Such a leveling process results from the doctrines of propositional revelation and plenary inspiration, which in his judgment are rationalizations. The Bible, although inspired by the Holy Spirit, cannot be elevated from its truly human authorship to the place where its divinity is a predicate of the inspired book or of supernatural truths.[9]

The Bible's human writers' witness has a decisive centralization, a concentration. "The knowledge which is the unmistakable aim of Scripture is the knowledge of faith which is life eternal."[10] So the interpretation and use of all Scripture must be governed by its unique purpose.[11] The Bible's witness is time-bound and offers no eternal truths, moral or otherwise. Its nature is not eternalizing or abstract, but related to salvation history.[12] The continuity of the church's creed is found not in a presupposition separate from the reading of Scripture, but through reading it and by taking seriously its witness to all its human aspects. Scripture cannot be understood in an abstract way, but only in terms of a witness concerning Christ and his salvation.[13] Berkouwer starts with a faith "totally different from intellectual assent."[14] Not even the kerygma is made up of timeless supernatural truths.[15]

With what categories, then, does Berkouwer work? Functional,

---

[9]G. C. Berkouwer, *Holy Scripture* (Grand Rapids: Eerdmans, 1975) 32.
[10]Ibid., 178, 179.
[11]Ibid., 183.
[12]Ibid., 188, 191, 253.
[13]Ibid., 263.
[14]Ibid., 54.
[15]Ibid., 32.

utilitarian categories replace ontological and logical ones. From 2 Timothy 3:16–17 he stresses the "functional character" of Scripture related to salvation and concrete wisdom for the future.[16] Its words can never be formally isolated, but are directed toward salvation. They point to the authoritative function of the written words throughout, written by men and coming to us with divine authority.[17] Berkouwer does not want his terms "organic inspiration" or "instrumental inspiration" understood as a theory. "But the real intention in the doctrine of Scripture is the interest in the peculiar and conscious functionality of man in the revelation of God."[18]

For Berkouwer the revelation is no longer in the Bible's logical assertions about ontological referents, realities, or beings. Revelation occurs or happens in the experience of salvation a sinner has as a result of reading or hearing the Bible's words, human, and time-bound though they are. In the reading of his *Man: The Image of God,* for example, we no more find out what man *is,* than we can learn about who God *is* in the Bible. The Bible, he says, tells us nothing about material or spiritual entities, body, or soul. He knows man only as he functions in relationship or out of relationship to God and knows God only in relationship to changing people.

What Berkouwer tends to overlook is that the redemptive value of the biblical witness is explicitly dependent upon its assertions of truth about reality. We need not make the choice between conceptual truth and functional value, indeed, we ought not. The reason the Bible can lead us to a saving experience with the living Word is that its teachings are true of the real Christ who redeems. Its truths lead us away from idols to the living Christ. "If Christ has not been raised, our preaching is useless and so is your faith. . . . your faith is futile, you are still in your sins" (1 Cor 15:14, 17). Fortunately Berkouwer sees the connection of utility to fact in reference to Christ's resurrection.[19] Unfortunately, he does not see this to be the case in other biblical teachings, and his general ascription of relativism to Scripture makes it difficult for a reader to make an exception for its permanent truthfulness regarding the fact of Christ's resurrection.

Berkouwer's universal generalizations about the time-bound character of human thought may have proved too much. Why should the Bible's teachings about its redemptive purpose be true for all times and cultures? As Geoffrey Bromiley puts it, "Why should any-

---

[16]Ibid., 142
[17]Ibid., 149.
[18]Ibid., 154.
[19]Ibid., 253.

thing in Scripture be relevant to this age and place when all of it was written for other ages and places?"[20] Clearly, Berkouwer imposes on himself and others an either/or of timeless truth and contingency which is unnecessary.

Having insisted that Scripture has but one purpose, Berkouwer has not sufficiently defined what is included and what is not in the witness to Christ and his salvation. Is the Bible's teaching about creation, providence, common grace, church and state, and things to come necessary to salvation? It seems obvious that the Bible intends to teach some things in addition to the possibility of a personal encounter with Christ. It teaches what in fact happened in the past, the significance of historical events, divine guidance in all the events of history and the affairs of nations, and things to come.

Unfortunately, Berkouwer leaves the believer in Christ and the Bible without a reason for his hope (1 Pet 3:15). He thinks no other support is needed than the witness of the Spirit in internal experience, so that the Bible is not accepted merely in an objective, abstract way. However, Christians need not choose between objective truth of Christianity and subjective indications of personal participation in its benefits. Appeals to illumination by the Spirit cannot settle questions of the text or canon or the validity of the Christian religion. Bernard Ramm helpfully explains, "The *testimonium* validates one's personal participation in redemption; evidences validate the objective religion of the gospel."[21] Hence, Ramm warns against a cavalier attitude toward evidence. "The *testimonium* is a certification of our personal adoption. But Christianity is also an objective religion of God. Christian evidences are to objective religion what the *testimonium* is to personal religion."[22]

III. HELMUT THIELICKE'S EXISTENTIAL CATEGORIES

Like Berkouwer, Thielicke denies that revelation may be equated with the thesaurus of Holy Scripture, thinking that static propositions loose the active fire of revelation.[23] Furthermore he considers the categories of our world of objective experience to be alien to God.

---

[20]G. Bromiley, "Review of *Holy Scripture*," *Christianity Today* (November 21, 1975) 44.

[21]B. Ramm, *Witness of the Spirit* (Grand Rapids: Eerdmans, 1959) 119.

[22]Ibid.

[23]H. Thielicke, *The Evangelical Faith* (Grand Rapids: Eerdmans, 1974, vol. 1; 1977, vol. 2), 2. 8.

Since divine revelation comes from without, it cannot be verified by our formal criteria. God's true presence is sought, as in Barthianism, in Jesus Christ only.[24]

Revelation takes place, however, not merely in the events of Jesus' life, but in their appropriation or actualization now. Thielicke's theology of actualization consists of a new interpretation of the truth (Christ) while the truth remains intact. Unlike conservatives who cut the ill-fitting garment of traditional matter to suit themselves, Thielicke reinterprets it for his contemporaries. And unlike liberalism, he tries to avoid bringing the truth under him and making himself its norm. Rather, Thielicke summons his hearers to live "under the truth."[25]

To do theology is to reproduce and re-present the truth expressed in the past in a new way for present day questions and situations. The theologian's task is "to actualize Christian truth, or better, to set it forth in its actuality and to understand it afresh thereby. To that extent theology is by nature, and not merely in its pedagogical implications, historical. It has nothing whatever to do with timeless truth."[26] God is Lord of the wording of his Word. Even in the incarnation we do not have a fixed ontological status, but we hear about God and receive him in the form of stories.[27]

Like Kant, Thielicke can know nothing as it is in itself, but only as it is refashioned by his forms and categories of apprehension[28] (which he assumes to be totally different from the way things are). Thielicke cannot know his own being, for substance is what the thing means for the one who handles it. Neither can he know the divine being or attributes, as constituents in God himself. For him, divine attributes are merely "modes of the subject who resolves upon these relationships." By speaking of God as the active subject, he tries to avoid divesting God of his transcendence as much relational thinking does. Rather, he claims God's being is in his becoming, not in a being for itself apart from and behind this becoming.[29]

Orthodox trinitarianism affirms the three personal distinctions within the Divine Being, but Thielicke regards questions about the Divine Being out of order. The questions which "come to actualization" in the doctrine of the Trinity have to do with God's relation to

---

[24]Ibid., 2. 13; 1. 26–27.
[25]Ibid., 1. 27.
[26]Ibid., 1. 23.
[27]Ibid., 2. 105, 115.
[28]Ibid., 2. 118.
[29]Ibid., 2. 125, 127.

his Word through which he binds himself to man and enters into relationship with him.[30] In the salvation event are three stages. "Here is God in action: God the Creator, God the Redeemer entering into solidarity with His creatures, and God the Holy Spirit present in the creative work of His Word." In the threefoldness of the forms of encounter, Thielicke thinks he is always dealing with the one God.[31]

Some interesting statements about categories come out in Thielicke's attempted defense of his views against the charge of Sabellian modalism. Although his view seems closer to the Sabellian modes of relating to man than to the modes of existence within the divine being, Thielicke insists that he does more than present God only phenomenologically and in terms of our own categories and criteria. The creative Word is the subject of the encounter and as such is not conditioned by our consciousness. "If God is the Father who creates the world, the Son who redeems it and the Spirit who makes himself present to it, this is not due to the world and its state." How does Thielicke know this? He assumes that the categories of the human consciousness are not alien after all, so that they cannot know God. He explains, "The consciousness to which he discloses himself is also created by him and influenced by his Spirit."[32] In the end, then, Thielicke seeks not to believe that the essential Trinity and the revelational Trinity have to be set in total antithesis. And finally he calls for not only an existentialist, but also a realistic interpretation of even the most abstract and remote of trinitarian formulae.[33]

To the extent that Thielicke's doctrine of the Trinity is orthodox, he has been inconsistent with his own existentialist and relational way of knowing. To the extent that he remains consistently within his own approach to knowing, he cannot affirm that God is either one or three *in himself.* But somehow Thielicke's assertion that God is one seems to apply to God as he is in himself, not just to his relations with his creatures. If Thielicke can know that God is one, he can know on the same basis that God exists (as well as relates), in three persons. The reliable basis for knowing either the oneness or the threeness is propositional revelation originating with God and given through men verbally and plenarily inspired by the Holy Spirit. By eliminating cognitive concepts of revelation and inspiration, Thielicke has eliminated the primary basis upon which we may test the spirits to see whether they are of God (1 John 4:1–3). The people who met God according to

---

[30]Ibid., 2. 133.
[31]Ibid., 2. 135.
[32]Ibid., 2. 179.
[33]Ibid., 2. 181, 183.

biblical sources knew not only that an unknown something acted and spoke, they knew his changeless being-personal Spirit (Exod 3:14; John 4:24), and attributes—holiness and love (1 Pet 1:15-16; 1 John 4:8). God relates to us faithfully in holy love because he is in himself, as he has said, holy love. And God is changelessly holy love; he is not holy love only when so relating to Thielicke. His being is not limited to the becoming of his activities in relation to man. Before man or the earth was formed, he existed in all his magnificence.

Neither Kant nor Thielicke need presume that the categories of conceptual thought are alien to the Creator of the mind or the universe he created for man to intelligently know and rule. If God is not so totally other that he cannot disclose himself to the human consciousness, he is not so totally other that he cannot reveal himself to the minds of prophetic and apostolic spokesmen. Or if God is so infinitely removed from intellectual categories, he must also be unrelated to man's non-rational consciousness.

IV. JOHN BRIGHT'S "BIBLICAL" CATEGORIES

Bright joins the chorus of those who deny that the Bible conveys propositionally revealed truths in verbally inspired words. The former professor of OT at Union Theological Seminary, Virginia, looks behind the diversity of the biblical writers for their common faith, "to lay hold of the structure of belief that underlies and informs them, and of which they are all in one way or another expressions."[34]

The conventional rubrics of systematic theologians—God, man, sin, salvation, etc.—force the biblical materials into a Procrustean bed of organization foreign to its nature, according to Bright. What is presented is not biblical theology, he claims, but something abstracted from it. In contrast his inductive method descriptively sets forth in the Bible's own terms "the essential, normative content of the faith of the Old Testament and the New, respectively."[35] In spite of the enormous difficulties philosophers have found in trying to derive an ought from an is, Bright naively imagines his induction to be normative. And paradoxically while denying that there is any "timeless truth" he seeks to express the changeless kerygma of the Bible, arguing that the theology of the biblical word can address all situations.[36]

---

[34] J. Bright, *The Authority of the Old Testament* (Grand Rapids: Baker, 1967) 124.

[35] Ibid., 125

[36] Ibid., 159, 173.

Bright properly stresses the importance of the historical context in biblical interpretation and imagines that systematic theology assumes its positions *a priori* and seeks proof texts. Systematics, he thinks, cites passages in a mechanical way because of the belief that the Bible was fully inspired and authoritative in all its parts.[37] Apparently he has not read systematic theologian Bernard Ramm's *Protestant Biblical Interpretation,* with its emphasis on the grammatical, historical, cultural contexts, but not liberalism's historicism with a vengeance.

Does Bright find any unity of teaching at all in the works of different writers in different historical settings of the OT? Israel's faith, he says, does not center on a doctrine of God or ethical teachings, but an understanding of history as the theater of God's purposive activity. Offering a theological interpretation of history, the OT is so diverse in its expressions, that it can by no means be reduced to a harmonious system of doctrine.[38] Nevertheless, biblical theologians can search behind its variety of expression to find a commonly held structure of believing and a characteristically Israelite understanding of reality.[39]

A few of the essential features have to do with election, the sovereign and exclusive lordship of Yahweh over his people, the understanding of reality expressed in the concept of covenant, a note of promise, and a confident expectation for the future.[40] Why, if "The Old Testament in all its diversity hangs together about a coherent, though never systematically articulate structure of belief,"[41] cannot one think, as well as preach, upon this coherence to the point of spelling it out? Systematic theology need not be imagined a matter of *a priori* assumptions. The data of biblical theology may stand in judgment upon the alternative theological claims.[42]

Another biblical theologian, Brevard Childs of Yale, also considers the approaches of both liberals and conservatives rationalistic, abstract, or fragmentary. The required position for understanding the Bible, he says, is to stand at the Bible's "point of standing" to put ourselves within the world of the Bible, and to understand it in its own categories.[43] From within the biblical world, Childs's sources find a

---

[37] Ibid., 48.

[38] Ibid., 130–1.

[39] Ibid., 131.

[40] Ibid., 131–6.

[41] Ibid., 136.

[42] See my theological workbook, *Decide for Yourself* (Downers Grove: Inter-Varsity, 1970).

[43] B. S. Childs, *Biblical Theology in Crisis* (Philadelphia: Westminster, 1970) 45.

concrete Hebrew mentality in contrast to the abstract, rationalistic, and theoretical Greek mentality.[44] Biblical theologians, he reports, have documented two different approaches to life. The decisive word-form in the language of the Bible is not the substantive, as in Greek, but the verb, the word of action. So the thought of the Bible is not substantive, neuter, and abstract, but verbal, historical, and personal.[45]

Although some regard these to be mutually exclusive approaches to life, they need not be. The Bible explicitly includes both Hebrew and Greek languages. It avoids the Greek philosopher's views of Being as impersonal, impassive, and inactive and teaches that the living Lord is changeless in being, attributes, and purposes. Far from immobile, the God of the Bible lives and acts in harmony with his immutable nature. He is faithful, true to himself, self-consistent. He cannot deny himself. Even Greek philosophers may have had some truth from the creation and common grace, but they seriously suppressed and distorted the divine immutability by confusing it with immobility.

The God of Scripture must be as sharply distinguished from the process theologians' God who is ever changing. If God is essentially dependent on the world and its evolutionary processes, he also is relative, time-bound, and unworthy of our worship.[46] Even the unbelieving can clearly see God's "eternal power and divine nature" (Rom 1:20) for God has made it plain to them (1:19). Contemporary process theology, like the ancient Greek inactive Being, results from suppression of general revelation.

To distinguish the living God from an immobile God of Greek philosophy, is not to dismiss all ontology or metaphysics. Endless paradoxes and contradictions result from trying to begin with the Greek's passive principles and move to the God who preserves, governs, judges, promises, calls, convicts, regenerates, converts, baptizes into the body of Christ, indwells, leads, guides, teaches, comforts, gives gifts, endues with power, and grants spiritual fruit. But a poor starting point does not justify dismissal of all conceptual thinking in theology. Rather, we start again with a biblical view of God's dynamic activities in harmony with his changeless attributes and purposes. Then the paradoxical muddles diminish.[47]

---

[44]Ibid., 45.

[45]Ibid., 45–46.

[46]D. G. Bloesch, *Essentials of Evangelical Theology* (San Francisco: Harper and Row, 1978), 1. 27–28.

[47]J. O. Buswell, Jr., "The Place of Paradox in Our Christian Testimony" *Journal of the American Philosophical Association* 16 (March 1964) 88–92.

Furthermore, biblical sentences include both substantives and verbs. More attention may need to be given to divine activities than has been customary, but complete sentences require both noun and verb and a balanced theology requires both. The pendulum may be swinging away from knowledge of substantive entities toward dynamic relationships and processes. At another time it may swing to the enduring entities. A biblical approach to theology can hardly regard them mutually exclusive. By means of divine revelation we may know God's acts and we may know the God who acts; we experience his loving relationship with us and we may know who it is that is relating. We know that he is faithful love, steadfast love, unchangeably loving, just, wise, and holy. Biblical teaching focuses not only on what God *does* but also on who God *is*. God told Moses to say, "I Am" has sent you (Exod 3:14). The psalmist and writer of Hebrews both stress the fact that though everything else grows old like a garment, God is the same; he changes not (Ps 102:25–27; Heb 1:10–12). Jesus told the woman at the well that God is spirit (John 4:24). "Although spoken for a practical purpose," said W. G. T. Shedd, "it is also a scientific definition." The noun "spirit" occurs first in the sentence for emphasis. Putting ourselves in the historical milieux, long before Kant's skepticism of knowing about things in themselves, the Scriptures clearly teach that the God who acts, hears prayer, and receives worship, is not flesh and bones (Luke 24:39), but an invisible, spiritual being.

Biblical teaching also spotlights Jesus' being as well as his doings. He did not say, "How am I coming across or relating?" His great concern was, "Who do people say the Son of man is?" (Matt 16:13). Frequently he said people should know that "I am" (John 8:23, 58; 13:19). He came from God and was one with the Father (John 8:42; 10:30). Hebrews explains, "The Son is the radiance of God's glory and the exact representation of his being" (Heb 1:3). What Jesus did on earth as man is crucial; what Jesus was, and is, is equally crucial. In speaking of Christ, the Bible does not limit itself to the categories of becoming, process, relating, loving, and functioning; it also utilizes the ontological categories of being.[48] The sufficiency of Christ's atonement, Athanasius argued, depends on who he *is*.

The Bible refers not only to particular persons, but also to people universally. "Adam" may designate mankind as well as the first man. Under condemnation are all Jews and all Gentiles (Rom 1–3). Universally, all people from all times and all cultures have sinned. Hence it is not unbiblical to speak of a doctrine of man or sin.

---

[48]See A. W. Klem, "D. M. Baillie on the Person of Christ," *BETS* 7 (Spring 1964) 45–52.

The Bible utilizes logical categories in referring to both being and becoming, such as the laws of identity, excluded middle, and noncontradiction. If Israel's election is by grace, then it is no longer by works; if it were, grace would no longer be grace (Rom 11:6). Paul teaches here that grace is grace and not nongrace; Israel's election cannot be on the basis of both grace and works; and since it is by grace, the contradictory notion that it is conditioned on works must be false.

The Bible also utilizes syllogistic reasoning (Gal 3:15-17). The structure of argument behind this passage could be expressed in two premises and their conclusion: (1) no duly established covenant is a covenant that can be set aside; (2) the Abrahamic covenant is a duly established covenant; and (3) therefore the Abrahamic covenant is not a covenant that is set aside by the law which came 430 years later.

Since the Bible sets a precedent for using basic laws of logic in its reasoning, the systematizing of biblical teaching with the help of logic cannot be condemned *a priori*. Both systematic theology and biblical theology are valuable and need each other. On the one hand, systematic theology must emphasize the unity of the Bible's teachings on given subjects, without disregarding the varied historical contexts in which those teachings appear. On the other hand, biblical theology must emphasize the diversity of presentations by different writers at different times without destroying the unity. Viewed in this way, the disciplines complement each other.

Biblical and systematic theology worked together, as Gerald Bray effectively showed, at Chalcedon:

> We have already argued that the ontological quest of the early church arose from an Old Testament view of God. In the same way, the need to express the reality of the incarnate Christ arose from, and was governed by, New Testament requirements. Chalcedon did not adopt philosophy; it took some basic philosophical words and forged a theology based on Scripture. Its logic is a systematization of the logic inherent in Scripture, not a philosophical corruption of primitive texts. For that reason, although it may be simplified for mass consumption, it can never be replaced. Ontological christology is part of the biblical revelation which cannot and must not be compromised in the name of historical and/or cultural relativism.[49]

Not only the doctrine of Christ, but also the doctrine of the Trinity arises from a coherent account of carefully exegeted biblical materials. B. B. Warfield expressed it well.

---

[49]G. E. Bray, "Can We Dispense with Chalcedon?" *Themelios* 3 (January 1978) 2-9.

The doctrine of the Trinity is given to us in Scripture, not in formulated definition, but in fragmentary allusions; when we assemble the *disjecta membra* into their organic unity, we are not passing from Scripture but entering more thoroughly into the meaning of Scripture.[50]

V. CONCLUSION

Baumer's book, with which this chapter began, ends its survey of *Modern European Thought* with a dismal chapter on "The Decline of the West." A chorus of experts despair of survival. However, Baumer discovered a consensus among humanists: "European civilization, if it was to survive, had to discover new roots, a new center for creative life." Jaspers cut deeper. "Civilization would be reconstructed only if and when man—individual man—discovered his selfhood, and thus gained the perspective and the power to resist dominion by apparatus." The hope for public improvement lay ultimately, not in expertise, but in "the very being of man," and in "the widening of his horizons by a return to metaphysics."[51]

While others at last are seeing the meaninglessness of life without knowledge of dependable being, many evangelicals are still trying to think exclusively in categories from the world of change. People reacting from *Future Shock* have had enough of John Dewey's functionalism or pragmatism, Sartre's existential nausea, and Esalen's encounter groups. In the name of God and his Word, evangelicals must offer more than another fluctuating experience. We must present and display an enduring experience founded on changeless *truth* about *reality*, about the ultimate *Being*, about the living and faithful Lord of all.

---

[50]B. B. Warfield, "Trinity," *International Standard Bible Encyclopedia* (Grand Rapids: Eerdmans, 1949), 5. 3012.

[51]Baumer, *Modern European Thought*, 512–13.

PART
FOUR

PASTORAL THEOLOGY

19

The Positive Case for the Ordination of Women

E. Margaret Howe

The present situation concerning women and leadership roles in the church[1] is one of inconsistency and confusion. Under the guise of "biblical viewpoint," myths are being perpetrated by the church which encourage congregations to deny to women the honor and dignity of their being. These myths encompass both sociological and theological issues. There is, for example, the concept that sexuality is in some way

---

[1] I have found the following books of particular significance in this discussion: C. K. Barrett, *The First Epistle to the Corinthians* (New York: Harper and Row, 1968); K. Stendahl, *The Bible and the Role of Women* (Philadelphia: Fortress, 1966); P. K. Jewett, *Man as Male and Female* (Grand Rapids: Eerdmans, 1975); D. Williams, *The Apostle Paul and Women in the Church* (Van Nuys, CA: *BIM*, 1977); D. R. Kuhns, *Women in the Church* (Scottdale, PA: Herald, 1978); Letha Scanzoni and Nancy Hardesty, *All We're Meant to Be* (Waco, Texas: Word, 1974); Virginia Mollenkott, *Women, Men and the Bible* (Nashville: Abingdon, 1977); Mary Daly, *The Church and the Second Sex* (New York: Harper and Row, 1968). Writers such as Elizabeth Elliott, Ruth Graham, George Knight, and Larry Christenson, have enabled me to identify the thought patterns which are currently influencing some sections of the Christian community. Robert K. Johnston has provided a significant contribution to the debate by concentrating attention on the hermeneutical problems involved and by offering guidelines which would lead towards consistency in evangelical thought. See "The Role of Women in the Church and Home: An Evangelical Testcase in Hermeneutics," *Scripture, Tradition, and Interpretation,* W. W. Gasque and W. S. LaSor, eds. (Grand Rapids: Eerdmans, 1978) 234–59.

evil, and that female sexuality is more debased than that of the male. This is sometimes linked with the idea that a woman is primarily a sex object and that she only assumes wholeness and personhood as she relates to the male. The male, on the other hand, is complete in himself. Furthermore, the woman is often represented as being a constant source of temptation to a man, while the reverse is seldom considered. As such, she is cast in the role of the temptress, enticing men from holy living to the pursuit of sensual pleasure. If the male is overcome by her charm, she must bear the guilt. Clearly neither revelation nor logic could be adduced in support of such theses.

Another myth which basically influences these issues is that concerning the essential nature of God. The Genesis creation narratives state that, "God created man in his own image" (Gen 1:27). Although the continuation of this verse reads, "male and female created he them," clarifying that the image of God is represented in the complementary nature of men and women, that word "man" is frequently interpreted in a sexual rather than a generic sense. The male of the species, it is claimed, is most truly representative of God. This understanding is confirmed by OT imagery which represents God as "father." Those passages in the Hebrew Scriptures which typify God as "mother" are overlooked,[2] and the image is interpreted as though in some mystical sense it were the reality.[3] The sexuality of God is therefore stressed, rather than his personhood. Similarly, significance is given to the fact that Mary gave birth to a *male* child who was to be called "Son of the Most High" (Luke 1:32). That this was not theologically necessary is overlooked.[4] Indeed the theological rationale would point in another direction, for the atonement sacrifice in Judaism was to consist in the offering of the female of the species, so that the maleness of Jesus presents some difficulties as well as some reassurances.[5] Certainly we are in the realms of mythology when we conceptualize God as male, rather than female, just as we would be if we considered him to be female rather than male. The being of God transcends the limitations of sexuality.

The influence such thinking has had upon the present debate is far reaching. Because God is male, only the male may represent him. The Jewish priesthood was exclusively male, it is argued, and Jesus chose

---

[2] E.g. Isa 49:15.

[3] Cf. C. S. Lewis, "Priestesses in the Church?" *God in the Dock* (Grand Rapids: Eerdmans, 1970) 236–8.

[4] Cf. P. K. Jewett, "Why I Favor the Ordination of Women," *Christianity Today* (June 6, 1975) 10.

[5] S. Katz, "Christology: A Jewish View," *SJT* 24 (1971) 196.

twelve men to carry out his mission of evangelism and teaching. The issue of priesthood is a pertinent one. The priest represents God to the people in pronouncing forgiveness. This forgiveness comes about on the basis of the sacrificial system. But the reformed tradition regards the death of Jesus as the ultimate sacrifice, offered once on behalf of all, never to be repeated. With the end of the sacrificial system there comes about the end of this aspect of the priestly function. The church as a whole now assumes the responsibility of pronouncing forgiveness.[6] The fact that the Hebrew Scriptures speak of women as prophets but nowhere as priests is thus irrelevant to the discussion, unless perhaps it could be linked significantly with the fact that the church is "built upon the foundation of the apostles and prophets,"[7] whereas the Jewish community was built upon the prophetic and priestly functions. The NT teaching concerning the priesthood of all believers[8] indicates that the complementary function of the priest, that of representing the people before God, is also shared by the believing community. In any case, representing God to the people and the people to God is only one aspect of the ministerial function. The minister also represents the church to the world. And as the church is frequently described as the "bride" of Christ in the NT, a woman might well communicate this symbolism more effectively than a man.[9]

In order to jettison the accumulated debris of the ages, it is necessary to turn to the pages of Scripture. Even here caution is needed. It is possible at the level of translation for errors of judgment to be made, so that what is printed in the English text may perchance reflect the value judgment of the translator, rather than the intention of the original writer. For example, Paul commends to the church in Rome, "our sister, Phoebe, a deaconess of the church in Cenchreae" (Rom 16:1, RSV). The word used in Greek is actually not deaconess but deacon (the feminine form of the word was not in use at this time). It would perhaps have been better to retain the word *deacon,* so that it would be clear to the reader that the office referred to is identical to that held by men.[10] However a further and more disturbing problem

---

[6]Matt 18:18; Jas 5:16.

[7]Eph 2:20.

[8]1 Pet 2:5, 9; Cf. Exod 19:6; Rev 1:6; 5:10.

[9]Cf. P. K. Jewett, "Why I Favor the Ordination of Women," 9.

[10]F. F. Bruce, in a personal letter, "I do not care for the appointment of women as deaconesses, because when that term is used it so often implies some inferiority to deacons. . . . Let them be called deacons, as Phoebe was" (November 2, 1978).

arises here. The same word is used in Colossians to describe Epaphras (1:7), Paul (1:25), and Tychicus (4:7). In these three latter instances, the RSV translates the word as "minister." To be consistent then, the RSV should have rendered Rom 16:1, "our sister Phoebe, a minister of the church at Cenchreae." The prejudice which prevented such a translation is reflected also in Kittel's *Theological Dictionary*.[11] H. W. Beyer, in his consideration of διάκονος, lists its occurrence in Romans 16:1 separately from its occurrence in the other passages referred to above. Beyer questions whether in this one instance the reference is to a fixed office or whether it is merely an acknowledgment of Phoebe's services on behalf of the congregation. The issue is presumed not to be viable in the instances in which a man is named. Beyer has worked back from his own concept of a woman's role to the biblical text, and in so doing has done a great disservice to NT scholars.[12]

Similar bias can be found in the RSV translation of Rom 16:7, where ἐπίσημοι ἐν τοῖς ἀποστόλοις is translated "*men* of note among the apostles," rather than "people of note among the apostles." This does not permit the average reader to discern that there is uncertainty whether the second person named is a female (Junia) or a male (Junias).[13] The translator has assumed (without conclusive evidence) that the person referred to is male, and has confirmed this assumption by excluding any possible female reference in the qualifying clause which follows. The translator has decided on *a priori* grounds that a woman, in his opinion, could not have been an apostle, and has therefore precluded that possibility from becoming apparent in the text. The reader of the English Bible is frequently misled also in the rendering of the word γυναῖκας in 1 Tim 3:11. The KJV and many popular modern renderings (NEB, NIV, Living Bible, Good News, etc.), translate this word as "wives" rather than "women," so that the instructions given are understood as having reference to the wives of deacons rather than to women deacons. This kind of translation bias may well be "unworthy of the age in which we live," but it must nevertheless be taken into consideration.

Among the inconsistencies with which this debate is riddled is the matter concerning the role of women as teachers. "I do not permit a

---

[11] *TDNT*, 2. 88-93.

[12] The KJV is even more devious here. Phoebe is described only as a "servant" of the church in Cenchrae, thus concealing the true nature of her office; while Epaphras, Paul, and Tychicus are described as "ministers" in Col 1:7, 25; 4:7.

[13] Cf. F. F. Bruce, *The Epistle of Paul to the Romans* (Grand Rapids: Eerdmans, 1963) 271.

woman to teach," the author of the Pastorals boldly writes.[14] Leaving the source critical issues aside, this has generally been interpreted as meaning that a woman must not occupy a pulpit to deliver the formal sermon in a Sunday gathering of the congregation. Naturally this would preclude her from the ordained ministry of the church. But carried to its logical conclusion, if we are to take the saying at face value and without regard to the rest of Scripture, this dictum actually prohibits much more than that.

The teaching ministry of the church cannot be limited in this way to one sacred location or time period. And if we view this ministry in its wider context, it becomes apparent that those churches which have denied to women the pulpit and the salary, have yet drawn heavily upon the teaching ministry of women. The great hymns of the church which instruct and inspire, include among their number those written by women such as Fanny Jane Crosby, Charlotte Elliott, and Frances Ridley Havergal. A vast volume of Sunday School literature, written to instruct student and teacher alike, has been master-minded by women under the guidance of the Holy Spirit. Countless books and magazine articles written by women have been used by God to instruct, edify, convict, and reprove men. And most churches pursue a Sunday school program staffed predominantly by women. Is such a teaching ministry as this for some reason excluded from the Pastoral rubric? So that a woman may in fact "teach," but not from the pulpit? And if so, by whom have these contours been drawn?[15] Finally, there are many churches which, while denying to women the pulpit and ministerial office in the secure environment of the home country, will yet commission women to act in the role of apostle, evangelist, and teacher in the stressful environment of the foreign mission field, where the responsibilities are often heavier and the financial remuneration is slight. When the danger is passed and the church well established, do we then appoint only men to the ministry?

It is situations such as these which lay the church open to the strong suspicion that ulterior motives are responsible for the exclusion of women from ministerial positions. Once the Bible verse has been quoted, it is interpreted and reinterpreted according to the color of

---

[14]I Tim 2:12.

[15]Some churches attempt to overcome such inconsistencies by claiming that women may teach women. In 1 Tim 2:12 they read ἀνδρός as the object of διδάσκειν as well as of αὐθεντεῖν and therefore exclude women only from teaching men. Other churches permit a woman to teach also preadolescent boys, assuming that Timothy as a child was taught by his mother and grandmother. Both of these interpretations are open to question.

the local congregation. "I do not permit a woman to teach" becomes, "We do not permit a woman to preach," or "We do not permit a woman to be paid for teaching," or "We do not permit a woman to teach in America." Yet while embracing attitudes such as these, the church has piously sought to present to the world an appearance of holding to scriptural guidelines. Is it only coincidence that Sunday school teachers are not paid for their ministry, while those who teach from the pulpit are generously rewarded for their work? Is it a matter of chance that the position which carries with it honor and respect and a title is open exclusively to men, while those offices which are background ministries, carrying little recognition, may be cheerfully designated to women? Does the Bible really imply that a woman may be as fully involved in the ministry of the church as a man, but may not receive the honor and recognition and financial remuneration that he receives? If this text is indeed an ontological injunction forbidding a woman to teach in a church context, then let women be withdrawn completely from the teaching ministry of the church. But if, in the light of other Scripture, it becomes apparent that women do have a significant leadership role to fulfill, then let the church be consistent in apportioning honor.

Much of the confusion characterizing the modern debate has arisen from a lack of understanding concerning the relationship between structure and function in the early church. When we speak of the ordination of Christian ministers, we are speaking of the appointment of certain individuals to leadership roles, in recognition of their gifts and calling. These leadership roles, however, are not clearly defined in the NT. Various titles are used, apostle, bishop, deacon, elder, prophet, and so on; various functions are indicated, preaching, teaching, baptizing, healing, and so on; and guidelines are given concerning the qualities of character to be looked for in those who aspire to such position. But little indication is given concerning the precise nature of any such ministry. For example, the offices of deacon and bishop are thought by many to have been foreshadowed in the division of duties mentioned in Acts 6. "Serving tables" is often taken as a reference to the ministry of a deacon, while "prayer and the ministry of the word" is understood as defining the function of a bishop. However, Stephen, designated to the former category, was apparently involved for the most part in a ministry of teaching.[16] The sermon attributed to him by Luke is one of the most perceptive and significant of all those recorded in the Book of Acts.[17] Philip, appointed to "serve

---

[16] Acts 6:8–10.
[17] Acts 7:1–53.

tables," was involved in a ministry of preaching and baptizing.[18] If Acts 6 is to be taken as definitive for the role of deacon, then we must acknowledge that women serving as deacons in the early church were involved in a ministry which included that of teaching, preaching, and baptizing. If we do not take Acts 6 as definitive of this role, then we must acknowledge that the NT is silent on the issue and the local church must assign content to the office. But let it not then claim that its authority is the Word of God.

Similar confusion surrounds the role of prophet in the early Christian community. Again the problem is one of lack of clear differentiation in the NT documents, but the guidelines which are available demonstrate conclusively that prophecy was an activity which convicted nonchristians and edified Christians, and that Paul considered this activity to be possibly the most significant contribution a person could make during a formal gathering of the church (1 Cor 14:1–25). It would be reasonable to suppose, then, that Philip's daughters (Acts 21:9) were involved in a ministry of preaching and teaching. This would be in accord with the Hebrew Scriptures, "Your sons and daughters shall prophesy" (Joel 2:28). Paul, therefore, had no qualms about the fact that women in Corinth were prophesying in mixed gatherings of the church.[19] His only concern was that in so doing they should maintain their sexual identity as women, and that this should be reflected in their manner of dress, just as a man in a similar position should preserve his identity as a man, and this should be reflected in his manner of dress. A woman appointed to a leadership position in the church is not adopting a male role; nor, on the other hand does she stand before the congregation as a sex object. A woman leading public worship does so in relation to God, not in relation to a man. Her hair and shoulders are to be covered because in the redemptive order she stands before God as man's equal, not as the object of man's desire. Thus the veil is a symbol of her "authority," authority invested in her by God as a result of the redemptive work of Christ in whom "there is neither male nor female" (Gal 3:28). In the light of these careful instructions, it would be presumptuous to argue that Paul's later comments in this letter (14:34–35) preclude a woman from ordination on the basis that she is not permitted to speak in the church. Whatever the situation Paul has in mind here, it is clearly not one which concerns a woman's right to lead public worship.

Confusion has also arisen from the Pastoral injunction concerning women "exercising authority" over men. It might well be cautionary

---

[18] Acts 8:26–40.
[19] I Cor 11:2–16; cf. C. K. Barrett, *First Epistle to the Corinthians*, 247–58.

to re-examine the essential nature of Christian leadership. While it is true that Jesus gave to his disciples authority to preach and to heal,[20] and that Paul could claim authority granted to him be exercised on occasion in the context of strong admonition and church discipline,[21] it is also true that Jesus explicitly commanded his disciples that they were not to "lord it" over people, as did certain secular leaders. In contradistinction to these, the disciples of Jesus were to note that Jesus himself was among them as a servant, and that, "a servant is not greater than his master."[22] Peter specifies that leadership in the church does not give license for "domineering over" other people.[23] As the basic pattern for leadership appears to be one of *service,* it is hard to see in what sense an ordained woman would be "exercising authority" over a man in a way which would be unacceptable. Some might also reconsider this aspect of the relationship between husband and wife which is so frequently brought into the discussion. Jesus said, "I am among you as he who *serves.*"[24] If the husband is to base his relationship to the wife on this pattern, then the woman will be the one who gives direction to the marriage, and the man will be the one who contributes support.[25] This would re-establish the pattern reflected in Genesis 3 where the woman is the one who is consulted about a decision which affects both husband and wife, and it is she who initiates the course of action.[26] One should bear in mind, however, that the more basic NT principle is one of *mutual* submission, and this needs to be reflected in the church structure no less than in the family unit. Leadership which makes an exclusive claim to the decision-making process rather than functioning on the basis of mutual submission is unbiblical whether it is exercised by a man or a woman, and whether it functions in the church unit or that of the home.

For more specific guidance concerning the essential nature of Christian leadership, attention must be given to the relationship between charismatic endowment and the ordination of ministers. The sparse evidence the NT offers relating to church structure seems to

---

[20]Matt 10:1–7.

[21]1 Cor 5:3–5; 2 Cor 10:8.

[22]Luke 22:24–27; John 16:20.

[23]1 Pet 5:3.

[24]Luke 22:27.

[25]This is not out of harmony with 1 Cor 11:3 if "head" is understood as "source." Cf. C. K. Barrett, *First Epistle to the Corinthians,* 248–9.

[26]Cf. J. M. Higgins, "Anastasius Sinaita and the Superiority of the Woman," *JBL* 97 2 (1978), 253–6.

indicate that structure is subservient to task. The principal task of the church in community is to edify its diverse membership. The medium through which this is to be accomplished is that of spiritual gifts. These are distributed variously throughout the congregation, without respect to sex. There is not the slightest hint in the relevant Scriptures that those gifts which would equip for leadership positions (preaching, teaching, prophesying, etc.) will be restricted to men, while those equipping for other ministries (giving of money, practicing hospitality, demonstrating love, etc.) will be bequeathed on women. The apostle states unequivocally that the Holy Spirit distributes gifts to each one as *he* wills.[27] The recipient of a gift (and no Christian is excluded) has a responsibility to use that gift for the *common* good. The example of the human body is used to clarify this point. In a body there are both diversity and unity. The gifts are different, but the purpose for which they are given is the same. They are all intended as a means of upbuilding the body as a unit. If a person has the gift of prophecy, that person is under an obligation to use that gift for the upbuilding of the entire congregation, not for some section differentiated by sexual characteristics. If gifts equipping for leadership positions are distributed *by God* to women, what higher authority does the church have for denying to women their expression?

In drawing conclusions from this data, it is necessary to recognize that some anomalies arise from the nature of the source material. It is not clear from the NT documents which ministries required official ordination and which were considered a part of the lay ministry of the church. Official titles are unclear, and the nature of each office is open to speculation. The title *elder,* for example, may well have been a general designation for the offices of bishop and deacon, rather than an indication of a third category of ministry. The title of *minister,* which is commonly in use today, is imprecise. Apostles, bishops, and deacons are all ministers of the church, and the word may be used with reference to any of these offices.

For this reason, caution must be exercised in offering a rationale for the present day position of the church with respect to ordination. To say that a woman may not be ordained as a minister because she is not permitted to teach, is to perpetuate inadequate argumentation. Women are designated as deacons in the NT, and they are designated as prophetesses. Both of these ministries involve teaching. To exclude a woman from the ministry on the basis that the OT priesthood was exclusively male, is to overlook the indications that the NT ministerial model approximates more closely to that of the Hebrew prophet than

---

[27]1 Cor 12:11.

that of the Jewish priest. To withhold ordination from women on the premise that God is best represented by a male figure, is to perpetuate the misconception that God partakes of human sexuality and is male.

If women are represented in the NT as fulfilling functions known to be associated with leadership positions, it is reasonable to assume that they were in fact appointed to the offices associated with such activities, and that they bore the same titles as those assigned to men in similar ministries. This assumption is confirmed by the evidence of the NT itself. Although there are some passages which give us pause for thought, these are few in number. The overwhelming impression communicated by the Pauline writings is that the Pauline communities affirmed the leadership role of women as being both theologically viable and practically effective.

Those who claim that the present day church is not suppressing women's gifts, need to look more honestly at the situation. If women have gifts relating to administration, decision making, preaching, and teaching, and yet are excluded from roles in which these can be effectively exercised, then the church is definitely suppressing the gifts of women. Those who claim to be reaffirming "the historic Christian position,"[28] need to analyze carefully the nature of that position. Unknowingly, they may well be perpetuating the traditions of men rather than implementing the purposes of God.

---

[28]G. W. Knight, "The New Testament Teaching on the Role Relationship of Male and Female," *JETS* 18 2 (1975) 82.

20

The Negative Case Against the Ordination of Women

Robert L. Saucy

In seeking to set forth the negative case against the ordination of women, it is necessary at the outset to clarify the limited meaning of ordination in this particular context. According to biblical usage, ordination as a public recognition and appointment was practiced for a variety of functions including the seven in Acts 6 and the sending of Paul and Barnabas as missionaries in Acts 13. Understood in this broad biblical usage it is not our intention to argue for the exclusion of women from ordination. Our concern is directed only to the question of the ordination of women to the function of elder or bishop as the highest authoritative position of the church.

I. THE SUBORDINATION OF WOMEN

There are three passages in the New Testament which would appear to have a direct bearing on this issue. The first two concern activities of women in the church while the third relates to a certain propriety of dress. It is important for the question before us to note that in each of these passages the primary concept is the maintenance of a certain order between man and woman in the church.

In 1 Corinthians 14:34–35 Paul writes, "Let the women keep silence in the churches; for they are not permitted to speak, but let them subject themselves, just as the Law also says. And if they desire to learn anything, let them ask their own husbands at home; for it is improper for a woman to speak in church" (NASB). To seek to explicate the specific nature of the silence enjoined here by the apostle is beyond the scope of our discussion. Perhaps it is best explained in the context as a reference to the discussion and judgments of prophecies given in the church (cf. v. 29). The church at this time may have also had the congregation divided with the men on one side and the women on the other as in the Jewish synagogues. The asking of questions by the women to their husbands on the other side would certainly have produced disorder. It goes without saying that a knowledge of the cultural setting would be necessary for the proper understanding of this injunction.

The primary point of this instruction however, whatever its exact nature may have been, was that by its observance women would "subject themselves" according to the law, which as Bruce suggests probably has reference to the creation narratives of Genesis 1 and 2.[1] In other words, to fail to obey this particular injunction in this situation would be a failure on the part of the women to subject themselves according to the law of God.

The words "subject themselves" come from the Gr verb ὑποτάσσω which literally means "to order under." It signifies a subordination, but carries no necessary concept of a personal inferiority of the one in the subordinate position. This is evident in its use for the people of Israel who are subordinate to David (Ps 143:2 LXX), the members of the church to their church leaders (1 Cor 16:16), and even Jesus to his parents (Luke 2:51).

Turning to Paul's instructions in 1 Timothy 2:11–12 we find the same basic concern for the proper order between man and woman. This time it is expressed in relation to the function of teaching. "Let a woman quietly receive instruction with entire submissiveness. But I do not allow a woman to teach or exercise authority over a man, but to remain quiet" (NASB). Again the primary issue is not teaching *per se* for it is obvious that women performed this function in the church with propriety under the right circumstances (e.g. Titus 2:3–4). The issue is teaching in a way which would negate the characteristic of "submissiveness" and in so doing "exercise authority over a man." The word "submissiveness" is the noun form of the same Gr word mentioned previously denoting an "ordering under," while the Gr word used for the prohibition against exercising authority over a man signifies domineering over someone.[2] Again the apostle's instruction was designed to preserve a proper order between man and

---

[1]F. F. Bruce, *I and II Corinthians*, New Century Bible (London: Marshall, Morgan and Scott, 1971) 136.

[2]BAG, 120.

woman. The action prohibited was such which would have negated this order.

The third passage with direct bearing on this issue involves the discussion of the head covering in 1 Corinthians 11. Again the emphasis is on an order between man and woman in which man is said to be the "head" of the woman. It is beyond the scope of our task to enter into a full discussion of the meaning of the word "head" (κεφαλή). Though it may well denote origin here in Paul's usage, implying as Schlier notes, "one who stands over another in the sense of being the ground of his being,"[3] the resulting order is also present. Barrett aptly ties these two thoughts together when he concludes concerning the various headships mentioned in this passage, "thus a chain of originating and subordinating relationships is set up: God, Christ, man, woman."[4]

From these passages that refer directly to the relation of man and woman in the church we are compelled to conclude that the apostle clearly teaches a fundamental order in the church, one in which the woman is ordered under the man. It is exactly the same order which is found in other passages relative to the husband and wife in the home (cf. Eph 5:21ff.; Col 3:18-19; 1 Pet 3:1-7). We would reiterate with emphasis that this order concerns function and role. It in no way implies personal superiority anymore than do the orders between parents and children, citizens and government, or people and church leaders.

II. THE ORDER BETWEEN MAN AND WOMAN IN CREATION

When we examine the Scriptures concerning the rationale for the order between man and woman we find that whenever reason is given for this order it is found in the relationship of man and woman in the creation account (1 Cor 11:3ff.; 1 Tim 2:13). In one instance the apostle mentions the deception of the woman in the fall (1 Tim 2:14). But that is only added after primary reference has already been made to the order of creation.

The creation of man and woman is given to us in two complementary accounts. In Genesis 1 man and woman are viewed in their relationship to their Creator and the rest of creation. Here the emphasis is upon their absolute equality as human beings before God. Both par-

---

[3]H. Schlier, "κεφαλή," TDNT 3. 679.
[4]C. K. Barrett, *The First Epistle to the Corinthians* (New York: Harper & Row, 1968) 249.

take equally in the divine image and in the mandate of rulership over the rest of creation (1:26–28).

In the more detailed account of the second chapter we find the creation of man and woman in relationship to each other. It is from this account that the Scriptures draw the rationale for an order between man and woman. Two truths are highlighted in this account which are later made the basis of an order between man and woman. The first is simply the order of creation, man is created before woman (Gen 2:18–23). Paul refers to this both in 1 Corinthians 11:8 and 1 Timothy 2:13. An additional thought of the woman originating from the man is added in the Corinthian passage. The second truth noted is the fact that woman was created "for the man's sake" (1 Cor 11:9; cf. Gen 2:18–23). In the Genesis account she is referred to as "a helper suitable for him" (2:18, 20). That the word "helper" does not connote personal inferiority is evident from its use for God as the helper of man. It merely points to the functional role of woman as the complementary helper of man. It is always from these two fundamental truths concerning the relation of the man to the woman in the creation account that the apostle draws his basis for an order between man and woman in the church.

Now this is especially significant in the light of the frequent assertion today that anything other than a pure egalitarian relationship is the result of the entrance of sin and the perversion of God's design. Redemption from sin and its power is thus said to include the abolishment of any order between man and woman which smacks of subordination. Contrary to this interpretation, as we have seen, the Scriptures ground the relationship between man and woman in God's good creation before the Fall. To be sure sin has brought discord into this order as it has in all of God's cosmos. Harshness and self-centered injustice have frequently replaced the divinely intended operational principle of love. But sin is never cited as the cause of the order itself. God's statement to fallen woman in Genesis 3:16 that her husband would rule over her is not the source of the order, nor is it ever cited in later Scripture as such. It rather points to the fact that with the entrance of sin and the obvious disruption of the man-woman order in the Fall, the divine order remains but sin's effect will now be experienced within the order.

Redemption from sin works to negate these disruptive elements and restore the principle of love to the order, but it does not abolish the order itself which was a prior part of the good creation. As Conzelmann comments in his discussion of I Corinthians 11, "... the order of salvation does not abrogate the order of the world."[5]

---

[5]H. Conzelmann, *I Corinthians* (Philadelphia: Fortress) 188, n. 75.

III. THE ORDER OF MAN AND WOMAN IN REDEMPTION

Much of the contemporary discussion of the relation between man and woman turns on one's understanding of the apostle's statement in Galatians 3:28: " . . . there is neither male nor female; for you are all one in Christ Jesus." Proponents of the ordination of women frequently appeal to this text as evidence that redemption abolishes all order between man and woman. All of the references which manifestly teach such an order must give way by some means of interpretation to this clear statement of theology according to this view. Examination of this passage, however, demonstrates that it is far from a clear statement which abolishes all order between man and woman. All would certainly have to agree that some distinction yet remains between the sexes. Since that is true, the interpretive question is: What is the distinction between male and female which is overcome in Christ? To phrase it another way in light of the apostle's statement "for you are all one in Christ Jesus," what is the "oneness" which male and female share in Christ? We would like to suggest several thoughts which indicate that the answers to these questions do not concern the functional order between man and woman at all. Rather the issue, as in the other two pairs mentioned, concerns spiritual status before God.

1. This is suggested first of all by the context of this verse as well as the entire Book of Galatians. The issue in the church at Galatia was the theological question of the place of the law, specifically circumcision, and the basis of acceptance with God. The immediate context surrounding verse 28 makes this abundantly clear when we note the following phrases (italics added):

v 26 " . . . you are *all sons of God through faith in Christ Jesus.*"
v 27 " . . . *all* of you who were *baptized into Christ have clothed yourselves in Christ.*"
v 28 " . . . you are *all one in Christ Jesus.*"
v 29 " . . . if you *belong to Christ,* then you are *Abraham's offspring, heirs according to promise.*"

The thrust of these statements is the truth that all are equally sons of God; all are equally clothed with Christ; all are equally heirs of the promise. Nothing whatsoever is said about all being equal functionally in the church or for that matter in the home or in the state. To impart the issue of the functional orders of human society into this passage is to impute a meaning not justified by a valid contextual exegesis. There is therefore no more basis for abolishing the order between man and woman in the church from Galatians 3:28 than for abolishing an order between believing parents and children or believing citizens and rulers. For they are all in one Christ in or out of the organization of the church.

2. A second point to note which is corroborative of the fact that spiritual standing is the issue in 3:28 is the fact that all three of the examples of distinctions which are transcended in Christ involved religious distinctions in the time of the NT.

It is not necessary for us to elaborate at great length the position of women in ancient Judaism. While there are statements praising the virtuous and righteous woman, these are outweighed by statements and practices which demonstrate that women were considered personally and religiously inferior to men. Jeremias sums up the evidence when he says,

> We have therefore the impression that Judaism in Jesus' time also had a very low view of women, which is usual in the Orient where she is chiefly valued for her fecundity, kept as far as possible shut away from the outer world, submissive to the power of her father or her husband, and where she is inferior to men from a religious point of view.[6]

The apostle's concern with Judaizing tendencies at Galatia suggests that his audience would have been largely conditioned with this attitude toward women. And even though, according to Oepke, there was a greater measure of freedom the further west one went toward Greece and Rome, even in these cultures women were still considered less than men.[7]

The same personal and religious inferiority was assigned to slaves in comparison to free men. Rengstorf writes:

> For Judaism in the time of Jesus as for the Greek world, the slave was on a lower level of humanity. . . . In the cultic sphere this meant that the slave was subject to cultic obligations only to a limited extent. At this point the slave was like a wife, his cultic subordination being thus strongly emphasized. Above all, however, slaves were ethically inferior, being subject to the law only to a limited degree.[8]

Finally, the "Greek," who is here the equivalent of the Gentile as opposed to the Jew, definitely stood on inferior religious ground. In the view of Rabbinic Judaism, the non-Israelite was a stranger to God, being far from him. Gentiles including their families, houses, and

---

[6]J. Jeremias, *Jerusalem in the Time of Jesus* (Philadelphia: Fortress, 1962) 375. Cf. also A. Oepke "γυνή," TDNT 1. 781-4.

[7] Ibid., 777.

[8]K. H. Rengstorf, "δοῦλος," TDNT 2. 271.

lands were unclean.[9] The visible evidence of this thought in New Testament times was the Outer Court of the Gentiles which according to Josephus was separated from the inner areas of the temple precincts by a five foot wall. Gentiles with an offering were permitted beyond this wall, but only to a place between the Court of the Gentiles and the Court of Women. Beyond the Court of Women were still the Court of the Sons of Israel and the Court of the Priests.[10]

Certain aspects of the distinction between Jews and Gentiles had been rightfully grounded in the outworking of God's salvation history. The apostle himself notes that the Gentiles had been "without God in the world" and "far off." But now they have been "brought near by the blood of Christ" (Eph 2:12–13). They are now equally as near as the Jew so as to form "one new man" in Christ (2:15). This theology of unity in the Book of Ephesians is the same theology which the apostle presses home to the Galatian church. In Christ Jew and Gentile share the same spiritual standing.

The recognition of these spiritual differentiations which existed in the historical situation between Jew and Greek, slave and free man, and male and female make it all the more evident that it is the transcending of these differences which Paul has in mind in Galatians 3:28. In this connection one is reminded of the frequently quoted prayer in which the Jewish man gives thanks to God that he has not made him a woman, a Gentile, or a slave, the very three categories mentioned by the apostle.

3. One further evidence of this interpretation may be gleaned from the specific words which the apostle uses in this verse, namely "male" and "female." When we examine the passages that clearly refer to an order between man and woman we find that in every instance the terms used are "man" and "woman" or in the context of marriage "husband" and "wife." The latter terms, "man" and "woman" or "husband" and "wife," translate the Gr words ἀνήρ and γυνή while "male" and "female" come from ἄρσην and θῆλυς.

The immediate question that arises is, why, if the apostle is speaking of the functional relationship in Galatians 3:28, does he not use the language which he uses in every other passage? Why does he not say, "there is neither man nor woman" in Christ rather than "male" and "female"? If, as many say, he is giving the ideal of egalitarianism here

---

[9]Cf. A. Bietenhard, "People, Nation, Gentiles, Crowd, City," *The New International Dictionary of New Testament Theology* (Grand Rapids: Zondervan, 1976) 2. 791-2.

[10]M. Barth, *Ephesians 1-3*, The Anchor Bible (Garden City: Doubleday, 1974) 283.

and only commanding subordination of the woman as a temporary
provision in deference to the patriarchal culture, why does he not
make this clear by using the same words for both that we might
recognize that the ideal is designed to ultimately transform the temporary practice?

We would suggest that the change of terms is deliberate and sup-
portive of the fact that the issue of Galatians 3:28 is not the functional
relationship between man and woman, but rather their relationship
before God. The terms ἄρσην and θῆλυς (male and female) denote a
strong emphasis on sex and are used together to express emphatic
sexual distinction.[11] Ἀνήρ and γυνή (man and woman), on the other
hand, denote man in relation to woman in terms of their dominant
characteristics.[12] This latter meaning is obviously more appropriate
when the functional roles of man and woman are under consideration; for it is in function, especially in relation to each other, where the
dominant characteristics of each would be particularly applicable.

This concept is further supported when we go back to the Genesis
record. In Genesis chapter 1, where we argued earlier that man and
woman are seen in relation to God and the rest of creation, they are
called "male" and "female" (Gen 1:27; זָכָר, נְקֵבָה or ἄρσην, θῆλυς). In
Genesis 2, however, where we find the creation of man and woman in
relation to each other and the first marriage the words "man" and
"woman" are used (Gen 2:22–24 אִישׁ, אִשָּׁה or ἀνήρ, γυνή). Therefore
when the apostle uses the terminology "male" and "female" in Galatians 3:28 he is using the language of Genesis 1 and we would suggest
has the theology of this chapter in mind. As we have indicated, in his
day, as has probably been the case in all times since the entrance of
sin, the personal equality of man and woman was denied. By virtue of
greater strength man has often exerted himself sinfully treating
woman as an inferior being rather than an equal person before God.
It is this effect of sin which the apostle affirms is overturned through
redemption. In Christ male and female stand on equal terms spiritually before God even as they did in the good creation.

If our interpretation based on this verbal usage is correct, it is one
more evidence that the apostle in Galatians 3:28 is concerned with the
spiritual standing of man and woman before God. He is not con-
tradicting what he said in other places concerning an order between
man and woman in the church, as well as in the home, based upon the
order of creation from Genesis 2.

We therefore conclude that a proper interpretation of this verse,

---

[11]A. Oepke, "ἀνήρ," TDNT 1. 362.
[12]BAG 65–66, 167.

based upon the context, the historical-cultural situation, and the words used, does not support an egalitarian abolishment of the functional order between man and woman which is clearly taught in other passages. The argument based upon this verse which is frequently set forth that since true Christianity was ultimately influential in the abolishment of slavery, it was likewise intended to finally abolish all distinction between man and woman founders on at least two counts. First, the relationship involved in slavery and that between man and woman can never be viewed as analogous in Scripture. The latter is grounded in God's creation, the former is not. Second, while slavery as such was abolished, the principle of an order between employer and employee yet remains as a very legitimate application of the biblical injunctions to both slaves and masters.

If Galatians 3:28 does not teach the abolishment of the order of man and woman in salvation, there would appear to be no didactic support in Scripture for such a position. If such is the case, we are left with the alternative of accepting Paul's clear teaching of an order based upon his understanding of the biblical teaching of the relationship of man and woman in creation, or denying his interpretation in favor of our own better understanding of man and woman based upon contemporary anthropological, sociological, psychological, or political knowledge. It is difficult to see how one who accepts the apostle as an inspired teacher of faith and practice can refuse his teaching on the implication of the creation account of Genesis 2.

Evidence for the ordination of women is sometimes claimed from the terminology applied to women in the NT church. The appellations "fellow workers," "διάκονος" or "deacon," and "prophetess" are all on occasion applied to women who ministered in the church. It is beyond the scope of this presentation to discuss each instance involved save to say that none of these can be shown to refer to the highest authoritative office of the church.

Finally, the OT example of Deborah is set forth as a clear case of woman leadership (Judg 4:4–5:31). May we say in this regard that there may be instances when the regular pattern of God's order may have to be temporarily set aside due to unusual circumstances. When, for example, the husband and father is absent, the woman of the house assumes the headship of the family. So it would appear, there may be unusual circumstances when male leadership is unavailable for one reason or another. At such times God may use women to accomplish his purposes even as he used Deborah.

We would conclude therefore that the Scriptures teach the absolute personal equality of man and woman as human beings in the image of God. They just as clearly teach a basic pattern of functional order applicable to the church which is grounded in God's good creation. The different roles assigned to man and woman must never be allowed to negate their absolute personal equality. But likewise, their personal equality cannot be used to abolish the functional order between them. Obedience to the Word of God necessitates upholding both of these truths in our attitudes and actions within the church.

INDEX

Development, 144; in
  Pauline thought,
  195–207
Dipolar theism, 21–22.
  See also Process theol-
  ogy
Dispensationalism,
  163–76
Dogmatics, 6–7, 12
DuBois, W. E. B., 153
Dutch Reformed
  Church, 84–85
Dynamism, recovery of
  (task of systematic
  theology), 10–12

Election, 81–115,
  218–19
Ellisen, Stanley, 175–76
Equal ultimacy, 90–91
Eschatology in dis-
  pensationalism,
  168–76
Existential categories,
  256–59
Existentialist
  philosophies, 231
Exodus, 120–21
Experience, Kant's limi-
  tation of categories to
  sphere of, 235–36,
  238, 242–43

Faith and reason, 53–55
"Female," 283–84
Figures of speech,
  167–68
Filioque clause, 71, 72
Ford, Leighton, 137–38
Functional categories,
  254–56

Gatti, Enzo, 118
"Generate," 69–70
Gereformeerde Kerken
  van Nederland,
  85–88
German Christianity,
  145

Gese, Hartmut, 182–83
Gifts for leadership po-
  sitions, 275
Grace: Wesleyan con-
  ception of free, 99;
  Lutheran conception
  of, 106–13
Grace Unlimited (Pin-
  nock), 102–03
Grafting in (of Israel),
  211, 215, 216
Gregory of Nyssa, 70
Growth in Pauline
  thought, 195–207

"Hardening" of Israel,
  217–23
Hartshorne, Charles,
  15, 23
Hick, John. See *Myth of
  God Incarnate* (Hick)
Historical continuity (in
  Paul), 204
Historical-critical
  method, 45, 59–65,
  181, 185–86, 189
Historical method
  (Christology), 43–50
Hoeksema, Herman,
  86–87
Holiness, Wesley's sys-
  tem of, 74–75, 97–98
Holistic concept of
  biblical theology,
  188–89
Holy Spirit, 67–79

Ignatius, 68–69
Immediacy, revela-
  tional, 203
Immutability of God,
  38, 39–40
Impassibility of God,
  39, 41
Incarnation, 122;
  viewed as myth,
  57–65
Irenaeus, 69
Israel, God's intentions
  for, 209–27

Israel and Judah, de-
  struction of, 121–22

Justin Martyr, 69

Kant, Immanuel, 7–8,
  233–50
Käsemann, Ernst, 47
Keswick conventions,
  75
Knowledge, problem of
  religious, 231–50

Ladd, George Eldon,
  78
Language of liberation,
  dangers in, 136–39,
  142, 148–49
Larson, Bruce, 252–54
Liberalism, theological,
  132–33
Liberation, theology of,
  117–50
Literal interpretation,
  166–73
Logos (process theol-
  ogy), 23–25, 32–34
Luke, 200
Luther, Martin, 72–73,
  108–09, 140
Lutheranism and elec-
  tion, 105–15

"Male," 283–84
"Man," 283–84
Melanchthon, Philipp,
  4, 6, 8, 109
Methodius, 69–70
Miranda, José, 119
Monarchians, Dynamic,
  33
Myth of God Incarnate
  (Hick), 58–63

Naturalistic theism. *See*
  Process theology
Natural science, 245–